THE MICHAL AFFAIR

Hebrew Bible Monographs, 3

Series Editors
David J.A. Clines, J. Cheryl Exum, Keith W. Whitelam

Editorial Board
A Graeme Auld, Francis Landy, Hugh S. Pyper, Stuart D.E. Weeks

The Michal Affair

From Zimri-Lim to the Rabbis

Daniel Bodi

in collaboration with Brigitte Donnet-Guez

Sheffield Phoenix Press

2005

First published in hardback, 2005
First published in paperback, 2006

Published by Sheffield Phoenix Press
Department of Biblical Studies, University of Sheffield
Sheffield S10 2TN

www.sheffieldphoenix.com

A CIP catalogue record for this book
is available from the British Library

Typeset by Forthcoming Publications
Printed by Lightning Source

ISBN 1-905048-17-3 (hardback)
ISBN 1-905048-74-2 (paperback)
ISSN 1747-9614

CONTENTS

Abbreviations vii

Introduction 1

Chapter 1
A POLITICAL READING OF THE MICHAL STORY:
THE TRAGEDY OF MICHAL AS A CRITIQUE OF THE
ISRAELITE MONARCHY AND THE PREFIGURATION OF ITS END 5
1. Introduction 5
2. Fragments of the Michal Tradition and Considerations about Methodology 6
3. Love as an Emotion and as Political Allegiance in the Michal Tradition 11
4. Michal Sides with David against her Father 22
5. Saul Severs David's Bonds of Kinship with the Royal Family 28
6. David Re-establishes his Ties with the Royal Family 34
7. David the King and Michal the Intractable Queen 40
8. David Exterminates the Last Members of Saul's Dynasty 53
9. Conclusions 58

Chapter 2
THE DAUGHTERS OF SAUL AND THE DAUGHTERS OF ZIMRI-LIM 64
1. The Historical Problem: Saul Offers his Two Daughters to David 64
2. The Daughters of Zimri-Lim: A Mari Analogy 68
3. The Suicide Motif in Mari and in One Greek Tragedy 78
4. The Marriage Gift or Counter-Gift in Israel and Mari 80
5. The Two Daughters of Hatshepsut Given to the Same Prince 83
6. Conclusions 85

Chapter 3
MICHAL IN RABBINIC LITERATURE 88
1. Introduction 88
2. Emotional Aspects of Michal's Marriage with David 89
3. Legal Aspects of David's Marriages with Saul's Daughters 91
4. Abrabanel's Interpretation 94

5. David's Apparent Humility 96
6. One Hundred Foreskins as a Counter-Gift 97
7. David and the Military Conflicts 98
8. Michal Saves David's Life 100
9. The Problem of the Teraphim 102
10. Michal's Marriage with Palti 103
11. Was Michal's Marriage with Palti Legal? 104
12. Doeg the Edomite's Treachery 105
13. David's Supposed Letter of Divorce (*gṭ*) 106
14. The Invalidity of Michal and Merab's Marriages with Palti and Adriel 109
15. David Demands the Return of his Wife Michal 110
16. Was it Legitimate for David to take Michal Back? 111
17. David's Dance before the Ark and the Dispute with Michal 116
18. The Conflict 118
19. The Ark at Obed-Edom's House 121
20. David's Fault 123
21. David's Guilt according to the Talmudic Literature 126
22. Did Michal Have Children? 130
23. The Equation of Eglah with Michal 131
24. The Five Sons of Michal or of Merab? 133
25. The Michal–Rachel Analogy 135
26. Michal as an Exceptionally Beautiful Woman 137
27. Michal as a Strong-Willed Woman 138
28. Michal, a Pious Woman Wearing Phylacteries and Studying the Torah 138
29. Michal as David's Wife in the World to Come 141
30. Michal a 'Helpmate Opposing' David 142

Conclusions 143

Bibliography 146
Index of Select References 162
Index of Authors 166

ABBREVIATIONS

ABL	R.F. Harper, *Assyrian and Babylonian Letters* (14 vols.; London: British Museum; Chicago: University of Chicago Press, 1892–1914)
AEM	*Archives épistolaires de Mari* (Archives royales de Mari, XXVI; Paris: Editions Recherche sur les Civilisations, 1988)
AB	Anchor Bible
ABD	David Noel Freedman (ed.), *The Anchor Bible Dictionary* (New York: Doubleday, 1992)
AfO	*Archiv für Orientforschung*
AHw	Wolfram von Soden (ed.), *Akkadisches Handwörterbuch* (3 vols.; Wiesbaden: Otto Harrassowitz, 1965–81)
AJSL	*American Journal of Semitic Languages and Literatures*
ANEP	James B. Pritchard (ed.), *Ancient Near East in Pictures Relating to the Old Testament* (Princeton: Princeton University Press, 1954)
ANET	James B. Pritchard (ed.), *Ancient Near Eastern Texts Relating to the Old Testament* (Princeton: Princeton University Press, 1950)
AOAT	Alter Orient und Altes Testament
AOS	American Oriental Series
ARM	Archives royales de Mari
ARMT	*Archives royales de Mari, Textes*
AS	Assyriological Studies
BETL	Bibliotheca ephemeridum theologicarum lovaniensium
b.	*Babylonian Talmud*
Bib	*Biblica*
BibOr	Biblica et orientalia
BZ	*Biblische Zeitschrift*
BZAW	Beihefte zur *ZAW*
CAD	Ignace J. Gelb *et al.* (eds.), *The Assyrian Dictionary of the Oriental Institute of the University of Chicago* (18 vols.; Chicago: Oriental Institute, 1956–)
CAT	Commentaire de l'Ancien Testament
CBQ	*Catholic Biblical Quarterly*
CDA	J. Black, A. George and N. Postgate (eds.), *A Concise Dictionary of Akkadian* (Wiesbaden: Otto Harrassowitz, 2000)
CH	Codex Hammurabi
EA	El Amarna
ErIsr	*Eretz Israel*
EThL	*Ephemerides theologicae lovanienses*

ETR	*Etudes théologiques et religieuses*
EvTh	*Evangelische Theologie*
HALOT	L. Koehler, W. Baumgartner, J.J. Stamm, B. Hartmann, Z. Ben-Hayyim, E.Y. Kutscher and Ph. Raymond (eds.), *The Hebrew and Aramaic Lexicon of the Old Testament* (trans. M.E.J. Richardson; 5 vols.; Leiden: E.J. Brill, 1994–2000)
HSM	Harvard Semitic Monographs
HSS	Harvard Semitic Studies
HTR	*Harvard Theological Review*
HUCA	*Hebrew Union College Annual*
IBK	Innsbrucker Beiträge zur Kulturwissenschaft
IDB	George Arthur Buttrick (ed.), *The Interpreter's Dictionary of the Bible* (4 vols.; Nashville: Abingdon Press, 1962)
IEJ	*Israel Exploration Journal*
Int	*Interpretation*
IOSCS	International Organization for Septuagint and Cognate Studies
JANES	*Journal of the Ancient Near Eastern Society of Columbia University*
JAOS	*Journal of the American Oriental Society*
JBL	*Journal of Biblical Literature*
JCS	*Journal of Cuneiform Studies*
JESHO	*Journal of the Economic and Social History of the Orient*
JJS	*Journal of Jewish Studies*
JNWSL	*Journal of Northwest Semitic Languages*
JSOT	*Journal for the Study of the Old Testament*
JSOTSup	*Journal for the Study of the Old Testament*, Supplement Series
JTS	*Journal of Theological Studies*
KAT	Kommentar zum Alten Testament
LAPO	Littératures anciennes du Proche-Orient
LD	Lectio divina
LXX	Septauagint
MARI	*Mari annales de recherches interdisciplinaires*
NEB	*New English Bible*
NIV	*New International Version*
NJPS	New Jewish Publication Society Version
OBO	Orbis biblicus et orientalis
OLZ	*Orientalistische Literaturzeitung*
Or	*Orientalia*
OTL	Old Testament Library
PEQ	*Palestine Exploration Quarterly*
RA	*Revue d'assyriologie et d'archéologie orientale*
RAI	Rencontre assyriologique internationale
RB	*Revue biblique*
REJ	*Revue des études juives*
RSV	Revised Standard Version
SBT	Studies in Biblical Theology
SSN	Studia semitica neerlandica

THAT	Ernst Jenni and Claus Westermann (eds.), *Theologisches Handwörterbuch zum Alten Testament* (Munich: Chr. Kaiser, 1971–76)
ThLZ	*Theologische Literaturzeitung*
TOB	Traduction œcuménique de la Bible
UF	*Ugarit-Forschungen*
UISK	Untersuchungen zur indogermanischen Sprach- und Kulturwissenschaft
VAB	Vorderasiatische Bibliothek
VT	*Vetus Testamentum*
WMANT	Wissenschaftliche Monographien zum Alten und Neuen Testament
y.	Jerusalem Talmud
YOS	Yale Oriental Series
ZA	*Zeitschrift für Assyriologie*
ZAW	*Zeitschrift für die alttestamentliche Wissenschaft*
ZDMG	*Zeitschrift der deutschen morgenländischen Gesellschaft*

Introduction

The Michal tradition concerning Saul's daughter and David's first wife contains several aspects which make it akin to the best ancient Greek tragedies. Its dramatic qualities, skilful use of irony, wordplays and intrigue all contribute to making it a downright masterpiece of ancient Hebrew literature.

In the present work, the Michal story will be analyzed by juxtaposing several interpretative methods: historical-critical analysis with elements of rhetorical criticism coupled with the comparative method followed by rabbinic interpretations. This research produces a surprising result: modern historians as well as rabbis in the Talmud and midrashic commentaries make a similar judgment concerning David and reasons for his desire to become Saul's son-in-law. Behind his attitude of apparent self-effacing modesty lurks his political opportunism and unbridled ambition. Historical-critical exegesis as well as Talmudic interpretations reveal David's guilt in respect to his dance in front of the ark in 2 Samuel 6. For the last two thousand years, the careful reading of biblical texts dealing with the figure of David in his relationship with his first wife Michal reaches the same conclusion: he is not exactly the man he pretends to be.

The first chapter will defend the thesis according to which the compiler of the biblical text has used the story of the tragic destiny of a Hebrew princess in order to deconstruct royal ideology and debunk the abuses of the nascent Israelite monarchy. The redactor is denouncing the new institution by depicting the guilty behavior of the first two kings of Israel, Saul and David, and revealing their merciless power-struggle. Caught in the political power-play between her father and her husband, Michal serves as a mirror for these two men whose political ambitions merge into the same image which she serves to reflect. It appears to be a unique phenomenon in ancient Near Eastern literature that the story of a woman should become a vehicle for a trenchant critique of the monarchic institution, the power-struggle and the cruelty it entails. The Michal story is a conclusion of Saul's story but it does not founder in the tenebrae without grace like the latter. The effort to transcend unjust human relationships and the strictures of patriarchy gives the tragedy of Michal particular value. It presents an exceptional theological contribution by expressing a faith in God that transcends the will for power and domination. The Michal story allows one to elaborate a biblical theology fully conscious of the patriarchal bias that the biblical texts contain and to reveal and denounce patriarchal-political and religious justification. Through biblical texts that describe the victims of oppression speaks a prophetic voice calling the readers to recognize and to affirm the human dignity that is implied in their faith in God.

The second chapter draws a comparison between Saul offering his two daughters Merab and Michal as wives to David, and the unhappy fate of two daughters of Zimri-Lim, the Bedouin and tribal king of Mari in northern Syria. Zimri-Lim gave his two daughters Kirûm and Šimātum to the same man, his vassal Ḫāya-Sūmû, in order to spy on him and to increase control of his political moves. The Mari Royal Archives dating from the eighteenth century BCE provide a significant historical precedent for the transaction between Saul and David involving two daughters offered to the same man. Apparently this was somewhat common behavior among tribal kings. Moreover, Mari texts provide the first occurrence in ancient Near Eastern texts of a divorce instigated by a woman: Zimri-Lim's daughter Kirûm was unhappy about the way her husband treated her. Although Ḫāya-Sūmû performs the public gestures signifying the divorce from Kirûm, it was she herself who insisted on the divorce by repeatedly asking to be released from her miserable state and unhappy marriage. Being a royal princess and daughter of the most powerful ruler in that region she probably took advantage of a particular stipulation in Old Babylonian marriage laws allowing a woman to obtain a divorce. Nevertheless, a woman divorcing a man remains an extremely rare thing for the epoch.

The third chapter offers an analysis of the Michal story in the light of rabbinic interpretations from the Talmud and midrashim. The basic rabbinic documentation dealing with the figure of Michal has been collected and translated into French by one of my doctoral students Brigitte Donnet-Guez and other participants of my graduate seminar on 'David's Wives'. They were then checked against the Hebrew originals and translated into English by myself. Whenever an English translation of rabbinic texts was available, however, I drew on it. For the sake of comparison, I have deliberately structured the presentation of rabbinical material to follow as closely as possible the biblical sequence of the Michal story as presented in the first chapter.

A few words of explanation are necessary concerning the rabbinic interpretative method. The literary genre called 'midrash' (from the Hebrew root *dāraš* meaning 'to explore [the Scripture]') best characterizes rabbinic literature. It represents a form of 'creative exegesis' and constitutes the category *par excellence* of traditional Jewish interpretation of the Scripture. The midrash pays close attention to every detail of the Hebrew text and even finds meaning in the blanks between the Hebrew characters.[1] In rabbinic literature,

1. This calls to mind Jacques Derrida's unorthodox orthography of the term *Différance*, which he spells with an *a*. In Derrida's deconstructive reading of texts as the search for the

chronological considerations and historical perspectives are of secondary importance. Contrary to historical-critical scholarship, for the Doctors of the Law the Torah already existed at the time of the first kings of Israel. This fact prompts the rabbis to engage in numerous discussions concerning the legal aspects of marriages between Merab, Michal and David. Moreover, the rabbis shortcut historical perspective and project laws and customs from their own times on to the nascent Israelite monarchy. The rabbis mentioned in the Jerusalem and the Babylonian Talmuds lived and wrote down their discussions between the first and sixth centuries CE. In respect of Michal, Saul and David, the rabbis occasionally bring into play references to the Sanhedrin. This supreme council of Jewish elders with its seat in Jerusalem was founded at the earliest in the second century BCE. It is therefore a blatant anachronism to imply that it could have existed already in the time of Saul and David. Moreover, one midrash attributes knowledge of the Greek language to David! Here rabbis at the beginning of the Christian era are ascribing to David their own multilingual culture and habits. While respecting the meaning of the original Hebrew text, the rabbinic interpretation nevertheless remains in the service of a theological hermeneutic. One major principle of rabbinic interpretation says that 'there is neither before nor after in the Torah'.[2] Here the term 'Torah' is taken to include not only the Pentateuch but also the rest of the Scripture. This principle allows the rabbis to solve most of the chronological difficulties which they did not fail to detect in the biblical texts. The fundamental theological interpretation of the rabbis implies that God included the entire Torah in his initial creative Word. The chronology is therefore of secondary importance.

One highly imaginative midrash of the Haggadic[3] type (akin to legendary accounts) concerning the blessing provoked by the arrival of the ark in the house of one of David's servants, Obed-Edom, amounts to a fairy tale: all the women in Obed-Edom's household experience exceptional fertility rates

trace, the track or spoor of that which is absent, he defines it in the following manner: '*Différance* is the systematic play of differences, of the traces of differences, of the spacing by means of which elements are related to each other. This spacing is the simultaneously active and passive (the *a* of *différance* indicates this indecision as concerns activity and passivity...) production of the intervals without which the "full" term would not signify...' (J. Derrida, *Positions* [trans. Alan Bass; Chicago: University of Chicago Press, 1981], p. 27). In 1986, my teacher Edward L. Greenstein at Jewish Theological Seminary in New York, entitled one of his lectures, 'Midrash as an Early Form of Deconstruction'.

2. See J. Neusner, *History and Torah* (New York: Schocken Books, 1965), p. 22, on the 'flattening of history' in rabbinic literature.

3. *Haggadah* (lit. 'tale, lesson') is the name given to those sections of rabbinic literature which contain homiletic expositions of the Bible, stories, legends, folk-lore, anecdotes and maxims. It is opposed to *Halakhah* (lit. 'step, guidance') designating those sections of rabbinic literature which deal with legal questions.

and give birth twice a month! Haggadic legends of this kind found in the midrashic commentaries make it necessary to read the rabbinic sources in a critical manner and to distinguish between the genres employed. Conscious of the problem, Judaism does not attribute the same value to all its sources and makes a sharp distinction between material that is normative and binding (*Halakhah*) and what amounts to stories useful for edification and entertainment (*Haggadah*).[4]

The interest of this chapter dealing with rabbinic interpretations of the Michal story is certainly not found in the historical light that it can shed on biblical texts. Rather, it reflects preoccupations of the two thousand-year-long rabbinic interpretative tradition and contributes to the history of Scripture interpretation. The rabbinic interpretations represent one major aspect of the so-called *Wirkungsgeschichte* as they illustrate the way in which the Michal tradition was read and received in Judaism. Furthermore, it provides the general public with a translation of medieval rabbinic commentaries that are often inaccessible outside narrow and rather specialized circles.

4. See further W.S. Towner, 'Form Criticism of Rabbinic Literature', *JJS* 24 (1973), pp. 110-18; A. Saldarini, '"Form Criticism" of Rabbinic Literature', *JBL* 96 (1977), pp. 257-74.

1

A POLITICAL READING OF THE MICHAL STORY: THE TRAGEDY OF MICHAL AS A CRITIQUE OF THE ISRAELITE MONARCHY AND THE PREFIGURATION OF ITS END*

1. *Introduction*

This study was prompted by the remarkable research tool concerning the Michal story provided by D.J.A. Clines and T.C. Eskenazi.[1] In this collection of essays on Queen Michal one is struck, however, by the absence of any reference to the polemic role of the Michal story in the context of the denunciation of the institution of the Israelite monarchy by the redactors of the 'Deuteronomistic Historiography'.[2] The fact that the Michal story can be read as a political intrigue seems not to have been adequately grasped nor applied to the interpretation of the texts dealing with her. A political reading of the Michal narrative brings to the fore the power-play between Saul and David which forms its main intrigue. Moreover, it shows how Michal's tragedy foreshadows that of the Israelite monarchy and underpins the negative assessment of this institution made by the Deuteronomistic historiographers.[3] In

* A shorter version of this chapter appeared in French, 'La tragédie de Mikal en tant que critique de la monarchie israélite et préfiguration de sa fin', *Foi et Vie* 96 (1996), pp. 65-105.

1. D.J.A. Clines and T.C. Eskenazi (eds.), *Telling Queen Michal's Story: An Experiment in Comparative Interpretation* (JSOTSup, 119; Sheffield: JSOT Press, 1991).

2. The hypothesis of Deuteronomistic Historiography (DtrH) as traditionally formulated by M. Noth in 1943, comprising the books of Josiah + Judges + 1–2 Samuel + 1–2 Kings, is nowadays seriously questioned; cf. A. de Pury, T. Römer and J.-D. Macchi (eds.), *Israël construit son histoire: L'historiographie deutéronomiste à la lumière des recherches récentes* (Geneva: Labor & Fides, 1996), pp. 9-120, for a résumé of the history of research.

3. F. Langlamet, 'Pour ou contre Salomon? La rédaction prosalomonienne de 1 Rois I–II', *RB* 83 (1976), pp. 321-79, offers a detailed analysis of the 'pro-' and 'anti-'monarchic redaction of the Succession Narrative. According to L. Delekat, 'Tendenz und Theologie der David-Salomo-Erzählung', in F. Maass (ed.), *Das ferne und nahe Wort* (Festschrift L. Rost; BZAW, 105; Berlin: Alfred Töpelmann, 1967), pp. 26-37 (26-27), 1 Sam. 11 and 12 reflect the negative attitude toward the monarch. See also H.J. Boecker, *Die Beurteilung*

this context, we will adduce some reasons why the episode in 2 Sam. 21.8-9, where David orders the killing of Michal's five sons, should be seen as an integral part of the Michal story.

Michal, Saul's daughter and David's first wife, is a lesser known character in the Bible. To affirm that she was indispensable to David in his accession to the kingship would be exaggerated. Nevertheless, she saved his life. This woman, however, remained in David's shadow, while Sarah, Rebekah, Rachel and Leah, the wives of the patriarchs, are much better known, to the point that some authors coined a new term for them, calling them the 'matriarchs'.[4]

2. *Fragments of the Michal Tradition and Considerations about Methodology*

By paying greater attention to the presence of the literary phenomenon of *inclusio*[5] in identifying the beginning and the end of a particular pericope, the following texts or fragments can be adduced as constituting an original Michal narrative:[6]

1. Michal's Love for and Marriage to David (1 Sam. 18.20-28)
2. Michal Saves David's Life (1 Sam. 19.10d-18a)
3. Michal Married to Another Man (1 Sam. 25.42-45)
4. Michal Brought Back to David (2 Sam. 3.12-16)
5. The Rupture in the Relationship between Michal and David (2 Sam. 6.16-23 + 1 Chron. 15.29)
6. The Massacre of Michal's Five Sons (2 Sam. 21.8-9).

Most of these passages have been amply treated in the above-mentioned collection of essays. While offering a history of research on the Michal story, in the course of our political reading of Michal fragments I will pay particular attention to features which have been omitted or hastily glossed over by previous commentators. These are important as they show how the Deuteronomistic redactor elaborates his critique of the monarchy and discredits the royal ideology in Israel.

der Anfänge des Königtums in den deuteronomistischen Abschnitten des 1. Samuelbuches: Ein Beitrag zum Problem des 'Deuteronomistischen Geschichtswerks' (WMANT, 31; Neukirchen–Vluyn: Neukirchener Verlag, 1969); M.C. Astour, 'The Amarna Age Forerunners of Biblical Antiroyalism', in *Studies in Jewish Languages, Literature, and Society: For Max Weinreich on his Seventieth Birthday* (The Hague: Mouton, 1964), pp. 6-17.

4. C. Chalier, *Les matriarches: Sarah, Rébecca, Rachel et Léa* (Paris: Seuil, 1985).

5. M. Anbar, 'La "reprise"', *VT* 38 (1988), pp. 385-98, finds this literary technique in use already in the composition of the Mari letters in the eighteenth century BCE. For its wide use in the Bible, see C. Kuhl, 'Die "Wiederaufnahme"—ein literarkritisches Prinzip', *ZAW* 64 (1952), pp. 1-11.

6. The name of Michal is first mentioned in the genealogical enumeration of Saul's children (1 Sam. 14.49-51).

Since Michal's story is part of David's, in order to analyze it one has to deconstruct the biblical narrative by applying to it what D.J.A. Clines calls a 'reading against the grain'.[7] Moreover, reading the story of David from the point of view of a minor character like Michal is another typical feature of deconstruction.[8]

The first four fragments of the Michal story, or, as H. Schulte termed it, the 'Michal Tradition',[9] emerge at strategic points throughout the main narrative of David's so-called 'rise to power' (1 Sam. 15–2 Sam. 5).[10] The latter, with sober realism, describes the devious ways by which a poor shepherd becomes a warrior in the service of Saul and eventually a tribal king. At the root of David's 'rags to riches' story, there is an original narrative which some scholars place at the end of the tenth or at the beginning of the ninth century BCE.[11] F. Langlamet considers five fragments of the Michal tradition (with the exception of the sixth one, i.e. 2 Sam. 21.8-9), as being predeuteronomistic as well.[12] He confirms the results of J.H. Grønbaek's analysis which attributed the tradition concerning Michal to what he called the *Grundschrift*.[13] In the elaboration of his critique of the Israelite monarchy, the Deuteronomistic redactor drew on an earlier Michal tradition because it contained elements that he could use in order to support his point of view.

The freedom which the narrator retains in respect to the main protagonists Saul and David is unique in the literature of the ancient Near East. It continues and develops into what is traditionally called the 'Succession Narrative' (2 Sam. 9–20 and 1 Kgs 1–2).[14] O. Kaiser dates the composition of this

7. Clines and Eskenazi (eds.), *Telling Queen Michal's Story*, p. 129.

8. The method of reading texts called 'Deconstruction' was first formulated by J. Derrida, *De la grammatologie* (Paris: Les Editions de Minuit, 1967), pp. 96-108 ('La brisure') = ET *Of Grammatology* (trans. G.C. Spivak; Baltimore: The Johns Hopkins University Press, 1975).

9. H. Schulte, *Die Enstehung der Geschichtsschreibung im alten Israel* (BZAW, 128; Berlin: W. de Gruyter, 1972), p. 146.

10. J.-H. Grønbaek, *Die Geschichte vom Aufstieg Davids (1. Sam. 15–2. Sam. 5): Tradition und Komposition* (Acta Theologica Danica, 10; Copenhagen: Munksgaard, 1971); R.A. Carlson, *David the Chosen King: A Traditio-Historical Approach to the Second Book of Samuel* (Stockholm: Almqvist & Wicksell, 1964); J. Conrad, 'Zum geschichtlichen Hintergrund der Darstellung von Davids Aufstieg', *ThLZ* 97 (1972), cols. 321-32.

11. O. Kaiser, 'David und Jonathan', *EThL* 66 (1990), pp. 281-96. According to T.N.D. Mettinger, *King and Messiah* (Lund: G.W.K. Gleerup, 1976), pp. 38-41, the narrative of David's rise to power stems from the time of the schism.

12. F. Langlamet, 'David, fils de Jessé, une édition prédeutéronomiste de l'Histoire de la Succession', *RB* 89 (1982), pp. 5-47 (7-9, 15, 19).

13. Grønbaek, *Die Geschichte vom Aufstieg Davids*, pp. 237-38.

14. It was L. Rost who spoke of the 'Succession Narrative', which he traced and analyzed in 2 Sam. 9–20 and in 1 Kgs 1–2. He argued for a continuous story formed by a

narrative between the eighth and sixth centuries BCE.[15] Here the often tragic family events of the House of David are subject to a detailed and circumstantial description. A series of crimes are committed provoking crises that radically undermine David's rule and maintain a persistent questioning on how to resolve the succession of the aging king. In fact, the institution of tribal kingship entails the question of dynasty. Through dramatic confrontations that oppose the sons to their father, the issue of succession is heightened.

While it is part of the account of the transfer of the ark to Jerusalem, Michal's intervention in 2 Sam. 6.16-23 (Fragment 5) represents a transition between 'David's rise to power' and the 'Succession Narrative'. The fact that there would be no descendant to unite the House of Saul with the House of David accentuates the intrigue. The account of the massacre of Michal's five sons—possible pretenders to the throne (Fragment 6)—is fittingly placed in the middle of the 'Succession Narrative'.[16]

Some scholars no longer consider the 'Succession Narrative' as a piece of historiography but rather as a narrative of a particular genre.[17] Moreover, recent research has shown that we do not have an account of 'David's rise to power'. Rather, the narrative deals with rivalry between two houses fighting for tribal supremacy, the House of Saul pitting itself against that of David. In this newer thematic conceptualization of traditional material, the narrative does not end with the establishment of a new capital in the City of David, but with Nathan's prophecy in 2 Samuel 7 bearing on the future of the Davidic

skilful joining of independent traditions to recount the history of the succession to David's throne, in *Die Überlieferung von der Thronnachfolge Davids* (BWANT, III/6; Stuttgart: W. Kohlhammer, 1926) = ET *The Succession to the Throne of David* (Historic Texts and Interpreters in Biblical Scholarship, 1; Sheffield: Almond Press, 1982).

15. O. Kaiser, 'Beobachtungen zur sogenannten Thronnachfolgeerzählung', *EThL* 64 (1988), pp. 5-20; A. de Pury and T. Römer (eds.), *Die sogenannte Thronnachfolgegeschichte Davids: Neue Einsichten und Anfragen* (OBO, 176; Freiburg: Universitätsverlag, 2000); J. Barton, 'Dating the "Succession Narrative"', in J. Day (ed.), *In Search of Pre-Exilic Israel* (JSOTSup, 406; London: T. & T. Clark International, 2004), pp. 95-106.

16. J.P. Fokkelman offered a study from a literary point of view in his work, *Narrative Art and Poetry in the Books of Samuel: A Full Interpretation Based on Stylistic and Structural Analyses*. I. *King David (II Sam. 9–20 & I Kings 1–2)* (SSN, 20; Assen: Van Gorcum, 1981); II. *The Crossing Fates* (SSN, 23; Assen: Van Gorcum, 1986); III. *Throne and City* (SSN, 27; Assen: Van Gorcum, 1990).

17. See, among others, R.N. Whybray, *The Succession Narrative: A Study of II Sam. 9–20 and 1 Kings 1 and 2* (SBT, 2/9; London: SCM Press, 1968); P.R. Ackroyd, 'The Succession Narrative (So-Called)', *Int* 35 (1981), pp. 383-96; D.M. Gunn, *The Story of King David: Genre and Interpretation* (JSOTSup, 6; repr. Sheffield: JSOT Press, 1989 [1978]), especially Chapter 2, 'Genre: Prevailing Views'; G. Keys, *The Wages of Sin: A Reappraisal of the 'Succession Narrative'* (JSOTSup, 221; Sheffield: Sheffield Academic Press, 1996).

dynasty.[18] In the present study, I use terms such as 'David's rise to power' and 'Succession Narrative' in a purely conventional way.

The narrative of David's rise to power and of his succession is not completely consistent as a result of various more ancient sources being joined to it. The opinion of L. Rost might still be valid: 'These sources are in every respect individual, independent creations which, by means of more or less skilful transitional formulas, are attached to, or embedded in the larger narrative'.[19] The Michal tradition might have been one such originally independent creation stemming from circles that wanted to preserve the memory of the first tribal king and of his family. Moreover, the considerable number of *hapax legomena* or rare terms that appear in these fragments would militate for the remote antiquity of the original Michal tradition.

Convinced of the necessity of forging a 'literary middle ground'[20] in biblical studies, the texts will be treated with some use of rhetorical criticism which is understood to belong to the general rubric of literary criticism.[21] The former has proven its heuristic value in facilitating fruitful theological reflection.[22] The present research has an avowed concern for theological applicability. Moreover, some affinity exists between the rhetorical-critical method where biblical texts are submitted to close reading and the traditional rabbinic method of interpretation as found in the Talmud and the midrash.

18. J. Vermeylen, 'La Maison de Saül et la Maison de David. Un écrit de propagande théologico-politique de 1 S 11 à 2 S 7', in L. Desrousseaux and J. Vermeylen (eds.), *Figures de David à travers la Bible* (LD, 177; Paris: Cerf, 1999), pp. 34-74 (53); *idem, La loi du plus fort: Histoire de la rédaction des récits davidiques de 1 Samuel 8 à 1 Rois 2* (BETL, 154; Leuven: Peeters, 2000); W. Dietrich (ed.), *David und Saul im Widerstreit: Diachronie und Synchronie im Wettstreit, Beiträge zur Auslegung des ersten Samuelbuches* (OBO, 206; Freiburg: Academic Press, 2004).

19. Rost, *The Succession to the Throne of David*, p. 4.

20. R. Alter, 'A Literary Approach to the Bible', *Commentary* 60 (1975), pp. 70-78. Alter criticized the tendency of professional biblical scholars to center their efforts either on narrow philological issues or on theology 'with no literary middle ground', so that essential aspects such as 'character, motive, and narrative design' go unnoticed. In his day, Alter called biblical scholars' attention 'to the artful use of language, to the shifting play of ideas, conventions, tone, sound, imagery, narrative viewpoint (and) compositional units' in biblical narratives.

21. Having been initiated into rhetorical criticism by my teacher Phyllis Trible, I tend to follow her version of it, which also implies that we will try to be sensitive to some feminist liberation aspects of the biblical texts; cf. P. Trible, *God and the Rhetoric of Sexuality* (Philadelphia: Fortress Press, 1978), Chapter 1, 'Clues in a Text', and *idem, Rhetorical Criticism* (Minneapolis: Fortress Press, 1994), pp. 5-87, for some guidelines on this method (with an abundant bibliography).

22. Cf. D.J.A. Clines, 'Story and Poem: The Old Testament as Literature and as Scripture', *Int* 34 (1980), pp. 115-27 (115), and the quote from *Luther's Correspondence* (trans. and ed. P. Smith and C.M. Jacobs; 2 vols.; Philadelphia: United Lutheran Publication House, 1918), II, pp. 176-77.

The third chapter of the present study serves to illustrate this point. Whenever the insights of historical criticism and the history of religions further our understanding of the text, we will make ample use of them. Moreover, as pointed out by an historian, 'Nothing is more unfair than to judge men of the past by the ideas of the present'.[23] In order to avoid this error we will use the comparative method (referring to Mari, El-Amarna, Egypt and Akkadian literature in general) in order to place biblical phenomena in their larger ancient Near Eastern context. As shown in the second chapter of this study, I use the historical-critical method and the comparative-contrastive approach in order to do justice to the specific historical and cultural setting in which biblical literature took shape and to secure its connection with other literatures of the ancient Near East with which the Bible forms a literary and cultural continuum. I therefore fully subscribe to what the historian Fernand Braudel called *la promiscuité des méthodes*, and reject totalitarian pretensions of a single method.

In the present form of the biblical narrative the Michal tradition represents only a minor plot within the larger story dealing primarily with David. Attempts which seek to transform Michal into a major character in the Bible do not do justice to the text. This feature establishes the following goals for the present study: (1) to recover the Michal tradition from the preserved fragments which mention her; (2) to make a contribution to the study of David's character from the point of view of his relationship with his wife Michal and her father Saul; (3) to analyze political implications of the union between Michal and David and show how the tragic side of their relationship serves the purpose of the redactor in his condemnation of the Israelite monarchy; (4) together with Chapter 2, to analyze the role of women in ancient Israel and in the ancient Near East;[24] (5) to provide a basis for a comparison between the broader historical and rhetorical-critical analysis of the Michal story and the rabbinical interpretations of it as found in the third chapter of the present study.

We will start from a common psychological observation: the behavior of a person may be compared to prismatic reflections. Each new relationship

23. Quoted in B.W. Tuchman, *The March of Folly* (London: Abacus, 1984), p. 4.

24. Cf. A. Brenner, *The Israelite Woman: Social Role and Literary Type in Biblical Narrative* (The Biblical Seminar, 1; Sheffield: JSOT Press, 1985). Assyriologists have published several studies on the role of women in the ancient Near East: J. Bottéro, 'La femme dans la Mésopotamie ancienne', in P. Grimmal (ed.), *Histoire mondiale de la femme* (Paris: Nouvelle Librairie de France, 1965), pp. 158-223; J.-M. Durand (ed.), *La femme dans le Proche-Orient antique* (RAI, 33; Paris: Editions Recherche sur les Civilisations, 1987); cf. also the two Strasbourg congresses devoted to the role of women in ancient Greece, E. Lévy (ed.), *La femme dans les sociétés antiques* (Actes des colloques de Strasbourg; Strasbourg: Université des Sciences Humaines de Strasbourg, 1983).

brings out a particular facet of one's personality.[25] Fortunately for our approach, David was not only a 'man according to YHWH's heart' (1 Sam. 13.14), but also a ladies' man.[26] Therefore, the study of David's numerous relationships with women allows us to gain insight into his character.[27]

David, loved by women, reminds us of one of the etymologies of his name (*dôd*) 'beloved'. The name that Nathan gave to Solomon in 1 Sam. 12.25—Jedidiah 'Beloved of the Lord'—would be in the same vein. This is why J.J. Stamm translates the name of David with 'Liebling', that is, 'beloved'.[28] The root of the name is *dwd* (so *dawid* or *dawd*). B. Halpern convincingly explains the second manner in which the name is understood as '(paternal) uncle', and its connection with the meaning "beloved"'. 'The "paternal uncle", or *dwd*, is the family member responsible for burial when a household is without direct heirs (*dwdw*, Amos 6.10). He is the nearest relation to whom the incest taboo does not apply, which is the reason the term also denotes one's "beloved"'.[29] The priority should be given to the first meaning, however, since no text spells David's name *dd*, as 'uncle' is sometimes written.[30]

Let us turn to the first fragment of the Michal tradition.

3. *Love as an Emotion and as Political Allegiance in the Michal Tradition*

Fragment 1. Michal's Love for and Marriage to David (1 Samuel 18.20-28):

> (20) Michal the daughter of Saul loved (*'hb*) David; and they told Saul, and the thing pleased him (*yšr hdbr b'ynyw*, lit. 'the thing was right in his eyes'). (21) Saul thought, 'Let me give her to him, that she may be a snare (*mwqš*[31]) for him, and that the hand of the Philistines may be against him'. Therefore Saul said to David, 'A second time (*bštym*) you shall now be my son-in-law'.

25. This principle has been aptly described by C.S. Lewis, *The Four Loves* (New York: Harcourt Brace Jovanovich, 1960), p. 92: 'In each of my friends there is something that only some other friend can fully bring out. By myself I am not large enough to call the whole man into activity.'

26. 'David est un homme à femmes'; so J. Kelen, *Les femmes de la Bible* (Paris: A. Michel, 1985), p. 88.

27. In her article 'Characterization in Biblical Narrative: David's Wives', *JSOT* 23 (1982), pp. 69-85, A. Berlin analyzed the relationship between David and the following women: Michal, Abigail, Bathsheba and Abishag.

28. J.J. Stamm, *Beiträge zur hebräischen und altorientalischen Namenskunde* (OBO, 30; Freiburg: Universitätsverlag, 1980), p. 25.

29. B. Halpern, *David's Secret Demons, Messiah, Murderer, Traitor, King* (repr. Grand Rapids: Eerdmans, 2004 [2001]), p. 269.

30. W. Dietrich, '*dāwīd, dôd* und *bytdwd*', *ThZ* 53 (1997), pp. 17-32.

31. In modern Israeli Hebrew the term *môqēš* is used in order to designate a military anti-personnel mine.

(22) And Saul commanded his courtiers, 'Speak to David in private and say, "Here, the king has delight in you, and all his courtiers love you (*'hb*); now then become the king's son-in-law"'. (23) And Saul's courtiers spoke those words in the ears of David. And David said, 'Does it seem to you a trifling matter (*hnqllh*) to become the king's son-in-law, seeing that I am a poor and a negligible (*nqlh*) man?' (24) And the courtiers of Saul told him, 'Thus and so did David speak'. (25) Then Saul said, 'The king desires no marriage present (*mhr*, "counter-gift") except a hundred foreskins of the Philistines, that he may be avenged of the king's enemies'. Now Saul thought to make David fall by the hand of the Philistines. (26) And when his courtiers told David these words, it pleased David well to be the king's son-in-law (*yšr hdbr b'yny dwd*, lit. 'the thing was right in David's eyes'). Before the time had expired (27) David arose and went along with his men, and killed two hundred of the Philistines; and David brought their foreskins, which were given in full number to the king, that he might become the king's son-in-law. And Saul gave him his daughter Michal for a wife. (28) Saul saw and knew that YHWH was with David, and Michal the daughter of Saul loved him (*'hbthw*).

a. *The Double Meaning of the Word 'Love' (*'hb*)*. This literary unit is easily identified, since the account begins and ends with the statement that Michal loved David. The Hebrew phrase (*wt'hb mykl bt š'wl 't dwd*) in v. 20 forms an *inclusio* with (*wmykl bt š'wl 'hbthw*) in v. 28.[32]

The beginning of the relationship between Michal and David stands in striking contrast to the moment of its definitive rupture in Fragment 5 where it is said that 'she despised him in her heart' (2 Sam. 6.16). As already noted by commentators, Michal's love twice stated has a special significance because it is the only instance in the Bible, apart from the Song of Songs, where it is explicitly said that a woman loved a man.[33] The reference, however, is not unique in ancient Near Eastern literature. A literary motif exists in Sumerian literature where a woman expresses her choice of the man she wants.[34]

32. In his article 'X, X ben Y, ben Y: Personal Names in Hebrew Narrative Style', *VT* 22 (1972), pp. 266-87 (269-72), D.J.A. Clines points out the usage and significance of particular formulations of biblical names. This fragment begins and ends with Michal's name.

33. In the Song of Songs the woman says five times in respect to the man she loves, 'he whom my *npš* loves', 1.7; 3.1, 2, 3, 4.

34. B. Alster, 'Marriage and Love in the Sumerian Love Songs with Some Notes on the Manchester Tammuz', in M.E. Cohen, D.C. Snell and D.B. Weisberg (eds.), *The Tablet and the Scroll: Near Eastern Studies in Honor of W.W. Hallo* (Bethesda, MD: CDL Press, 1993), pp. 15-27 (18): 'to judge from literary sources, it is equally clear that, at least in the world of poetry, the girl was not prepared to accept the choice without discussion. In view of the formalized way in which this issue is phrased, there are good reasons to believe that this does in some way reflect reality. A phrase is used according to which she would only accept "the man of my heart" (= choice, i.e., the man she loves), and this may well have been a phrase that had legal connotations (*mu-lu šà-ab-mu* "the man of my heart").'

According to one account, at the moment when David entered the service of Saul as a musician, the king 'loved him a lot' (*wy'hbhw m'd*) (1 Sam. 16.21). This is the first occurrence of the term 'love' found again at the beginning of Michal and David's relationship. At this stage there was no hostility between Saul and David. The first contact between the two men was positive. Her father's initial love for David probably encouraged Michal in her own feelings toward the young man. The relationship between Saul and David soon deteriorated, however. Victim of a morbid jealousy, Saul foundered into insanity. At the beginning, however, David assumed a therapeutic role with Saul: 'And whenever the evil spirit (*pneuma ponēron* LXX) from God was upon Saul, David took the lyre and played it with his hand' (1 Sam. 16.23). In the ancient Near East, a person's sickness is often explained as an attack by an evil spirit. In Akkadian, for example, an epidemic is indicated by the expression *qāt ili* ('the hand of god').[35]

In Mesopotamia, the goddess of war and love, Inanna/Ištar, was both revered and feared by the population on account of her unpredictability. She too was prone to murderous rage as reflected in war destructions which were also her specialty. For that reason the wise god Enki came to the help of the gods and the humans by creating a special cultic official called g a l a, who was both a priest and a singer in charge of lamentations. He had an instrument on which he played appeasing music, and chanted prayers and supplications in order to assuage the hot-tempered goddess.[36] This is an earlier example of music being used for therapeutic purposes. It is comparable to what David was doing with his lyre, namely, trying to relieve Saul's tormented mind.[37]

From the first contact between Saul and David, the reader wonders whether Saul will be able to maintain his position as leader of the Israelite tribes. David seems to possess better mental health and greater vigor to the point that one scholar wonders whether David's rise to power is not due to 'psychiatric' reasons as much as to his military exploits?[38] The young David shows such a surplus of vitality that he attracts different members of Saul's household: the father takes him into his service, the younger daughter falls in love with him, and the son Jonathan develops a friendship which becomes legendary. Nothing is said of the attitude of the other sons of Saul, Abinadab and

35. *CAD*, Q, 1982, p. 186 *qāt ili*, 'a calamity, a specific illness'.

36. S.N. Kramer, 'BM 29616: The Fashioning of the *gala*', *Acta Sumerologica* 3 (1981), pp. 1-9.

37. R. Harris, 'Inanna-Ishtar as Paradox and a Coincidence of Opposites', *History of Religions* 30 (1991), pp. 261-78 (266 n. 26).

38. See R. North, 'David's Rise: Sacral, Military, or Psychiatric?', *Bib* 63 (1982), pp. 524-44; D.V. Edelman, *King Saul in the Historiography of Judah* (JSOTSup, 121; Sheffield: JSOT Press, 1991).

Malchishua, towards this happy intruder. David immediately appears too popular not to raise suspicious jealousy in Saul.

The term 'love' is thus a key word in the first fragment of the Michal tradition. It reappears in v. 22, where it is said that all the servants of the king, that is, the high-ranking members of the court, love David.[39] In this way the double meaning of the word 'love' is indicated: love as an emotion and as a political allegiance. The political connotation of the term 'love' is well attested both in the Bible and in ancient Near Eastern literature. It can stand for political loyalty, partisanship, or even a diplomatic or commercial contract.[40] Thus in 1 Kgs 5.15, Hiram the king of Tyre is described as having always loved (*'hb*) David. In a letter written four centuries prior to the time of David by a Canaanite city-king, the term 'love' is used to describe factional loyalty to rival leaders. In EA 138.71-73, one reads, '(The city of Byblos). Half of the city loves the sons of 'Abdi-Aširti (the instigator of rebellion) and half of it (loves) my Lord (the king of Egypt and legitimate sovereign)'.[41] El-Amarna Akkadian terms for 'love' (*râmu/ra'āmu* and *ra'āmūtu*) are functional equivalents of the Hebrew *'hb*.[42] In another El-Amarna letter (EA 17.27-28), Tušratta, the king of Mitanni, writes to the Pharaoh, 'My father loved you, and you in turn loved my father. In keeping with this love, my father [g]ave you my sister'.[43] As pointed out by W. Moran, 'by the Amarna period "love" (*râmu/ra'āmu* and derivatives) had become part of the terminology of international relations'.[44]

Moreover, the Neo-Assyrian vassal treaties offer a striking parallel to the biblical expression *'hb knpšw*. In 1 Sam. 18.1 it is said that Jonathan 'loved David as himself' (*wy'hbw yhwntn knpšw*). In Assyria, the vassals convoked by Esarhaddon (680–669 BCE) to ensure loyalty to his successor Assurbanipal

39. The title *'bd hmlk*, referred not to a low-ranking official but to a higher ranking member of the court. This is clear not only from biblical evidence (e.g. 2 Kgs 22.12; 2 Chron. 34.20; 2 Kgs 25.8), but also from surviving Israelite and other Northwest Semitic seals inscribed with this title after proper names; cf. P.K. McCarter, *I Samuel* (AB, 8; New York: Doubleday, 1980), p. 158. Z. Zevit, 'The Use of *'ebed* as a Diplomatic Term in Jeremiah', *JBL* 88 (1969), pp. 74-77.

40. See W.L. Moran, 'The Ancient Near Eastern Background of the Love of God in Deuteronomy', *CBQ* 25 (1963), pp. 77-87; J.A. Thompson, 'The Significance of the Verb LOVE in the David–Jonathan Narratives in 1 Samuel', *VT* 24 (1974), pp. 334-38.

41. Akkadian text EA 138.71-73: *'anūma ālu mišilši rā'im ana mārē 'Abdi-Aširti u mišilši ana bēlīya'*, in J.A. Knudtzon, *Die El-Amarna-Tafeln* (VAB, 2; Leipzig: J.C. Hinrichs, 1915), I, pp. 582-83.

42. For a long list of El-Amarna examples, see J.A. Knudtzon, *Die El-Amarna-Tafeln* (= EA) (Glossary), II, pp. 1493-94.

43. W.L. Moran, *The Amarna Letters* (Baltimore: The Johns Hopkins University Press, 1992), p. 41.

44. Moran, *The Amarna Letters*, p. xxiv n. 59.

(668–627 BCE) are told *kî napšatkuna la tar'amani* ('you will love [Assurbanipal] as your *napištu* [cf. Hebrew *npš*]').[45] The text in 1 Sam. 18.3 goes on to say that Jonathan made a pact (*krt bryt*) with David because he loved him as his *npš*. This means that Jonathan made a political contract with David in the midst of the power-struggle between David and Saul. Similarly, Assurbanipal required an oath of 'love' from his vassals and high officials to assure their loyalty before he went to war against his brother Šamaš-šumukin who rebelled against him in an attempt to make Babylon an independent city-state.[46] Moreover, David calls Jonathan his 'brother' in 2 Sam. 1.26 (*'ḥy*), although they had no filial relationship. This is significant, since it is now recognized that ŠEŠ.MEŠ = *aḫu* (*aḫḫū*) ('brother') and *aḫḫūtu* ('brotherhood') are technical Akkadian terms for 'treaty partners'.[47]

To Saul's chagrin, it is 'all Israel and Judah who love (*'hb*) David' (1 Sam. 18.16), meaning that the tribes in the north as well as those in the south pledged him political allegiance. Recognizing this state of affairs, Saul comes to fear David as a dangerous political rival (1 Sam. 18.15, 28).[48] Saul's fears are understandable since his own position was dependent on prestige and ascendancy over the same tribes. At this stage, David's reputation was beginning to surpass his own. David had become a great military leader or chief (cf. 2 Sam. 6.21 *ngyd*). In the skilful unfolding of this complex political drama the ambiguous verb *'hb* is used at several critical points, all of which

45. Cf. D.J. Wiseman, 'The Vassal Treaties of Esarhaddon', *Iraq* 2 (1958), pp. 1-99 (49-50) (= IV 266-68).

46. E. Gerstenberger, 'Covenant and Commandment', *JBL* 84 (1965), pp. 38-51.

47. M. Fishbane, 'The Treaty Background of Amos 1:11 and Related Matters', *JBL* 89 (1970), pp. 313-18 (314). S. Schroer and T. Staubli, 'Saul, David und Jonathan—eine Dreieckgeschichte?', *Bibel und Kirche* 51 (1996), pp. 15-22, had revived a nineteenth-century interpretation made by the French playwright André Gide (*Saül* [Paris: Gallimard, 1896]) of a supposed homosexual relationship between David and Jonathan which prompted Saul's jealousy. This interpretation is not the most probable one as shown by M. Zehnder, 'Exegetische Beobachtungen zu den David-Jonathan-Geschichten', *Bib* 79 (1998), pp. 153-79.

48. Saul's outburst of jealousy was prompted by the dance (*śḥq*) and the song of the women, 'Saul has slain his thousands, and David his ten thousands' (1 Sam. 18.7). If this couplet is understood as an example of 'synonymous parallelism', the variations 'thousands//ten thousands' are simply a decoration and are not to be taken literally. If it is understood as 'progressive parallelism', the second element says something significantly different from the first: David is a greater warrior than Saul. Scholars are still debating over the correct understanding of this Hebrew verse. To push the irony to its extreme, it is possible that Saul too had difficulties in determining the kind of parallelism this couplet was meant to be. As noted by D.M. Gunn (*The Fate of King Saul* [JSOTSup, 14; Sheffield: JSOT Press, 1980], p. 149 n. 8), one of the beauties of this parallelism is that the poetry becomes yet another element of ambiguity thrown into Saul's path. We do not know with what degree of mischievous intent (if any) the couplet was coined and paraded.

are pregnant with political significance.[49] In my opinion the recognition of the fact that the term 'love' can stand for an emotion as well as for a political allegiance is of crucial importance for the correct understanding of this story. It sets the stage and foreshadows Michal's tragic love. In the first excerpt, the term 'love' appears three times and at key moments. Michal's tragic love for David is born in the shadow of political meaning of the term 'love'. In spite of rising tensions and occasional outright animosity between the two men, the daughter of Saul loves her father's rival. The love as an emotion felt by Michal will be sacrificed by her father who exploits it in order to get rid of his political adversary. The happiness of his daughter is a trifling thing for Saul. She is trapped in their power-struggle.

The literary structure reflects the numerous obstacles that Michal's love has to overcome. There are two relationships which are intertwined: that of Michal who loves David which forms the outer ring and the relationship between Saul and David 'who are making a deal' which forms the inner ring:

wt'hb mykl bt š'wl 't dwd	v. 20a
wygdw lš'wl wyšr hdbr b'ynw	v. 20b
wyšr hdbr b'yny dwd lhtḥtn bmlk	v. 26b
wmykl bt š'wl 'hbthw	v. 28b

In the first sentence the name of Saul separates Michal from David (v. 20a). In the last sentence in this section (v. 28), the obstacles having been successfully overcome, Michal's name follows immediately after that of David (*wyr' š'wl wyd' ky yhwh 'm dwd wmykl bt š'wl 'hbthw*, v. 28a-b).

Yet she is called the daughter of Saul. Her love is under the shadow of her father's name and the transaction made by the two men, the inner ring being established between the twice repeated expression, 'the thing was right (*yšr*) in (Saul's and David's) eyes'.

b. *The Double Meaning of the Word 'Right'* (yšr). There is profound irony in the use of the term *yšr*. This Hebrew verb means 'to be right, to be just', while the noun form represents the term *par excellence* used to designate the innocent believer who trusts in YHWH.[50] In the case of Saul it describes just the

49. So Thompson, 'The Significance of the Verb LOVE', p. 338. Cf. also P.R. Ackroyd, 'The Verb Love—*'AHEB* in the David–Jonathan Narrative—A Footnote', *VT* 25 (1975), pp. 213-14 (213): 'What is of greater interest in 1 Samuel...is the subtlety of an author or compiler who, in drawing together older traditions, binds them skilfully into a larger unity by the use of link words and overtones of meaning'. For the etymology of the Hebrew root 'love' see D. Winton Thomas, 'The Root *'āhēb* "Love" in Hebrew', *ZAW* 57 (1939), pp. 57-64.

50. See Ps. 11.7: '(YHWH) loves righteous deeds (*ṣdqwt*); the upright (*yšr*) shall behold his face'; Ps. 107.42: 'Let the upright (*yšrym*) see and rejoice, and every evil man clap shut his mouth' (cf. M. Dahood, *Psalms* [3 vols.; Garden City, NY: Doubleday, 1970], III,

opposite: his murderous intentions toward David. By making the marriage present a hundred dead Philistines, Saul hopes to entice David to his death.

The expression *yšr b'ynw* reminds us of the last sentence in the book of Judges: *bymym hhm 'yn mlk byśr'l 'yš hyšr b'ynw y'śh* ('In those days there was no king in Israel; every man did what was right in his own eyes', Judg. 21.25). This example of 'canon conscious redaction'[51] suggests that now that there is a king in Israel the situation is not really better. The *inclusio* between the twice repeated *yšr b'ynw* implicates both Saul and David in this critique of the monarchy as an institution and the merciless power-struggle which it generates. It is no accident that the term *yšr* is used in the context of the emerging Israelite monarchy. In the ancient Near East, this term carries a socio-political connotation as well. The oriental monarch was supposed to assure justice, often expressed by the terms *yšr* or *mšr*.[52] In eighteenth-century BCE Babylon, Hammurabi is said to have been divinely appointed in order 'to make justice prevail in the land' (*mīšaram ina mātim ana šūpîm*, *CH*, I 32–34). In describing his rule, Hammurabi boasts, *kittam u mīšaram ina pî mātim aškun* ('I made the land speak with justice and truth', *CH*, V, 20).[53] In an Old Babylonian letter from Tell Šemšāra on the Lower Zab, Išme-Dagan, the elder son of Šamši-Addu, reproaches the local governor with committing an unjust act with the potential consequence that the *pî mātim* or 'public opinion' might turn against the unjust ruler.[54] One of the cardinal duties of a 'just king' (*šar mīšarim*) as defined in Mesopotamian collections of laws is that he must rule with 'righteousness' (*kittu*) and 'justice' (*mīšaru*).[55]

p. 80); Ps. 112.2: 'His descendants will be mighty in the land, the generation of the upright (*yšrym*) will be blessed'. See also G. Liedke, '*jšr*', in *THAT*, I, pp. 790-94.

51. The expression comes from G.T. Sheppard, 'Canonization: Hearing the Voice of the Same God in Historically Dissimilar Traditions', *Int* 36 (1982), pp. 21-33.

52. H. Cazelles, 'De l'idéologie royale', *JANES* 5 (1973), pp. 59-73; W.G. Lambert, 'Nabukadnezzar King of Justice', *Iraq* 27 (1965), pp. 1-11; J.-G. Heintz, 'Note sur les origines de l'apocalyptique judaïque à la lumière des "Prophéties akkadiennes"', in F. Raphaël *et al.* (eds.), *L'Apocalyptique* (Etudes d'Histoire des Religions, 3; Paris: Geuthner, 1977), pp. 77-87 (81-82); S.M. Paul, 'Unrecognized Biblical Legal Idioms in the Light of Comparative Akkadian Expressions', *RB* 86 (1979), pp. 231-39.

53. Lit. 'I placed truth and justice in the mouth (of the people of) the land'; cf. M.E.J. Richardson, *Hammurabi's Laws: Text, Translation and Glossary* (The Biblical Seminar, 73; Semitic Texts and Studies, 2; Sheffield: Sheffield Academic Press, 2000), pp. 29 and 41 (P3). See also G.R. Driver and J.C. Miles, *The Babylonian Laws Transliterated Text, Translation, Philological Notes, Glossary* (Oxford: Clarendon Press, 1955), II, pp. 12-13. The laws of Hammurabi are called 'the just laws' (*dinat mīšarim*, *CH*, XXIV, 2).

54. J.-R. Kupper, 'L'opinion publique à Mari', *RA* 58 (1964), pp. 79-82 (80 n. 3, with bibliography; and p. 82). Kupper renders the expression *pî mātim* with 'public opinion'

55. *CAD*, M/II, 1977, pp. 116b-119a. On *mē/īšaru(m)* in Mesopotamian laws, see J.J. Finkelstein, 'Some New *Misharum* Material and its Implications', in H.G. Güterbock

The notion of just rule is not limited to Mesopotamia. It is found in the Northwest Semitic domain as well. Closer to Israel, in the Phoenician inscriptions dating from the tenth century BCE, King Yehimilik of Byblos is designated as *mlk ṣdq* and *mlk yšr*.[56] In Egypt too, the Pharaoh is not supposed to rule arbitrarily. He lives under the obligation to maintain *ma'at* ('truth, justice, righteousness, right order') in the land. Thus it is said of the Pharaoh, 'Thy speech is the shrine of truth (*ma'at*)'.[57] Both Saul and David have banalized the meaning of the concept of *yšr* by using the royal office for private ends. They have failed in their obligation to uphold royal rectitude. In the sixth century BCE, the prophet Jeremiah reminds one of the last descendants of the Davidic dynasty in Jerusalem of the same obligation, 'Do justice and righteousness (*'św mšpṭ wṣdqh*)' (Jer. 22.3).

This cardinal virtue of oriental monarchy was already lacking at the beginning of this institution in Israel. A prophetic letter from Mari dating from the eighteenth century BCE attests to the great antiquity of the requirement that Northwest Semitic tribal chiefs conduct themselves ethically.[58] A prophet of the god Adad in Ḫalab addresses the Bedouin tribal king Zimri-Lim, asking him to provide justice to people who have been oppressed or wronged:

> *[i]-nūma ḫablum u ᶠḫabi[ltum] išassikkum izizzma dinšu ušdin*
>
> If a man or a woman who were wronged appeal to you, stand up and render them justice (lit. judge his case).[59]

and T. Jacobsen (eds.), *Studies in Honor of Benno Landsberger* (AS, 16; Chicago: The University of Chicago Press, 1965), pp. 233-46; *idem*, 'The Edikt of Ammiṣaduqa: A New Text', *RA* 63 (1969), pp. 45-64; F.R. Kraus, *Ein Edikt des Königs Ammi-ṣaduqa von Babylon* (Leiden: E.J. Brill, 1958); *idem*, 'Ein Edikt des Königs Šamšu-iluna von Babylon', in Güterbock and Jacobsen (eds.), *Studies in Honor of B. Landsberger*, pp. 225-31.

56. H. Donner and W. Röllig, *Kanaanäische und aramäische Inschriften* (3 vols.; Wiesbaden: Otto Harrassowitz, 1973–79), I, no. 4, pp. 6-7; II, pp. 6-7 (commentary). Philo of Byblos mentions two divinities called Ṣuduk and Mišôr, which testify the divinization of these ancient royal prerogatives; see M. Liverani, 'Ṣuduk e Mišôr', in *Studi in onore di Eduardo Volterra* (Rome: Giuffrè Editore, 1969), VI, pp. 55-74. The West Semitic terms *yšr* and *ṣdq* are functional equivalents of Akkadian *kittu* and *mīšaru*.

57. Quoted in H. Frankfort, *Kingship and the Gods* (Chicago: The University of Chicago Press, 1948 [repr. 1978]), p. 51. On *ma'at* as attribute of kingship, see pp. 51-52, 149. Cf. also H. Brunner, 'Gerechtigkeit als Fundament des Thrones', *VT* 8 (1958), pp. 426-28. The author has pointed out that the Egyptian throne was mounted on a pedestal identical to the Egyptian hieroglyph for *ma'at*. He ingeniously suggests that this might be the background of the biblical line, 'Righteousness and justice are the foundation of thy throne' (Pss. 89.14 [Heb. 15]; 97.2; Prov. 16.12; 20.28 [LXX]; 25.5).

58. See M. Anbar, 'Aspect moral dans un discours « prophétique » de Mari', *UF* 7 (1975), pp. 517-18 (517).

59. *CAD*, H, 1956, p. 16 *ḫablu*, adjective 'wronged'. Cf. *CH*, xl, 73: *purussē mātim ana parāsam ḫablim šutēšurim*, 'to pronounce legal decisions for the country, to provide

The 'ring' construction of the section in 1 Sam. 18.20a-28b calls our attention to the dynamic of the relationship between the two men. It allows us to understand better David's court language of self-effacement before the king. His answer, 'I am a poor and a negligible man', is more than just an expression of Oriental courtesy. Rather, it is a sign of David's prudence. He is careful not to appear too eager to marry into the royal family because of what such a desire might suggest about his political ambitions. Yet the thing was 'right' in his eyes. He clearly saw it as an opportunity to become the king's son-in-law. The term 'bridegroom' or 'son-in-law' (*ḥtn*), appears five times in this fragment, underlining what is at stake in this transaction.[60] In 18.26 it is explicitly stated that the offer 'pleased him well'. Michal, being the daughter of the king, is a status symbol. Marriage to her gives David a claim to membership in the royal house of Israel, a relationship which he will use later, as king of Judah, to justify his succession to the northern throne as well (cf. 2 Sam. 3.12).

If we are to judge from Egyptian and Edomite parallels, David's marriage to a princess from the royal family would make him legitimate successor to the throne. David's marriage to Michal can be compared to that of the Egyptian general Ḥaremḥab (c. 1335–1308 BCE) with the Egyptian princess Mutnodjme. In the transition between the Egyptian eighteenth and the nineteenth dynasties, the military chief Ḥaremḥab, who was of obscure origin, married an old princess of royal blood with the intention of bringing legitimacy to the royal throne into his House.[61] 'It is known that general Ḥaremḥab, who founded the nineteenth dynasty, married a princess of royal

justice for the oppressed'. YOS, 9, 62.9: *muštēšir ḫablim u ḫabiltim*, 'who provides justice for the oppressed, male or female' (Nidnūša of Dēr). On the verb *izuzzum*, see D. Bodi, *Petite grammaire de l'akkadien à l'usage des débutants* (Paris: Geuthner, 2001), §124.

60. P.D. Miscall, 'Michal and her Sisters', in Clines and Eskenazi (eds.), *Telling Queen Michal's Story*, pp. 246-60 (249). The denominative *htḥtn* can be translated as 'offer one's self as a *ḥtn*'. It involved a payment of a 'counter-gift' (*mhr*) mentioned in 1 Sam. 18.25a (cf. also Gen. 34.12; Exod. 22.16), to the bride's father. It is on the basis of this *mhr* which he paid to Saul that David would later claim Michal back in 2 Sam. 3.14b. On the comparison between the Hebrew *mhr* and Akkadian *terḫatum* in Mari texts and in the Hammurabi Laws, see below, Chapter 2.

61. J.H. Breasted, *Ancient Records of Egypt*. III. *The Nineteenth Dynasty* (Chicago: University of Chicago Press, 1906), p. 17 par. 28. See also p. 14 par. 22: 'To make his claim on the crown legitimate, he next proceeds to the palace of the princess, Mutnezmet, the sister of Ikhanaton's queen, Nefer-nefruaton-Nofretete, who, although, advanced in years, was a princess of the royal line, and is therefore recognized as her husband'. While Breasted thought that Ḥaremḥab stemmed from an 'old monarchical house of Alabastronpolis' (p. 13), A. Gardiner, *Egypt of the Pharaohs* (Oxford: Oxford University Press, 1961), p. 242, rejected this view, saying that 'his parents are unknown, and there is no reason to think that royal blood flowed in his veins…'

blood, with the clear intention of ensuring that he would have legal royal offspring. Ḥaremḥab's deed was undoubtedly no exception.'[62]

In Mesopotamia as well, in Sumerian times, Gudea (c. 2200 BCE) became king of the city-state of Lagash owing to his marriage to one of the daughters of his predecessor Urbaba.[63]

As evidence of the accomplished task Saul demands a hundred Philistine foreskins. According to an accounting addition which transforms the one hundred foreskins (1 Sam. 18.25) into two hundred (v. 27), the narrator probably wanted to show that the son of Jesse not only fulfills the required conditions but fulfills them doubly and in so doing reveals his eagerness to become part of the royal family.[64]

By practicing circumcision the Israelites maintained a cultic-religious contrast to all other nations which did not practice it. In this context Saul's explicit demand for the killing of the 'uncircumcised' gives his proposal a religious sanction.[65] He disguises his murderous intentions under the religious cloak of a quasi-YHWH war. Saul's tendency to manipulate religion for his personal ambitions is manifest in 1 Samuel 15. Coupled with the use of the term *yšr*, which, as noted, has a religious connotation, a double irony emerges in the transaction between Saul and David. The literary form of the *inclusio* implicates both men in the same abuse of religion. These two men have a utilitarian attitude toward their religion. Significantly enough, this 'amoral note' is present in almost all the fragments of the Michal and David story. Saul and David behave as men beyond good and evil.

Most likely out of embarrassment toward his Greek readers who were uncircumcised like the ancient Philistines, Josephus says that Saul required six hundred Philistine heads (*Ant.* 6.10.2). The ancient Egyptians knew the practise of emasculating the vanquished enemies, cutting off their genitals as 'war trophies'. Ramses III (1182–1151 BCE) boasts that his warriors took 12,555 pieces of the cut off genitals (*qrnt*) from their enemies as war

62. C.J. Bleeker, 'The Position of the Queen in Ancient Egypt', in International Congress for the History of Religions, *The Sacral Kingship: Contributions to the Central Theme of the VIIIth International Congress for the History of Religions (Rome, 1955)* (NumenSup, 4; Leiden: E.J. Brill, 1959), pp. 261-68 (266); see also T. Ishida, *The Royal Dynasties in Ancient Israel: A Study on the Formation and Development of Royal-Dynastic Ideology* (BZAW, 142; Berlin: W. de Gruyter, 1977), p. 73.

63. J. Renger, 'The Daughters of Urbaba: Some Thoughts on the Succession to the Throne during the 2. Dynasty of Lagash', in B.L. Eichler (ed.), *Kramer Anniversary Volume* (AOAT, 25; Neukirchen–Vluyn: Neukirchener Verlag, 1976), pp. 367-69.

64. In 1 Sam. 18.27, the MT has 'two hundred foreskins'. Both LXX Vaticanus and Lucianic versions have 'one hundred'. The issue is decided by 2 Sam. 3.14, where the lower number is cited; so McCarter, *I Samuel*, p. 316.

65. So H.W. Hertzberg, *I and II Samuel: A Commentary* (OTL; Philadelphia: Westminster Press, 1962), p. 162.

trophies.[66] The Egyptian word (*qrnt* = [*qernet*]) is used in order to designate one of the characteristics of the phallus of foreign, that is, non-Egyptian ethnic groups like the 'Sea Peoples', as being uncircumcised.[67] For some scholars the Philistines might have been part of the 'Sea Peoples'[68] and this Egyptian perception of them would agree with the way the ancient Hebrews spoke of the Philistines as 'the uncircumcised ones'.[69]

In Mesopotamia, the Annals of Sennacherib (704–681 BCE) mention a similar custom of cutting off male genitals as war trophies:

> *pagrī qurādīšunu kīma urqīti umallâ ṣēra*
> *sapsapāte unakkisma baltašun ābut kīma bīni qiššê simāni*
>
> With the corpses of their (the enemy's) warriors I filled the plain as with grass,
> (Their) testicles I cut off, and tore out their private parts like ripe cucumbers
> (lit. cucumbers of the month of Siwan, i.e. June).[70]

One author finds the reason for David's particular ambition and eagerness to be linked to royalty in his family. Being the youngest of seven (1 Chron. 2.13-15) or eight sons of Jesse (1 Sam. 16.8-11; 17.12), he could not count on

66. See G. Widengren, 'Quelques remarques sur l'émasculation rituelle chez les peuples sémitiques', in *Studia orientalia J. Pedersen dicata* (Copenhagen: E. Munksgaard, 1953), pp. 377-84 (383). E. Meyer, *Geschichte des Altertums* (2 vols.; Stuttgart: J.G. Gotta, 1909), I, §167, takes the word *qrnt* as a foreskin and not as a 'Phallustasche', a sort of special leather pocket which the Lybians used in order to cover their genitals, as attested in texts and iconography.

67. A. Erman and H. Grapow, *Wörterbuch der aegyptischen Sprache* (Leipzig: J.C. Hinrichs, 1931), V, pp. 60-61, relate Egyptian *qrnt* ('Vorhaut') to the Hebrew term for foreskin, *'rlh*. See also R. Hanning and P. Vomberg, *Wortschatz der Pharaonen in Sachgruppen* (Hanning-Lexica, 2; Mainz: Verlag Philipp von Zabern, 1999), p. 323, who understand *qrnt* as '(unbeschnittener) Phallus (bes. als Kriegstrophäe)'; note also p. 757, where *qrnt* is understood to refer to the foreskin of an uncircumcised phallus, which can stand for a 'trophy' ('Beute').

68. D.B. Redford, *Egypt, Canaan, and Israel in Ancient Times* (Princeton, NJ: Princeton University Press, 1992), Chapter 9, 'The Coming of the Sea Peoples'.

69. However, W. Westendorf ('Beschneidung. A.', in W. Helck [ed.], *Lexikon der Ägyptologie* [Wiesbaden: Otto Harrassowitz, 1975–], I, pp. 727-29 [728 n. 9]), thinks that the Sea Peoples were circumcised as over against the Lybians, who were not and quotes Urk. III 54. The text he quotes, however, was translated by N.-C. Grimal, *La stèle triomphale de Pi('nkh)y au Musée du Caire* (Cairo: Publications de l'Institut Français d'Archéologie Orientale, 1981), p. 178 n. 529, who points out that the term used is (*'m'w*) a *hapax* which can mean either 'impure' or 'uncircumcised'. The text says that the various lords from the north could not enter the royal palace because they were uncircumcised and they ate fish, both features being an abomination for the Pharaoh.

70. D.D. Luckenbill, *The Annals of Sennacherib* (OIP, 2; Chicago: The University of Chicago Oriental Institute Publications, 1924), p. 46 col. VI, ll. 9-12. My translation follows that of G. Widengren and of *CAD*, Q, 1982, p. 314; *CAD*, S, 1985, p. 269. *CAD*, S, p. 167, however, translates *sapsapu* with 'lower lip'.

an inheritance.[71] David was poor indeed. Moreover, the symbolic importance of his marriage with Michal is pointed out by the words of David himself, 'Does it seem to you a trifling matter (*hnqllh*) to become the king's son-in-law, seeing that I am a poor and a negligible (*nqlh*) man?' (1 Sam. 18.23). No one takes such an offer for a trifle. Both men view Michal as a means to an end. To her father she is welcome bait which will cause the elimination of his rival. For David the marriage with Michal is an opportunity to further his own cause. For Michal it is the commencement of her tragedy. The ultimate irony is that her love for David is going to become the cause of her ruin.

D.M. Gunn identified a chiastic structure in 1 Sam. 18.20-26, which emphasizes the fact that at the end Saul is no better off than at the beginning of the transaction:

A The thing pleased him (Saul)
  B Saul thought...'let the hand of the Philistines be against him'
    C Saul speaks to David
  B′ Saul thought to make David fall by the hand of the Philistines
A′ And it pleased David to be the king's son-in-law.[72]

Saul's scheme related in this episode achieves the opposite of what he intended. It enhances David's fame as an intrepid warrior and allows him to become an official member of the royal family. The success which accompanies David is taken as a 'proof' by Saul's anxiety-stricken mind that 'YHWH was with David' (v. 28). The success of a scabrous affair, however, is not necessarily a sign of divine blessing. With time one is able to sort out and distinguish the shades in human actions. 'It is grace, says Pindar, grace that transforms everything into honey for humans, gives authority to error and makes us believe what is unbelievable... It is the sequel of days that allows one to discern what is true.'[73]

4. *Michal Sides with David against her Father*

Fragment 2. Michal Saves David's Life (1 Samuel 19.10d-18a):

(10d) And David fled and escaped (*wdwd ns wymlṭ*). (11) That night Saul sent messengers to David's house (*byt dwd*) to watch him and to kill him in the morning. But Michal, David's wife, told him, 'If you do not save (*mlṭ*) your life tonight, tomorrow you will be killed'. (12) So Michal let David down through the window (*wtrd...b'd hḥlwn*); and he went, fled and escaped (*wylk wybrḥ wymlṭ*). (13) Michal took a household idol (teraphim) and laid it on the

71. P.K. McCarter, 'The Historical David', *Int* 40 (1986), pp. 117-29 (119).

72. Gunn, *The Fate of King Saul*, p. 149 n. 10.

73. L. Desnoyers, *Histoire du peuple hébreu: des Juges à la captivité* (Paris: A. Picard, 1930), III, p. 385, quoting Pindar, a sixth-century BCE Greek lyric poet.

> bed and put a pillow of goats' hair[74] at its head, and covered it with clothes. (14) And when Saul sent messengers to take David, she said, 'He is sick'. (15) Then Saul sent the messengers to see David, saying, 'Bring him up to me in the bed, that I may kill him'. (16) And when the messengers came in, behold, the teraphim was in the bed, with the pillow of goats' hair at its head. (17) Saul said to Michal, 'Why have you deceived me thus, and let my enemy go (*wtšlḥy*), so that he has escaped (*mlṭ*)?' And Michal answered Saul, 'He said to me, "Let me go (*šlḥny*); why should I kill you?"' (18a) And David fled and escaped (*wdwd brḥ wymlṭ*)'.

In the present form of the text, the narrative follows immediately after Saul's fit of frenzy with the second attempt to nail David to the wall with his spear (1 Sam. 18.8-10a). Following such repeated scenes of Saul's morbid jealousy, David had to leave the royal court and take refuge in his house. He presumably thought that Saul was prey to another attack of jealous madness and that he would recover as usual. Saul's jealousy, however, is uncontainable as he plots to assassinate David. This episode heightens Michal's tragic condition. The power-struggle throws Saul into fits of paranoia. David has to be eliminated even if he is now his son-in-law and even if that would turn his daughter into a widow.

Despite the seriousness of the situation, this part of the story is told with considerable humor. Michal's ruse of the teraphim and the bedcloth is ingenious and humorous at the same time. Therefore, H. Gressmann described this fragment as *eine humoristische Anekdote*.[75]

The literary unit is defined by the two almost identical phrases which form an *inclusio*: 'and David fled and escaped' (*wdwd ns wymlṭ*, 1 Sam. 19.10d) and 'and David fled and escaped' (*wdwd brḥ wymlṭ*, 19.18a). While the first verb (*nws*) means 'to flee, to escape', the second one (*brḥ*) has a somewhat stronger connotation of fleeing like a homeless fugitive.[76] After Saul's second attempt to assassinate him, David has to abandon Saul's court. Saul sends messengers to Michal's house in order to kill David when he comes out in the morning. The way the conspirators wait in ambush without entering the

74. The meaning of the expression *k^ebîr hā'izzîm* in 1 Sam. 19.13, 'a pillow of goat's hair' (RSV), is doubtful. Since the LXX confused *kbyr* with *kbb* meaning 'liver', Josephus argued that Michal placed a half-living goat's liver in the bed to make the messengers believe that there was a breathing invalid beneath (*Ant.* 6.2.4).

75. H. Gressmann, *Die älteste Geschichtsschreibung und Prophetie Israels* (Die Schriften des Alten Testament, II/1; Göttingen: Vandenhoeck & Ruprecht, 2nd edn, 1921), p. 86.

76. In Jon. 1.3 it is said of Jonah who flees from God *wyqm ywnh lbrḥ tršyšh* ('Jonah rose up to flee to Tarshish'). Jonah has become a homeless fugitive. Isa. 15.5 gives the substantival form *bryḥh* ('her fugitives'), referring to homeless Moabites who flee from their homeland. See E. Jenni, 'Fliehen im akkadischen und im hebräischen Sprachgebrauch', *Or* 47 (1978), pp. 351-59.

house reminds the reader of a similar incident mentioned in Judg. 16.1-2, where Samson went to Gaza to see a harlot. The townspeople surrounded the place to ambush him, and during the night they made plans to kill him, without, however, storming the house. Samson stayed in bed with the prostitute until midnight (*ḥṣy hlylh*) when he escaped. As demonstrated by L. Köhler, there was a reason to feel safe at night in the shelter of a home and with a woman.[77] Owing to the Oriental taboo-like social customs, David was protected as long as he stayed with Michal in the house and the night was not yet over. Köhler cites a similar situation from the life of Mohammed when a group of men tried to kill him. He took refuge in the women's quarter of the house. As the assassins attempted to force their entry into the house a woman began to scream. Thereupon one of the attackers said, 'If we enter the house the whole of Arabia will soon know that we are those kind of heroes who pass by night over the walls of their neighbors, disturb the daughters of their kinsfolk in their sleep and profane the sacrosanct premises of the women'.[78]

German commentators describe this Oriental custom with the expression *Heiligkeit des Schlafes* (holiness of sleep), that is, during the night the neighbor should not be disturbed, his or her sleep being considered sacred.[79] In the two examples of the 'Sodomite Theme' in Genesis 19 and Judges 19,[80] the assault of the rapists occurred during the night, a breach of this Oriental custom that aggravated the offense. Setting these biblical stories in Genesis 19, Judges 19 and 1 Samuel 19 at night shows that something unusual is happening. One author calls this 'the atmosphere-charged potential of the night-time motif'. For 'apart from battle scenes in which armies make use of darkness for tactical purposes, the rule for normal life seems to have been: start a task early in the morning, continue during the day, and finish it in time to be home before darkness'.[81]

Just like Samson, David escaped while it was still night. It was a tactical move used in war conflicts. In warning David, Michal (who knows her father and is still presumably in touch with court informants), reveals Saul's plan to kill her husband.[82] Judging from the way the Mari king Zimri-Lim married

77. L. Köhler, 'Archäologisches', *ZAW* 36 (1916), pp. 21-28 (22).

78. S. Sprenger quoted by Köhler, 'Archäologisches', p. 22.

79. H.-J. Stoebe, *Das erste Buch Samuelis* (KAT, 8.1; Gütersloh: Gerd Mohn, 1973), p. 357.

80. S. Niditch, 'The "Sodomite" Theme in Judges 19–20: Family, Community, and Social Disintegration', *CBQ* 44 (1982), pp. 365-78.

81. W.W. Fields, 'The Motif "Night as Danger" Associated with Three Biblical Destruction Narratives', in M. Fishbane and E. Tov (eds.), *Sha'arei Talmon: Studies in the Bible, Qumran, and the Ancient Near East Presented to Shemaryahu Talmon* (Winona Lake, IN: Eisenbrauns, 1992), pp. 17-32 (21 n. 11).

82. H.-J. Stoebe, 'David und Mikal. Überlegungen zur Jugendgeschichte Davids', in J. Hempel and L. Rost (eds.), *Von Ugarit nach Qumran: Beiträge zur alttestamentlichen*

off his daughters to the same vassal in order to spy on him, it is plausible that Saul too expected Michal to provide him with information on David's whereabouts.[83] In this case, however, Michal shifted allegiance and passed the information to her husband. Her compact sentence reflects the urgency of the situation: 'If you do not escape tonight, tomorrow you are a dead man' (1 Sam. 19.11). The statement is followed by Michal's prompt action and David's immediate compliance: 'Michal let David down through the window (*wtrd*...*b'd hḥlwn*), and he fled and escaped' (v. 12). 'The three verbs for the one in Michal's breathless instructions underline David's single-minded attention to the crucial business of saving himself.'[84] Verse 12 corresponds almost verbatim to the action of the harlot Rahab who saved the Israelite spies in Josh. 2.15 (*wtwrdm*...*b'd hḥlwn*). The mention of the window anticipates 2 Sam. 6.16 (*b'd hḥlwn*) where Michal saw David through the window. In both fragments, here and in Fragment 5, the window represents a limit between inside and outside and therefore stands for a dangerous or liminal space between life and death. J.C. Exum captures some of its symbolism when she comments, 'By letting David out of the window—and Michal is the subject of all these verbs, *wtrd* ("let [David] down"), *wtšlḥy* ("you have let [my enemy] go"), *šlḥny* ("let me go")—Michal figuratively births David into freedom'.[85]

It is owing to his flight to freedom down through the window that David escaped death and saved his life. His house, which should normally be a place of shelter, threatened to become his tomb. David could save his life and continue his existence only by taking to the road. This sharp contrast could be taken as an illustration of a basic existential principle. In order to live it is necessary to have a point of reference, a place where one rests. It is just as necessary to go out of that place and to be ready to take risks. Etymologically the word 'to exist' comes from *sistere* ('to stand') and *ex* ('outside'). One exists only in 'ex-posing' oneself, that is, placing oneself outside, going beyond the limits of one's supposed security and reaching outside, transforming one's place into a base for departure and exploration of what is new and unknown. It is significant that most of the biblical history is presented under this dialectic tension or polarity between being on the road and living at home. There is the nomadic and errant existence of Abraham and the settlement in the promised land; on the one hand the Exodus from Egypt, the

und altorientalishcen Forschung Otto Eissfeldt zum 1 September 1957 dargebracht (BZAW, 77; Berlin: Alfred Töpelmann, 1958), pp. 224-43 (236).

83. For the analysis of the Zimri-Lim analogy, see Chapter 2 of the present study.

84. R. Alter, *The Art of Biblical Narrative* (New York: Basic Books, 1981), p. 120.

85. J. Cheryl Exum, 'Michal: The Whole Story', in *eadem*, *Fragmented Women, Feminist (Sub)versions of Biblical Narratives* (JSOTSup, 163; Sheffield: JSOT Press, 1993), pp. 42-60 (47).

departure into the Babylonian Exile, and on the other hand the biblical ideal of sedentary life 'every man under his vine and under his fig tree' (1 Kgs 4.25).[86]

It appears that the attitude of the story-teller is ambivalent toward Michal. She is portrayed as an energetic and cunning wife who comes to the aid of her husband. In the description of her ruse, successfully camouflaging David's absence by placing the teraphim in the bed, she is depicted as a devoted wife who renounces allegiance to her father in her devotion to her husband. Just like Rahab, the harlot from Jericho, Michal is courageous and resourceful, ready to take a risk in order to secure David's escape. Michal's use of these household idols, which the later tradition regarded as taboo, might indicate that the House of Saul, which the story-teller wanted to discredit, was implicated in idolatry. In 1 Sam. 15.23b, Samuel rebukes Saul, saying that his 'stubbornness is as *'wn wtrpym*, the iniquity of divination (through the teraphim)'. However, the incongruous designation *byt dwd* (v. 11) indicates that there is not much difference between Saul and David since household idols are found in the house of the latter as well. Since in his numerous wars David had the habit of consulting YHWH probably though oracular stones (*wrym wtmym*, Deut. 33.8)[87] and the ephod (1 Sam. 23.1-4, 9-12; cf. 28.6 where Saul consults the *wrym*), it is likely that the teraphim in David's house were used for divinatory purposes as well. Both the biblical references (Ezek. 21.26; Judg. 17.5; 18.14, 17) as well as Mesopotamian parallels tend to confirm the use of the teraphim in divination.[88] Elsewhere the teraphim designate household idols. This was a very ancient custom which did not disappear

86. A. Gounelle, 'La frontière. Variations sur un thème de Paul Tillich', *ETR* 67 (1992), pp. 393-401 (396).

87. W. Horowitz and V.(A.). Hurowitz, 'Urim and Thummim in Light of Psephomancy Ritual from Assur (LKA 137)', *JANES* 21 (1992), pp. 95-115.

88. On the different views concerning the nature of the teraphim, see the following articles: S. Smith, 'What Were the Teraphim?', *JTS* 33 (1932), pp. 33-36 (the author compares the teraphim with the Babylonian practice of burying small terracotta and copper figurines of deities under the floors or in walls of rooms where the sick might be treated; he derives the Hebrew word from *rp'* ['to heal'] and understands the teraphim as 'devil-drivers', that is, driving the sickness away); M. Greenberg, 'Another Look at Rachel's Theft of the Teraphim', *JBL* 81 (1962), pp. 239-48; G. Hoffmann and H. Gressmann, 'Teraphim, Masken und Winkorakel in Ägypten und Vorderasien', *ZAW* 40 (1922), pp. 75-137; C.J. Gadd, *Ideas of Divine Rule in the Ancient East* (Oxford: Oxford University Press, 1948), p. 95 (who adduced Akkadian parallels for the use of teraphim in divination); cf. also K. van der Toorn, 'The Nature of the Biblical Teraphim in the Light of the Cuneiform Evidence', *CBQ* 52 (1990), pp. 203-22 (213-14) (who sees the teraphim as ancestor figurines), and O. Loretz, 'Die Teraphim als "Ahnen-Götter-Figur(in)en" im Lichte der Texte aus Nuzi, Emar und Ugarit', *UF* 24 (1992), pp. 133-78 (with bibliography).

before the exile (2 Kgs 23.24). It appears that already in the time of Saul the possession of these household figurines, the teraphim, was considered wrong. Some commentators attempt to exculpate David saying that the house in question did not really belong to David but to Michal despite its being mentioned as *byt dwd*.[89]

There is a striking resemblance to the teraphim episode between Laban and Rachel in Gen. 31.32. Both Rachel and Michal were the youngest daughters. Both Laban and Saul were tricked. In both cases it was a situation of flight. R. Alter suggests that this allusion is meant to foreshadow a fatality shared by Michal and Rachel, who became the object of Jacob's unwitting curse because of theft.[90]

The deception of Saul's messengers with the help of the teraphim, and the readiness of Saul himself to be deceived, is narrated in such a way as to discredit the first king. It mocks Saul's blundering helplessness together with the ineptitude and obtuseness of his messengers. Because of his obsession, Saul alienates his own family in the effort to alienate them from David.

So far the relationship between Michal and David has literally and figuratively been a one-sided dialogue. First it was remarked twice that Michal loved David while all that could be safely inferred about his attitude toward her was that the marriage was politically useful. Now Michal vigorously demonstrates her love by her words and actions at a moment of crisis while the text envelops David in silence.[91]

After realizing that he was tricked, Saul, for the one and only time in the narrative, enters into direct discourse with Michal, 'Why have you deceived me thus, and let my enemy go?' (1 Sam. 19.17a). Here is a point of similarity between Saul's and David's relationship to Michal. David, too, only once directly addresses Michal in the narrative at the moment of the definitive rupture in their relationship in 1 Samuel 6 (Fragment 5). Michal is perceived as a woman who is acted upon but rarely spoken to.

In this episode Michal appears as a forceful initiator of action. In the following one she is perceived as an object acted upon, passed by her father from one man to another, in contrast to the energetic Abigail.

89. According to W. Caspari (*Die Samuelbücher* [KAT, 7; Leipzig: Deichert, 1926], p. 235), David acquired this house through marriage. In 1 Sam. 17.54, it is stated that David only had a tent (*'hl*).

90. See Alter, *The Art of Biblical Narrative*, p. 120; cf. Stoebe, 'David und Mikal', p. 237.

91. 'Michal betrayed her father in favor of her husband; and as an additional proof of her love, she offered freedom and space to David, instead of keeping him for herself; she preferred life to possession, even amorous possession.' So Kelen, *Les femmes de la Bible*, p. 90.

5. *Saul Severs David's Bonds of Kinship with the Royal Family*

Fragment 3. Michal Married to Another Man (1 Samuel 25.42-45):

> (42) And Abigail made haste and rose and mounted on an ass, and her five maidens attended her; she went after the messengers of David, and became his wife. (43) David also took Ahinoam of Jezreel; and both of them became his wives. (44) Saul had given Michal his daughter, David's wife, to Palti the son of Laish, who was of Gallim.

Fleeing Saul and his troop of three thousand men (1 Sam. 24.2), David, accompanied by only six hundred warriors (25.13),[92] roams the desert and leads the marginal life of a marauder and occasionally serves as a Philistine mercenary. This period of David's career resembles the life of the *'apiru* brigands from El-Amarna times.[93] The *'apiru* were a class of landless people and outlaws in exile who had run away from their overlord and roamed as marauders or mercenaries over vast parts of the Fertile Crescent. David's career follows a well-established pattern of traditional power-struggle between petty overlords in Syria and Canaan in the latter part of the second millennium BCE. Idrimi of Alalaḫ in northwest Syria (modern Tell Atchana) is a notable forerunner of this pattern. According to the inscription on his statue, dating from 1400 BCE, Idrimi was forced to take refuge with the *'apiru* when he was deposed from his position as king of Alalaḫ by a usurper. Like David, Idrimi is a younger brother whose ambition drives him to surpass his elders. With the help of the *'apiru*, he managed to re-establish his rule over Alalaḫ, a city north of Ugarit.[94] Idrimi's success confirms the divine favor he received through omens. For Idrimi as for David, personal triumph signifies divine election. Likewise, according to a series of El-Amarna letters (EA 74; 76; 79; 82; 84; etc.), 'Abdi-Aširta of Amurru (the latter term meaning 'West' in

92. Cf. 1 Sam. 22.2: 'And every one who was in distress, and every one who was in debt, and every one who was discontented, gathered to him; and he became captain over them'.

93. See M. Greenberg, *The Hab/piru* (AOS, 39; New Haven, CT: American Oriental Society, 1955), p. 76 n. 73; G.E. Mendenhall, *The Tenth Generation* (Baltimore: The Johns Hopkins University Press, 1973), pp. 135-36.

94. See G. Buccellati, '"La carriera" di David a quella di Idrimi re di Alalac', *Bibbia e Oriente* 4 (1962), pp. 95-99; N.P. Lemche, 'David's Rise', *JSOT* 10 (1978), pp. 2-25 (12); E.L. Greenstein and D. Marcus, 'The Akkadian Inscription of Idrimi', *JANES* 8 (1976), pp. 59-96. See also E.L. Greenstein, 'Autobiographies in Ancient Western Asia', in J.M. Sasson (ed.), *Civilizations of the Ancient Near East* (New York: Charles Scribner's Sons, 1995), IV, pp. 2421-32 (2425): 'The lengthy narrative of Idrimi's adventures in obtaining and securing his throne is unlike any Mesopotamian text and has its closest parallel in the Egyptian *Story of Sinuhe* and the biblical stories of Jacob, Joseph, Moses, Jephthah, David and Nehemiah'.

Akkadian and designating Canaan)[95] used the *'apiru* for his own purposes and placed Amurru among the leading states in Syria.[96] Geographically closer to David, Lab'ayu of Shechem and his sons transformed their city into a power to be reckoned with in Central Canaan with the help of the *'apiru* (EA 244; 246.6). It seems therefore that in his conflict with Saul, David follows a well-established socio-political pattern of action which different petty rulers in this region had already been using for several centuries.

In 1 Sam. 22.3-4 David takes refuge with the king of Moab of whom he asks protection for his parents. David's relationship with the king of Moab is natural in view of David's Moabite origins through Ruth, the mother of Obed, Jesse's father. Because David had a Moabite great-grandmother, he was barred from Israel's religious community.[97] In light of Deut. 17.15—'You may not put a foreigner (*nkry*) over you, who is not your brother'—David was not the best candidate for kingship in Israel. In later times this fact provoked lengthy discussions among rabbis in both Talmudim. The rabbis in the Jerusalem Talmud (*y. Sanh.* 2.3) argue that Nabal would have been a better royal candidate than David:

> Hezron had three sons as it is written, 'The sons of Hezron that were born to him: Jerahmeel, Ram, and Kelubai (*klwby*)' (1 Chron. 2.9). Jerahmeel was the eldest son. He committed, however, the error of marrying a pagan woman in order to adorn himself with her beauty as it is written, 'Jerahmeel also had another wife, whose name was 'Aṭarah.[98] She was the mother of Onam' (1 Chron. 2.26). [Her name] indicates the vanity that she brought into the house of her husband. Ram [the second son of Hezron] fathered Amminadab and [Amminadab] was the father of Nahshon; the latter begot Salma, who fathered Boaz, who married Ruth [the Moabite] (1 Chron. 2.10-11). I, Nabal, was born of Kelubai [the third son of Hezron] and therefore do not know a better genealogy in Israel.[99]

95. G. Dossin, 'Amurru, dieu cananéen', in M.A. Beek *et al.* (eds.), *Symbolae biblicae et Mesopotamicae F.M.Th. de Liagre Böhl dedicatae* (Leiden: E.J. Brill, 1973), pp. 95-98 (96): 'Si notre interprétation est exacte, à savoir que le dieu Amurru est le dieu de Canaan, le dieu cananéen, nous trouverons là une confirmation de la thèse selon laquelle au temps d'El-Amarna Amurru et Canaan étaient deux termes géographiques qui désignaient le même pays... Si notre lecture est bonne, il s'en suivrait que le dieu Amurru était considéré par les scribes mésopotamiens comme un dieu spécifiquement cananéen.'

96. See Moran, *The Amarna Letters*, p. 379, the index of letters mentioning 'Abdi-Aširta; H. Klengel, *Geschichte Syriens im 2. Jahrtausend v.u.Z.* II. *Mittel- und Südsyrien* (Berlin: Akademie Verlag, 1969), pp. 247-50, 'Abdiaširta und die Ḫāpiru'.

97. 'No Ammonite or Moabite shall enter the assembly of the Lord; even to the tenth generation none belonging to them shall enter the assembly of the Lord for ever' (Deut. 23.3).

98. The anthology of midrashim called *Yalquṭ Me'am Lo'ez*, commenting on 1 Sam. 25.2, picks up this clue and says, 'He married her in order to adorn himself'. Both comments are an example of midrashic exegesis based on a wordplay between *'ṭrh* the name of Jerahameel's wife meaning 'crown, diadem', and the verb *ht'ṭr* ('to adorn [oneself]').

99. *Talmud Yerušalmi* (Jerusalem: Shiloh, 5729 = 1968), p. 20a (Hebrew).

This would explain Nabal's words in 1 Sam. 25.10—'Who is David? Who is the son of Jesse?'—as well as the fact that Nabal is called a Calebite (*klby*) (1 Sam. 25.3). The rabbis in Babylon were aware of the objections raised by their colleagues in Palestine and have provided a lengthy legal discussion in order to rehabilitate David (in *b. Yeb.* 72b). Using a series of biblical quotations and establishing a very intricate relationship between different verses they succeed in 'deconstructing' the statement in Deut. 23.3 and conclude that an Israelite is permitted to marry a Moabite or an Ammonite woman; therefore David should be considered as a full-fledged Israelite.

David and his troop are roaming in the regions of Ziph (1 Sam. 23.14, 15, 19, 24; 26.1-2, corresponding to Tell Zif, 7 km southeast of Hebron), of Maon (1 Sam. 23.24-25; 25.1) or Khirbet Ma'în (14 km south of Hebron), and of Carmel (1 Sam. 25) or Khirbet el-Kirmil (2 km north of Maon). These three places seem to belong to the Calebite clan (Josh. 15.55; 1 Chron. 2.42-45). In view of David's problematic ancestry, the fact that Hebron and its region are connected with Abraham may play a role in providing David with some patriarchal connections: he walks in the steps of Abraham and like the illustrious ancestor respects the local customs of hospitality.[100] In Gen. 23.4 Abraham says that he is 'a foreigner and a sojourner' (*gr wtšb*) in this area of Hebron. His acquisition of a burial place for Sarah is a masterpiece of Oriental courtesy. The connection is maybe intended to intimate that David too acquired Nabal's property while respecting traditional customs of hospitality (see below).

In the first part of 1 Samuel 25, despite the theological filter and the euphemistic language, the nature of the work in which David and his band are involved is taken by many commentators as a form of racketeering: blackmail with the threat of violence in the background. David's troop is perceived as a self-constituted patrol force pressing their services on such wealthy flock owners as Nabal. When the latter refuses to pay, their reaction is that of a gang which has been denied its protection money.[101] What we have here is an ancient custom which survived among Arab tribes and communities of the region to this day. By paying 'protection money', an Arab tribe may shepherd its flocks peacefully under the protection of another tribe. It is called

100. A. Lemaire, 'Cycle primitif d'Abraham et contexte géographico-historique', in A. Lemaire and B. Otzen (eds.), *History and Traditions of Early Israel: Studies Presented to Eduard Nielsen* (Leiden: E.J. Brill, 1993), pp. 62-75 (65).

101. So W. McKane, *I and II Samuel: The Way to the Throne* (Torch Bible Commentaries; London: SCM Press, 1963), p. 152. P.R. Ackroyd, *The First Book of Samuel* (Cambridge Bible Commentary; Cambridge: Cambridge University Press, 1971), p. 195, states: 'On the face of it, what David is doing would today be called "running a protection racket". Those who respond to his demand for "gifts" are protected; those who do not are doomed.'

ḥawa ('Fraternity [tax]').[102] Nabal, a rich owner in the region of Hebron who has three thousand sheep and a thousand goats, refuses to pay. He dies hearing the news that his wife has provided food for David and his troop. He probably realized the nature of the threat that David represented. In 1 Sam. 27.8-9, as a Philistine mercenary, David reserved a particularly cruel treatment for the populations he fought against: 'And David smote the land, and left neither man nor woman alive, but took away the sheep, the oxen, the asses, the camels, and the garments...and David saved neither man nor woman alive...' (v. 11). Commenting on these verses, J. Vermeylen says, 'David's morality has its limits: He does not shrink either from lying [to the Philistines] or from committing atrocities'.[103]

Before settling in Hebron, in 1 Samuel 27 David is in the service of the Philistine king Achish from Gath at the moment when Saul is about to engage in a decisive battle against the Philistines.[104] The fact that David was a Philistine vassal is indisputable from a historical point of view. He appears as a traitor to the Israelite cause.[105] The final redaction of the text attempts to minimize this unpleasant fact without completely evacuating the suspicion that hovers over David's political conduct. An inscription found in Ekron and dating from the seventh century BCE bears the name of Ikaušu as chief of the city.[106] This name resembles that of Akish, and confirms the continuity of this non-Semitic name in the area over several centuries. As a vassal of the Philistines, David breaks away from Saul's fight against them and appears to be an opportunist, adroit in his alliances with the enemies of Saul.

As far as David's conduct towards Nabal in 1 Samuel 25 is concerned, one could propose a more positive reading. While the Masoretic text calls Nabal a Calebite (*klby*, 1 Sam. 25.3), the Syriac version plays with the root *klb* which means 'dog' while the LXX renders it with an adjective (*kunikos*) meaning 'dog-like'.[107] The versions show that from earliest times Nabal's rude refusal was perceived as churlish and as lacking in urbanity. Nabal is a rich farmer

102. J.-A. Jaussen, *Coutumes des Arabes au pays de Moab* (Paris: J. Gabalda, 1908), p. 102.

103. Vermeylen, 'La Maison de Saül', p. 67 n. 70.

104. During this battle Saul and his sons Jonathan, Abinadab and Malchishua perished (1 Sam. 31.2).

105. David's military service to the Philistine ruler Achish of Gath (1 Sam. 27.2) was bound to be seen as a wholesale betrayal of his Israelite tribes. Both Noth and Soggin point out that in the choice of means for the advancement of his own career David 'had few inhibitions'; M. Noth, *The History of Israel* (New York: Harper & Row, 1960), p. 181; J.A. Soggin, 'The Davidic–Solomonic Kingdom', in J.H. Hayes and J.M. Miller (eds.), *Israelite and Judaean History* (Philadelphia: Westminster Press, 1977), pp. 332-80 (345).

106. S. Gittin, D. Dothan and J. Naveh, 'A Royal Dedicatory Inscription from Ekron', *IEJ* 47 (1997), pp. 9-11.

107. The English word 'cynical' is derived from this Greek term.

with three thousand sheep and a thousand goats offering a feast for his shearers, and he yet refuses to give food to famished outsiders. He does not respect the ancient custom of hospitality which is sacred to the Orientals. Moreover, 1 Sam. 25.7 implies initially favorable contact between David's men and those of Nabal. Ancient Near Eastern literature has numerous references to a ritual of hospitality, with a highly coded pattern of behavior (see, e.g., the Myth of Adapa;[108] Ishtar's Descent to the Netherworld;[109] the Gilgameš Epic tablet II, where the savage and marginal Enkidu becomes used to urban life;[110] Inanna and Enki[111]). This 'anthropology of honor' linked to rites of hospitality permitting outsiders to integrate within a community follows this pattern: (1) in exchange of conventional words, carefully avoiding the offense of any party; (2) food, drink and some convivial moments are shared together; (3) the occasion of a toast often becomes a prelude to a challenge followed by a confrontation or verbal joust. Its goal is to judge the newcomer according to the norms of the community. His strength, courage, quick wit or any other quality may be put to the test. It is followed by an agreement and the acceptance of the newcomer.[112]

Referring to the Myth of Adapa and to Ishtar's Descent, A.D. Kilmer points out that the initial contact is crucial. If leniency is gained through manipulation of hospitality rules with flattery or humble supplication, the host will be bound to offer protection to the guest. The leniency consists in a friendly smile if not in a direct salutation. In the case of David and Nabal, 1 Sam. 25.7 implies initially favorable contact between David's men and those of Nabal. 'The salutation is as good as uttering an oath inasmuch as it commits the speaker. This is why a Bedouin may be silent to a stranger, or will question him before offering a salutation, and this is why a stranger may first approach a small child, for once the child has returned the salutation, the family may stand bound by the rule of hospitality.'[113] If this comparison is correct, Nabal would have been bound to respond favorably to the request of David's men, because his own shepherds have already practiced some form of bonding. David sends ten messengers with the specific salutation, 'Peace (*šlm*) be to you, and peace be to your house and peace be to all that you have'

108. See T. Jacobsen, 'The Investiture and Anointing of Adapa', *AJSL* 46 (1930), pp. 201-203.

109. A. Draffkorn Kilmer, 'How was Queen Ereshkigal Tricked? A New Interpretation of the Descent of Ishtar', *UF* 3 (1971), pp. 299-309.

110. A. George, *The Epic of Gilgamesh* (London: Penguin Books, 1999), pp. 101-107.

111. G. Farber-Flügge, *Der Mythos 'Inanna und Enki' unter besonderer Berücksichtigung der Liste der m e* (Studia Pohl, 10; Rome: Pontifical Biblical Institute, 1973).

112. J.-J. Glassner, 'L'hospitalité en Mésopotamie ancienne: aspect de la question de l'étranger', *ZA* 80 (1990), pp. 60-75.

113. Draffkorn Kilmer, 'How was Queen Ereshkigal Tricked?', p. 306.

(v. 6) and with the request for hospitality, that is, food and protection. David expected to receive these in return since he himself had, in the past, given hospitality and protection to Nabal's shepherds. Nabal's violent refusal is a breach of the traditional rules of hospitality. Abigail, however, having heard of David's plan to destroy Nabal and all that is his, rushes out to meet David and his retinue with all the trappings of hospitality: bread, wine, meat, and some grain and fruit. In v. 28 she says, 'Forgive the offense (*pš'*) of your handmaid'. The term is highly significant since it is used for the transgression of covenants taken under oath (Hos. 8.1; Jer. 3.13). In Amos 5.12, one commits a *pš'* when turning away a needy one at the gate.

In the concluding verses of 1 Samuel 25, we find David attempting to increase his power by marrying the widow of a high-ranking member of the clan that controlled Hebron (v. 42), as well as another woman from nearby Jezreel (v. 43). The fact that Abigail has no fewer than five ladies-in-waiting (1 Sam. 25.42), confirms that Nabal, her first husband, was no commoner. J.D. Levenson assumes that Nabal was the *r'š byt 'b* or *nśy'* of the Calebite clan, a status to which David lays claim through his marriage to Nabal's wife. 'It may well be that David picked a quarrel with Nabal with precisely such a marriage in mind.'[114] The political import of David's marriages has already been recognized by Levenson and Halpern.[115] Hebron is the historical and religious capital of Israel where the tombs of the patriarchs are found. David seems to pursue a well-defined political plan of action. From a geographical point of view he occupies important territory. Thereby the way is paved for David to become a prominent figure in the heartland of Judah. Abigail and Ahinoam constitute the beginning of David's harem to which other women are soon added. He now appears as an Oriental potentate. The women from his harem provide David with his first sons (2 Sam. 3.2-23). The idea of securing a sufficient number of sons as potential successors is already present in David's political action. Moreover David does not forget to establish political support groups with the elders of Judah by offering them presents

114. J.D. Levenson, '1 Samuel 25 as Literature and as History', *CBQ* 40 (1978), pp. 11-28 (27).

115. J.D. Levenson and B. Halpern, 'The Political Import of David's Marriages', *JBL* 99 (1980), pp. 507 18. The authors assume that Abigail, Nabal's wife, was in fact David's sister. Accordingly, in the course of tradition transmission, this fact was suppressed because it placed David in the position of an adulterer (an incestuous one at that) and deflated David's royal designation (p. 516). The value of this suggestion is limited because of too many assumptions. They assume that Ahinoam the Jezreelite was in fact Saul's wife (1 Sam. 14.50) whom David took from Saul and married first before marrying Abigail. They argue that this represents the background of Nathan's remark that YHWH gave David Saul's wives along with the kingship in 2 Sam. 12.8. Cf., however, Halpern, *David's Secret Demons*, p. 288: 'Ahinoam is probably Saul's wife or descendant. David took her later than is usually assumed.'

from the royal part of the spoil he collects during his numerous raids (1 Sam. 30.26-31). The investment produces significant dividends, since it is in Hebron that his supporters and the people of his tribe proclaim him as king. It is in Hebron that David establishes his headquarters with his wives and mercenaries, being officially recognized as 'king over the House of Judah' (2 Sam. 5.1-3). There he reigned 'seven years and six months' (2 Sam. 5.5; 2 Kgs 2.11).

As a response to David's increased political influence, Saul marries off Michal to somebody else. The move is clearly politically motivated, as it demonstrates that David has no bond of kinship with the royal family and hence no claim to the throne. What Michal feels about this transaction, or about David and his two new wives, we are not told. Her speechlessness reflects her powerlessness. She is a pawn in a political game between two unscrupulous males. Michal appears as a victim of the power-struggle raging between Saul and David. The Laban–Jacob tradition seems to be alluded to here. Just as Laban cheated Jacob in respect of his work for Rachel and Leah, Saul succeeds in cheating David in respect to Michal. Nothing about Saul seems to be definitive as he marries and remarries his daughter. In manipulating others, his only concern is to bolster his own position. The text is silent about Palti's feelings, and about the very identity of Michal's second husband. In the following episode (Fragment 4), however, Paltiel[116] will have a brief moment of revelation.

6. *David Re-establishes his Ties with the Royal Family*

Fragment 4. Michal Brought Back to David (2 Samuel 3.12-16):

> (12) And Abner sent messengers to David at Hebron, saying, 'To whom does the land belong? Make your covenant with me, and behold, my hand shall be with you to bring over all Israel to you.' (13) And he said, 'Good; I will make a

116. Palti in 1 Sam. 25.44 corresponds to Paltiel in 2 Sam. 3.15; cf. E.R. Dalglish, 'Palti', in *IDB*, III, p. 647; R.F. Johnson, 'Paltiel', in *IDB*, III, p. 647; L.S. Shearing, 'Palti', in *ABD*, V, p. 138. The name Paltiel means 'God is my deliverance'. Name formations with the root *plṭ* were relatively popular throughout Israelite history. In Num. 13.9, Moses sent a certain Palti, son of Raphu, a leader of the tribe of Benjamin with eleven other spies to survey the land of Canaan. In Num. 34.26, the name Paltiel is borne by a leader of the tribe of Issachar. Neh. 12.17 mentions a priest named Piltay. In Ezek. 11.1, 13, one finds the PN *Pelaṭ-Yahu* which can be translated as 'Yahweh's remnant'. But cf. J. Goettesberger, 'Zu Ez. 9.8 und 11.13', *BZ* 19 (1931), pp. 6-19, who translates the name with '*Jahwe lässt entrinnen*'. From an onomastic point of view the Hebrew name *Pelaṭ-Yahu* corresponds to similar Akkadian names such as *Riḫat* ^{d}*Anu* ('Anu's Remnant') and ^{d}*Nabû-riḫta-uṣur* ('Nabû, protect the remnant!'); cf. J.J. Stamm, *Die akkadische Namengebung* (MVAG, 44; Leipzig: J.C. Hinrichs, repr., 1968 [1939]), pp. 305, 288.

> covenant with you; but one thing I require of you; that is, you shall not see my face, unless you first bring Michal, Saul's daughter, when you come to see my face'. (14) Then David sent messengers to Ishbosheth Saul's son, saying, 'Give me my wife Michal, whom I betrothed at the price of a hundred foreskins of the Philistines'. (15) And Ishbosheth sent, and took her from her husband Paltiel the son of Laish. (16) But her husband went with her, weeping after her all the way to Bahurim. Then Abner said to him, 'Go, return'; and he returned.

After Saul's death a bitter civil war ensued between the House of Saul and the House of David (2 Sam. 3.1). The defeated dynasty still had its supporters. The political rivalry was rendered even more acute by old tribal antagonisms which threw the two main houses of the country against each other. The adversaries could only settle their differences by the force of arms. Reduced to occasional skirmishes, the civil war might have lasted a long time. Abner, Saul's commander-in-chief, decided which direction the conflict should take. Abner was too experienced and clear-sighted a general to maintain the hope of seeing the triumph of his weak master, Saul's son Ishbosheth. In 2 Sam. 2.8, Abner took Ishbosheth along and made him cross over the Jordan River to Mahanaim. This is an abuse of authority, perhaps a kidnapping, with the probable aim of preventing Ishbosheth from negotiating with David.[117] Moreover, by taking Rizpah, one of Saul's concubines for himself, Abner assumes the prerogatives of the true successor to his former master. In the ancient Near East, it is a recurrent pattern that the successor of a king appropriates the wives and concubines of his predecessor to himself. To violate the royal harem is not just an act of *lèse-majesté*, but also a public claim to the throne. A few years later, David's son Absalom would do the same thing by publicly sleeping with his father's concubines as a political act of claiming the crown for himself (1 Sam. 16.22). When the tribal king Zimri-Lim conquered Mari, he took over the entire harem of his predecessor Yasmaḫ-Addu. 'The capture of the royal harem and its integration into another harem seems to have been one of the fundamental characteristics of palace life in Syria in Old Babylonian times.'[118]

117. F.H. Cryer, 'David's Rise to Power and the Death of Abner: An Analysis of 1 Samuel xxvi 14-16 and its Redaction-Critical Implications', *VT* 35 (1985), pp. 385-94. According to J.-C. Haelewyck, 'La mort d'Abner: 2 Sam. 3.1-39', *RB* 102 (1995), pp. 161-92, Abner did not necessarily betray Ishbosheth—this is a version introduced by the Deuteronomist redactor. See also *idem*, 'L'assassinat d'Ishbaal (2 Samuel iv 1-12)', *VT* 47 (1997), pp. 145-53; T. Ishida, 'The Story of Abner's Murder: A Problem Posed by the Solomonic Apologist', *ErIsr* 23 (1993), pp. 109*-13*.

118. J.-M. Durand, 'Les dames du palais de Mari à l'époque du royaume de Haute Mésopotamie', *MARI* 4 (1985), pp. 385-436 (389). In the annex no. IV of the same article (p. 436), one finds the list of women in Zimri-Lims's harem that corresponds to the wives from Yasmaḫ-Addu's harem.

Ishbosheth rebukes Abner on account of Rizpah (2 Sam. 3.7) in an attempt to affirm his royal rights. Being just an 'operetta king', Ishbosheth is politically too weak effectively to oppose the strong man of the moment. The incident provokes a separation between Ishbosheth and Abner. The latter enters into direct negotiations with David proposing a military alliance.

Before complying with his request, David demands Abner first to give him back his wife Michal. She reappears at crucial moments in David's career.[119] The latter obviously needs the daughter of the former king in order to legitimize further his own kingship. Indirectly, this incident reveals the important social and political status which Michal possessed and which David wanted to control.[120] Michal has considerable political value for David. The fact that the daughter of the former king is married to Paltiel may inspire David's political enemies with some hopes. David's move does not seem to have been prompted by a sudden return of love for Michal. At the beginning of 2 Samuel 3 it is stated that David continued to increase the number of his wives and concubines. He marries a princess from Geshur. The marriage probably consolidated a political alliance allowing him to isolate further Ishbosheth. Geshur was an Aramean state north of Bashan (2 Sam. 3.2-5). In 1 Sam. 27.8 David made raids upon the Geshurites. The tribes he could not conquer he transformed into political allies through diplomatic marriages.

With his wives and concubines David has six sons in Hebron (2 Sam. 3.2-5). After he obtained the return of Michal, with whom he settled in Jerusalem, David continues to enlarge his harem by taking additional wives and concubines (2 Sam. 5.13). The verses that follow enumerate eleven sons who were born in Jerusalem without mentioning the daughters.[121] These details show how David, as he grew in riches and power, adopts the mores and customs of Oriental monarchs. The harem of a king constitutes one of his most precious possessions and reflects his power and political alliances by the number of women that it contains. By offering each other their daughters

119. The dynastic remarriage of David with the daughter of Saul was intended to underpin David's claim to Saul's former sovereignty over the tribes of northern and central Palestine; so E.L. Ehrlich, *A Concise History of Israel* (New York: Harper & Row, 1962), p. 34.

120. This state of affairs gives some credence to Morgenstern's hypothesis that ancient Israel practiced a *beena* method of access to kingship; cf. Morgenstern's articles, '*Beena* Marriage (*Matriarchate*) in Ancient Israel and its Historical Implications', *ZAW* 47 (1929), pp. 91-110, and 'Additional Notes on *Beena* Marriage (*Matriarchat*) in Ancient Israel', *ZAW* 49 (1931), pp. 46-58; *idem*, 'David and Jonathan', *JBL* 78 (1959), pp. 322-25. On the political importance of former wives of the king in Ugarit as well as in Israel, see M. Tsevat, 'Marriage and Monarchical Legitimacy in Ugarit and Israel', *JSS* 3 (1958), pp. 237-43.

121. Ph. de Robert, 'David et ses enfants', in Desrousseaux and Vermeylen (eds.), *Figures de David à travers la Bible*, pp. 113-37.

or beautiful women, ancient Near Eastern rulers sealed their political alliances. Women served as bargaining money. Another advantage of a harem was the increased number of descendants that could ensure the survival of the dynasty. Plans for an heir seem already to be well anchored in David's actions.

In this connection it is justified to speak of 'David's harem'. The existence of this institution in the Northwest Semitic domain is attested since the eighteenth century BCE. In the Mari royal palace in northern Syria, an entire sector of the building was isolated forming an independent entity which the Assyriologists and archaeologists consider to be the place of the royal harem. The Akkadian texts speak of the 'servants of the *tubuqtum*' literally meaning 'the space delimited by four corners'.[122] The term *tubqum* is therefore taken as the Akkadian word for 'harem'.

In the institution of the royal harem and the polygamy that it entails one should recognize a custom of ancient Near Eastern monarchs. The sarcastic remarks of modern commentators do not take into account the historical context and the political meaning of this social phenomenon. For example, at the beginning of the critical reading of Scripture, Pierre Bayle commented on David's propensity to multiply the number of women in his harem with an admirable understatement: 'One could not say that in respect to the pleasures of love, David had striven much to discontent his nature', while Voltaire in his article on 'The Philosopher' spoke of 'David's prodigious [sexual] incontinence'.[123]

The literary structure tells us how important Michal is for David. David's speech to Abner in 2 Sam. 3.13, forms a chiasmus with a single element at the center showing that this is the focal point of the speech.[124]

'Good; I will make a covenant with you;
but one thing I require of you; that is,
A You shall not see my face (*pny*),
B unless you first bring (*bw'*)
C Michal, Saul's daughter
B′ when you come (*bw'*)
A′ to see my face (*pny*)'.

122. See J.-M. Durand and J. Margueron, 'La question du Harem Royal dans le palais de Mari', *Journal des savants* (Oct–Dec 1980), pp. 253-80 (255); J.M. Sasson, 'Biographical Notices on some Royal Ladies from Mari', *JCS* 25 (1973), pp. 59-78.

123. Ph. de Robert, 'Bayle and Voltaire devant la Bible', in P.-M. Beaude and J. Fantino (eds.), *Le discours religieux, son sérieux, sa parodie en théologie et en littérature* (Paris: Cerf, 2001), pp. 139-53 (149).

124. So Gunn, *The Story of King David*, p. 78. On chiasmus in biblical and ancient literature, see the collection of articles in J.W. Welch (ed.), *Chiasmus in Antiquity* (Hildesheim: Gerstenberg Verlag, 1981).

The return of Michal with her second husband walking and weeping after her is remarkably suggestive. Paltiel is driven into despair by two men of power with whom he cannot contend: Abner and David.

In order to understand why Ishbosheth,[125] Saul's son, agreed to hand his sister over to the enemy of his House, as well as the legal claim on Michal which David made, one has to take into account the similar ancient Near Eastern laws which took a clear stance concerning marital cases like this one. As pointed out by Z. Ben-Barak,[126] a considerable number of Old Babylonian and Middle Assyrian laws state that if a husband be forced to leave his wife by an enemy against his will, his wife is allowed to remarry. The first husband upon his return receives his wife back while the sons born from the second marriage stay with the second husband, that is, they stay with their natural father. Hammurabi's Laws mention a similar situation:

> If a man has been taken captive (or has left surreptitiously *šalālu*), and there is no supply of food in the house, and his wife has entered someone else's house until his return and has given birth to sons, but then her husband comes back and rejoins his community, that woman shall go back to her first husband. The sons shall go after their father. (*CH*, 135)[127]

A. Finet points out that there are two Akkadian verbs—*šalālu* I, meaning 'to be taken captive, make spoil', and *šalālu* II—which in the passive or N conjugation means 'to leave surreptitiously or slide away'.[128] In this case it

125. A. Geiger, 'Der Baal in den hebräischen Eigennamen', *ZDMG* 16 (1862), pp. 728-32, argued that the term *bšt* ('shame') replaced original *b'l* and that it was a phenomenon limited to literature and not reflected in society. Presumably, the change was effected by theologians who were watching over the purity of Scripture and defaming a pagan god. This explanation was replaced by a newer one by M. Tsevat, 'Ishbosheth and Congeners: The Names and Their Study', *HUCA* 46 (1975), pp. 71-81 (76-77). Hebrew *bšt* related to Akkadian *baštu* is well attested in Babylonian and El-Amarna onomastics where it occurs as a constituent part of names, for instance, the Old Babylonian female name *mutibašti* ('My-Husband-is-My-*Baštu*'), cf. *CAD*, B, 1965, p. 143. In personal names *baštu* means 'dignity, pride, vigor', and often personifies a deity. It may also mean 'guardian angel'. Tsevat's thesis has been defended by G.J. Hamilton, 'New Evidence for the Authenticity of *bšt* in Hebrew Personal Names and for its Use as a Divine Epithet in Biblical Texts', *CBQ* 60 (1998), pp. 228-50.

126. See Z. Ben-Barak, 'The Legal Background to the Restoration of Michal to David', in Clines and Eskenazi (eds.), *Telling Queen Michal's Story*, pp. 74-90; B. Lang, 'Du sollst nicht nach der Frau eines anderen verlangen', *ZAW* 93 (1981), pp. 216-24; A. Finet, 'Hammu-rapi et l'épouse vertueuse', in M.A. Beek *et al.* (eds.), *Symbolae biblicae et Mesopotamicae F.M.T. de Liagre Böhl dedicatae* (Leiden: E.J. Brill, 1973), pp. 137-43.

127. Richardson, *Hammurabi's Laws*, p. 85.

128. A. Finet, *Le Code de Hammurapi* (Paris: Cerf, 1973), p. 86. This article in Hammurabi's laws makes a provision which is contrary to the law stipulated in Deut. 24.4, where it is stated that a divorced woman is not permitted to remarry her first husband

would indicate a husband who deserted his home and family. It parallels the way David 'slid away' from his home under the cover of night.

The same provision existed already in the Laws of Eshnuna (par. 29) dating from the nineteenth century BCE,[129] and is found in the Assyrian Laws as well, chronologically closer to the time of David.[130]

David's bloody reminder, 'Michal whom I betrothed with a hundred Philistine foreskins' (2 Sam. 3.14), is meant to stress the legal grounds on which he based his claim for Michal's return. According to the Near Eastern matrimonial laws, he had paid the full bridal price stipulated by her father, he was her first husband, and he left her under the constraints of a *force majeure*. Ishbosheth either had to comply with David's demand or break the basic law and custom of society. 'Its breach was liable to mark Ishbosheth as a ruler who attacked the legal foundations of society, and in consequence as unconcerned about social order and lawfulness in his kingdom.'[131] Here again David uses the ancient Near Eastern concept of *yšr* to his advantage.

There is a blatant contrast between David, who uses carefully weighed public words, and Paltiel, who expresses his grief through publicly visible action. The narrator contrasts the two men, Paltiel, who is emotional and caring, and David, who is cool and scheming. Paltiel is twice called Michal's man or husband (*'yš*), a title to which at least his feelings give him some claim. The word echoes ironically against David's use of *'šty* ('my wife') to designate a relationship with Michal that is legal but probably not at all emotional on his side.[132] This is the only time in the narrative when David calls Michal 'my wife'. The text is silent about Michal. We have no way of knowing whether she feels gratitude, love, pity or contempt for the weeping Paltiel. By being refractory to our curiosity about the emotional aspect of Michal's and David's relationship, the text provokes tension in the reader. It intimates in an oblique way that their feelings for each other are strained. The

if in the meanwhile she had belonged to another man. For the reasons of this biblical prohibition, see Y. Yaron, 'The Restoration of Marriage', *JJS* 17 (1966), pp. 1-11, and G.J. Wenham, 'The Restoration of Marriage Reconsidered', *JJS* 30 (1979), pp. 36-40. According to Wenham, to take back one's initial wife equals committing incest!

129. R. Yaron, *The Laws of Eshnunna* (Jerusalem: Magnes Press, 1969 [2nd edn 1988]), p. 34: 'If a man has been [*made prisoner*] during a raid/or an invasion, or has been carried off forcibly (and) [*dwelt*] in another land for a l[ong] time, and another indeed took his wife and/she bore a son—whenever he returns, he will [*take back*] his wife'.

130. M. Roth, *Law Collections from Mesopotamia and Asia Minor* (SBL Writings from the Ancient World, 6; Atlanta: Scholars Press, 1995), pp. 170-71.

131. Ben-Barak, 'The Legal Background', p. 88. Ben-Barak points out that it was an official preoccupation of Oriental monarchs that their names should be synonymous with order, justice, and preservation of the law. See D.J. Wiseman, 'Law and Order in Old Testament Times', *Vox Evangelica* 8 (1973), pp. 5-21.

132. Alter, *The Art of Biblical Narrative*, p. 122.

story-teller leads us to the resolution of this tension in the following episode where their mutual attitudes are revealed in an outburst of rage and contempt. So far, we have noticed a systematic avoidance of verbal exchange between Michal and David. In an artful way we are led to share in the final explosion of their long suppressed rancor and antagonism.

7. *David the King and Michal the Intractable Queen*

Fragment 5. The Rupture in the Relationship between Michal and David (2 Samuel 6.16-23):

> (16) As the ark of YHWH came into the city of David, Michal the daughter of Saul looked out of the window (*b'd hḥlwn*), and saw King David leaping (*mpzz*) and whirling (*mkrkr*) before YHWH; and she despised him in her heart. (17) And they brought in the ark of YHWH, and set it in its place, inside the tent which David had pitched for it; and David offered burnt offerings and peace offerings before YHWH. (18) And when David had finished offering the burnt offerings, he blessed the people in the name of the Lord of hosts (*yhwh ṣb'wt*), (19) and distributed among all the people, the whole multitude of Israel, both men and women, to each a cake of bread (*ḥlt lḥm*), a meat portion (*'špr*), and a raisin cake (*'šyšh*). Then all the people departed, each to his house. (20) And David returned to bless his household. But Michal the daughter of Saul came out to meet David, and said, 'How the king of Israel honored himself (*nqbd*) today, uncovering himself (*nglh*) today before the eyes of his servants' maids, as one of the vulgar fellows (*rqym*) shamelessly uncovers himself'. (21) And David said to Michal, 'It was before YHWH, who chose me above your father, and above all his house, to appoint me as chieftain (*ngyd*) over Israel, the people of YHWH, and I will dance (*śḥqty*) before YHWH. (22) I will make myself yet more contemptible (*qll*) than this, and I will be abased in my eyes; but by the maids of whom you have spoken, by them I shall be held in honor (*kbd*)'. (23) And Michal the daughter of Saul had no child to the day of her death.

The end of 2 Samuel 6 describes the achievement of some of David's dynastic goals. He captures the Jebusite mountain stronghold and makes it the capital of the dynasty he founds. Finally, in a festive procession, he brings the religious object *par excellence* into 'the city of David': the ark of YHWH.[133] David's political-dynastic ambition receives religious legitimization here by being brought under the aegis of YHWH in this blending of politics and religion. As pointed out by J.R. Porter, Nathan's oracle with the promise of

133. See P.D. Miller and J.J.M. Roberts, *The Hand of the Lord: A Reassessment of the 'Ark Narrative' of 1 Samuel* (The Johns Hopkins Near Eastern Studies; Baltimore: The Johns Hopkins University Press, 1977). In the Akkadian historical accounts of the capture and return of divine statues or images, of which the ark is taken to be the Israelite equivalent, Miller and Roberts adduce numerous Mesopotamian parallels to the so-called 'ark narrative' and its underlying liturgy. See also R.A. Carlson, 'David and the Ark in 2 Samuel 6', in Lemaire and Otzen (eds.), *History and Traditions of Early Israel*, pp. 17-23.

an eternal dynasty in 2 Sam. 7.16 should be read as intrinsically connected with 2 Samuel 6.[134] 'The point of this document (2 Sam. 7) is that one particular son of David is to enjoy the privilege of divine sonship (v. 14a "I [YHWH] shall be his father, and he shall be my son")'.[135] The hope of perpetuating the dynasty held an important place in this celebration. In this episode, however, Michal is the cog that grinds and hinders the realization of David's projects. According to L. Rost, the 'Succession Narrative' begins with the Michal episode because it mentions the absence of an heir that would come from Michal and David.[136] Michal the daughter of Saul represents an important political link between David and the Northern Israelite tribes who remained faithful to Saul. As noted by various scholars, the ark narrative linked to the Michal episode leads to an expected child or ideal successor.

While David is experiencing the peak of his political career, Michal is at the opposite end: she enters the picture as an unhappy spectator. There is a detail about Michal which connects this episode with a previous one, the mention of her 'peeping' through the window (*b'd hḥlwn*, LXX *diekupten*, connects it with Fragment 2 in 1 Sam. 19.12, *b'd hḥlwn*).

The window can also have an ominous connotation. Comparable to other openings like the door, or the opening of the womb, the window represents a frontier between two spaces: the obscure and the luminous, the interior and the exterior, the included and the excluded. In the ancient Semitic world, these spaces being liminal as a frontier between two domains, they were perceived as a dangerous space of conflict. As attested in ancient Near Eastern literature and architecture, this liminal space symbolized the alternative between life and death. This is why at the entrance of ancient Near Eastern temples one finds the statues of guardian angels, in Akkadian called *lamassu*, whose role was to prevent nefarious forces from penetrating into the temple.[137] Moreover, at the highly critical moment of birth, on account of high

134. According to J.R. Porter, 'The Interpretation of 2 Samuel VI and Psalm CXXXII', *JTS* 5 (1954), pp. 161-73, the hope of a perpetuation of the dynasty held a central place in the celebration. K. Rupprecht, *Der Tempel von Jerusalem: Gründung Salomos oder jebusitisches Erbe?* (BZAW, 144; Berlin: W. de Gruyter, 1977), p. 63, however, sees the relationship of 1 Sam. 6 and 7 only on the editorial level. Nathan's oracle in ch. 7, along with the Michal episode and certain other additions to ch. 6, has 'the function of holding together the originally independent stories of David's rise, succession to his throne, and the ark'.

135. Mettinger, *King and Messiah*, p. 62.

136. L. Rost, 'Die Überlieferung von der Thronnachfolge Davids', in *idem*, *Das kleine Credo und andere Studien zum A.T.* (Heidelberg: Quelle & Meyer, 1965), pp. 119-253, especially p. 212: 'das Bindeglied mit der entthronten Familie der Sauliden, ohne Kinder blieb'; and p. 214: 'Michal, die Saulidin, und als solche das politische wichtige Bindeglied zwischen David und den Nordstämmen, blieb kinderlos'.

137. E.D. van Buren, 'The Guardian of the Gate in the Akkadian Period', *Or* 16 NS (1947), pp. 312-32 (312): 'the Guardians of the Gate whose duty it was to guard the

infant mortality, as the baby left the secluded space of the womb to face the daylight, the ancient Semites chanted incantations in order to ensure divine protection and save the child from attacks by demons, baby-snatchers. The first tablet of the Atraḫasīs Epic, dating from the eighteenth century BCE, was traditionally used as a birth incantation.[138] The gates of the cities had to be protected too. In the Myth of Adapa, one of the functions of the sage Adapa, who had magical powers, was to watch the bolt of the door of the city of Eridu in order to protect the inhabitants from danger.[139]

The literary motif of the 'woman at the window'[140] occurs several times in the Bible. In 2 Kgs 9.30, it has a morally negative implication, when Jezebel peeps through the window as a harlot would do (*wtšqp b'd hḥlwn*, LXX *diekupsen dia tēs thuridos*). In Judg. 5.28, we find a morally neutral implication where Sisera's mother waits at the window (*b'd hḥlwn nišqph*, LXX *dia tēs thuridos diekupten*). In Prov. 7.6, we find a 'positive' implication where in a double transposition the observant female wisdom teacher tries to 'entice' the senseless youth who walks in the street in the direction of the harlot's house (*bḥlwn byty b'd*, LXX *parakuptousa*).[141]

The motif of the 'woman at the window' originated in Babylonia and spread to Phoenicia, Cyprus, and Canaan. It corresponds to a sculptural motif known from ivory plaques from Arslan Tash, Nimrud, Khorsabad, Phoenicia, and Samaria.[142] It was known in the territory of ancient Canaan at least a

portals of the divine abode, to drive away any hostile force which might seek to penetrate into the sanctuary...'

138. See W.G. Lambert and A.R. Millard, *Atra-Ḫasīs: The Babylonian Story of the Flood* (Oxford: Clarendon Press, 1969).

139. See Adapa Fragment A, BRM 4.18: [*u*]*mišamma šigār eridu iššar* ('every day he watched the door-bolt of Eridu') in S.A. Picchioni, *Il poemetto di Adapa* (Assyriologia, 6; Budapest: Eötvös Loránd University, 1981), p. 129 (with commentary).

140. For a résumé of the research on this motif together with abundant bibliography and several drawings, see U. Winter, *Frau und Göttin: Exegetische und ikonographische Studien zum weiblichen Gottesbild im Alten Testament und in dessen Umwelt* (OBO, 53; Freiburg: Universitätsverlag, 1983), pp. 296-301, 'Die "Frau am Fenster"'. Cf. also W. Fauth, *Aphrodite Parakyptusa: Untersuchungen zum Erscheinungsbild der vorderasiatischen Dea Prospiciens* (Akademie der Wissenschaften und der Literatur, Abhandlungen der geistes- und sozialwissenschaftlichen Klasse, 6; Wiesbaden: K. Steiner, 1967); F. Neirynck, 'Parakypsas blepei. Lc 24,12 et Jn 20,5', *EThL* 52 (1977), pp. 113-52.

141. See W. McKane, *Proverbs* (OTL; Philadelphia: Westminster Press, 1970), pp. 334, and 359-65.

142. See C. Decamp de Mertzenfeld, *Inventaire commenté des ivoires phéniciens et apparentés découverts dans le Proche-Orient* (Paris: Boccard, 1954), nos. 847-61, 939-46, 982-85; J.W. Crowfoot and Grace M. Crowfoot, *Early Ivories from Samaria* (London: Palestine Exploration Fund, 1938), p. 29, plate XII, fig. 2; F. Thureau-Dangin, A. Barrois, G. Dossin and M. Dunand, *Arslan Tash* (Bibliothèque archéologique et historique, 16; Paris: Geuthner, 1931), I, p. 116; D. Barnett, 'The Nimrud Ivories and the Art of the Phoenicians', *Iraq* 2 (1935), pp. 179-210 (185); M.E.L. Mallowan, *Nimrud and its*

millennium before the time of Michal. The archaeological excavations at Byblos on the Mediterranean coast have revealed a building adjacent to the temple of the goddess of Byblos, contemporary to the Old Kingdom in Egypt (end of the third millennium BCE). The building had access to the courtyard of the temple. It had a double *loggia* or a covered balcony dominating the courtyard. The archaeologist responsible for the excavation suggests that the spectators gathered in the courtyard watching a particular scene where, from the balcony, women in the service of the goddess solicited the attention of passers-by.[143] This motif was also known to pre-Hellenic Greeks.[144] In 1927 Herbig suggested a relationship between this sculptural motif and the literary one known to the Greeks as *Aphrodite parakuptousa* ('Aphrodite Peeping-Out [a Window]', mentioned by Aristophanes and Plutarch) and to the Romans as *Venus prospiciens*, in which the goddess, like her sacred harlots, allures passers-by from her window.[145]

The 'woman-at-the-window'-motif also has a funeral connotation, as pointed out by G. Contenau[146] who sees in it an original connection with

Remains (London: Collins 1966), p. 2, plate V; J. Thimme, *Phönizische Elfenbeine: Möbelverzierungen des 9. Jahrhunderts v. Chr. Eine Auswahl aus den Beständen des Badischen Landesmuseums* (Bildhefte des Badischen Landesmuseums Karlsruhe; Karlsruhe: C.F. Müller, 1973), nos. 13-15; C.E. Suter, 'Die Frau im Fenster in der orientalischen Elfenbein-Schnitzkunst des frühen 1. Jahrtausends v. Chr.', *Jahrbuch der Staatlichen Kunstsammlungen in Baden-Württemberg* 29 (1992), pp. 7-28.

143. M. Dunand, *Fouilles de Byblos* (Paris: Geuthner, 1937), I, p. 334; *idem*, 'Review of J.W. Crowfoot and G.M. Crowfoot, *Early Ivories from Samaria*, 1938', *Syria* 20 (1939), pp. 379-80 (380).

144. In Enkomi on the island of Cyprus a bronze socle was found dating from the Mycenean times with a representation of a pair of women figures looking through the window; see A.S. Murray, A.H. Smith and H.B. Walters, *Excavations in Cyprus* (London: British Museum, 1900), plate III. The authors were among the first to relate this motif to the following Old Testament passages: Judg. 5.28; 2 Sam. 6.16; 2 Kgs 9.30.

145. R. Herbig, 'Aphrodite Parakyptusa', *OLZ* 30 (1927), cols. 917-22. H. Zimmern ('Die babylonische Göttin im Fenster', *OLZ* 31 [1928], cols. 1-3) argued that the motif originated in Babylonia and from there travelled to Israel, Phoenicia and Cyprus. He related the motif to the goddess ^{d}*Kilili ša apāti* 'Kilili of the windows' (cf. E. Reiner, *Šurpu: A Collection of Sumerian and Akkadian Incantations* [*AfO* Beiheft, 11; Graz: Im Selbstverlage des Herausgebers, 1958], p. 21, tablet III, l. 78). Zimmern assumed that the sacred harlots of Kilili, a form of Ištar, allured men from the window. He derived the name of the goddess from Akkadian *kililu* ('crown'), which the harlots made with their hair, and compared it with 2 Kgs 9.30 where Jezebel at the window 'adorned her head'. However, *CAD*, K, 1971, p. 357, translates *mušīrtu ša apāti* with 'who leans into the windows' and *ša apāta ušarru* with 'who leans into (the house) through the windows'. For a photographic reproduction see *ANEP*, p. 39, no. 131.

146. G. Contenau, *Manuel d'archéologie orientale depuis les origines jusqu'à l'époque d'Alexandre* (4 vols.; Paris: A. Picard, 1927–47), III, pp. 1334-35, fig. 838; IV, p. 2226.

death and Egyptian *mastabas* (tomb constructions). The woman would represent the dead person looking from the tomb through the hatch window which was built for the purpose of allowing the deceased to 'see' the visitors.

The motif of the 'woman at the window' associated with Michal announces the death of her relationship with David. Michal at the window also has a proleptic function. It anticipates the death of Saul's last descendants; she will bear no ideal heir who would unite the two royal families. Moreover, her presence serves to foreshadow the rest of the Deuteronomistic history with the death of the Israelite monarchy as an institution.

It seems that in the case of Michal there was a blending of two pictures: the negative one connected with seduction, which probably reflects the anti-Saulide stance, and a more neutral one, that of the 'waiting woman', like Sisera's mother waiting in vain for her son who died in combat (Judg. 5.28).[147] In world literature we often find the following equation: the widow = the husbandless woman = the enticing harlot.[148] What can be safely inferred from this image of Michal at the window is that she was practically a husbandless woman, an ever-waiting and neglected wife. Her subsequent words clearly reveal her resentment over David's indifference to her all these years, over the other wives he has taken, and perhaps, over being torn away from the devoted Paltiel.[149]

In the present form of the text, the story of the ark and that of Michal's childlessness appear as well-integrated narrative. Verse 20a provides a neat *inclusio* with the preceding ark narrative: v. 12 speaks of YHWH blessing the household of Obed-Edom (*wygd lmlk dwd l'mr, brk yhwh 't-byt 'bd 'dm*). In v. 20a, David himself blesses his household (*wyšb dwd lbrk 't-bytw*). Furthermore, v. 16b, 'and she saw king David leaping and dancing before YHWH (*wtr' 't-hmlk dwd mpzz wmkrkr lpny yhwh*), requires v. 14, 'and David danced before YHWH with all his might' (*wdwd mkrkr bkl-'z lpny yhwh*). Instead of speculating about the original position of the Michal story, it might be more useful to see what has been achieved by the juxtaposition of these

147. P.K. McCarter, *II Samuel: A New Translation with Introduction, Notes and Commentary* (AB, 9; Garden City, NY: Doubleday, 1984), p. 172. N. Poulssen, 'De Mikal-scène 2 Sam. 6, 16, 20-23', *Bijdragen: Tijdschrift voor Filosofie en Theologie* 39 (1978), pp. 32-58.

148. In *Alexis Zorba* (Paris: Plon, 1954), by N. Kazantzakis, the widow of the village is killed under the accusation that she has become a harlot (so also in the motion picture by N. Cacoianis, 'Zorba the Greek' with Anthony Quinn); cf. also J. Eisenberg and A. Abecassis, *Et Dieu créa Eve* (Paris: A. Michel, 1979), p. 227, 'Nous connaissons ces stéréotypes: la femme tentatrice, la femme séductrice, la femme qui ouvre la boîte de Pandore du Mal', and M.A. Fergusson, *Images of Women in Literature* (Boston: Houghton Mifflin, 1973). The fact that Michal had five sons with another man might have been interpreted in certain circles as harlotry in respect to David, her first husband.

149. So Alter, *The Art of Biblical Narrative*, p. 123.

two stories. The ark has a double symbolism. It can bring blessing but also death. During the transportation of this sacred object Uzzah died because he touched it (2 Sam. 6.6). David, angry at this unnecessary death, left the ark at Obed-Edom's house. However, realizing that Obed-Edom's house was blessed by YHWH, David quickly takes all the measures necessary to secure the same blessing for himself. However, the contrasting *inclusio* is highly significant. While in v. 12 YHWH is the agent who blesses Obed-Edom's house, in v. 20a David is the one who blesses his household. David appears as an inveterate opportunist, always ready to push YHWH's hand for the sake of personal aggrandizement and gratification. By bringing the ark into Jerusalem, David is accomplishing a major achievement in his internal policy. The main Yahwistic symbol is under his roof, representing the crowning of his life-long work for political supremacy over the Israelite tribes. YHWH, however, does not seem so docile and supportive of all of David's clever schemes. The ark also brings death to the relationship of David and Michal. It might be a mistake to assume that Michal's childlessness places only her in an unfavorable position; David might be an even greater loser:

> In the case of Michal the accession and sexuality themes are inseparably bound together. She is potentially both a sexual partner and a means of royal legitimation. Her failure in the one regard, she bears no child, entails David's failure in the other. There is to be no child who might have been that political convenience, a son of both houses.[150]

The motif of the absence of a royal descendant is quite common in world literature. The news of the childlessness of the queen fits well into the beginning of a narrative dealing with the succession to David's throne. The question of who will occupy David's throne is answered negatively so that the possibility of complication arises in a way similar to that known to us from the seventh book of Herodotus's *History* (7.1-3) or from Xenophon's *Anabasis*.[151]

Michal's childlessness is a major blow to David's dynastic and political ambitions. The verbal exchange between Michal and David is a master-piece of compactness, whipsaw sarcasm, assonance and double-entendre. It reflects the high-tension fusion of the personal and the political aspects of their relationship. The three key words are *glh*, *qll*, and *kbd*, which in the niphal form mean, 'to expose oneself, to dishonor oneself, to be honored'. In

150. Gunn, *The Story of King David*, p. 94. I reject the interpretation of G. Auzou, *La danse devant l'arche: Etude du livre de Samuel* (Paris: Editions de l'Orante, 1968), pp. 268-69, who uncritically indulges in a form of hero worship describing David in superlatives and denigrating Michal as an ill-humored woman, unable to enjoy David's success.

151. So Rost, *Succession to the Throne of David*, p. 85. The account of Xerxes' invasion of Greece begins with the issue of who is going to succeed King Darius.

v. 20, Michal ironically refers to David's 'enjoying honor' (*nkbd*), but implying the opposite, that he has dishonored himself. This is clear in the clause which immediately follows, 'by flaunting himself before the eyes of his servants' maids (*'šr nglh hywm l'yny 'mhwt 'bdyw*) as one of the vulgar fellows shamelessly uncovers himself!' The term *nglh* meaning 'to expose oneself', makes David an exhibitionist in the technical sense of the word. Michal, the offended and neglected wife, might be suggesting that David had earned a certain sexual honor with the maids. F. Crüsemann has argued that the above verses preserve the remnant of a popular derogatory joke about David's sexual incontinence.[152] Apparently, David's sexual-erotic propensity had become a subject of general gossip. Judging from the story of David and Bathsheba (2 Sam. 11–12),[153] and that of his children Amnon and Tamar (2 Sam. 13), the court of David was not lacking in infamous affairs.

The term used to designate David as 'one of the vulgar fellows', or 'nobodies' (*rqym*), stands in dynamic opposition to 'honored' (*kbd*). The same opposition occurs in El-Amarna Akkadian between 'empty' (*rīqa*) and 'heavy, important, honored' (*kabta*). In EA 1, the Pharaoh complains to the king of Babylon regarding the status of the messengers he has sent to Egypt: they are 'nobodies' (*rīqa*) in contrast to those who are honored, who should have been sent (EA 1.15, 18, *kabta*).[154] This implies a breach in international relations; their treaty is not properly honored. In EA 245.36, Akkadian *qalālu* and *kabātu* seem to correspond to their Hebrew cognates *kbd* and *qll* in our Fragment 5. In the former, Biridiya the vassal of Egypt bitterly complains to the Pharaoh of having 'diminished' him while having 'honored' his 'less important' fellow vassals called 'brothers' in the ancient Near Eastern covenant idiom: 'What have I done to the king, my lord [the Pharaoh], that he has treated me with contempt: *ia*$_8$*-qí-ìl-li-ni* and honored: *ia*$_8$*-ka-bi-id* my less important brothers?' In EA 88.46-47, Rib-Hadda of Byblos protests jealously to the Pharaoh that 'the messenger of the king of Akko is more honored than (my) messenger' (*mār šipri šar Akka kabbit ištu mār šipr*[*īya*]).[155] This opposition is part of the ancient Near Eastern 'anthropology of honor and shame',

152. F. Crüsemann, 'Zwei alttestamentliche Witze', *ZAW* 92 (1980), pp. 215-17; *idem, Die Widerstand gegen das Königtum* (Neukirchen–Vluyn: Neukirchener Verlag, 1978), p. 181: 'Formgeschichtlich muss die Michal-Scene als ein eigenständiges Stück, eine Art Apophtegma, angesehen werden, das sein Zentrum in einem recht derben Wort Davids hat, mit dem Davids—offenbar bekannte—erotische Betätigung angesprochen wird, von der ausgerechnet Michal ausgenommen bleibt'.

153. R.C. Bailey, *David in Love and War: The Pursuit of Power in 2 Samuel 10–12* (JSOTSup, 75; Sheffield: JSOT Press, 1990).

154. Moran, *The Amarna Letters*, p. 3 n. 6, and S.M. Olyan, 'Honor, Shame, and Covenant Relations in Ancient Israel and its Environment', *JBL* 115 (1996), pp. 201-18, especially p. 205 n. 11 on *qll* and *kbd*.

155. Moran, *The Amarna Letters*, pp. 161, 299.

used in the context of covenant relationships. Coupled with the opposition between *qll* and *kbd*, corresponding to Akkadian *qalālu* and *kabātu* which, as demonstrated by S. Olyan, also belongs to ancient Near Eastern covenant terminology, Michal might be implying that David's dance represents a breach of the covenant with YHWH.

The verb used in order to describe David's dance 'before YHWH' (2 Sam. 6.21, *śḥqty*; cf. also v. 5, *mśḥqym*) is highly significant. In certain contexts, *śḥq* can have an erotic connotation. The term being ambiguous and equivocal, if not outright obscene, F. Langlamet points out how several Greek versions employed considerable effort in order to circumvent, neutralize or substitute this bothersome term of the Masoretic text:

> 'To dance' in such a manner, if one may say so, between the divine Name and the relative proposition of which YHWH was both the antecedent and the subject (v. 21a), was not tolerable. It was a sort of sacrilege that had to be attenuated or prevented by substituting the more neutral term (*orchoumenon* = *rqd*) for *śḥq* which was too equivocal (G); it had to be exorcized or replaced with a benediction (G^B), or conjured by an oath (G^L).[156]

Moreover, already the Hebrew text seems to have been tempered by the redactors and scribes. According to the literary analysis of Schulte and Veijola, the expression *lpny yhwh* in v. 21, where David argues that he is dancing 'before YHWH', is a later Deuteronomistic addition which tones down David's crude allusion and transforms his reply into an expression of piety.[157]

In Gen. 26.8, Abimelech looking through the window (*wyšqp…b'd hḥlwn*) sees Isaac engaged in 'love-play' or 'love-making' (*ṣḥq*) with Rebekah and understands immediately that she is his wife and not his sister.[158] In Gen. 39.14, 17, disappointed by not being able to bring Joseph into her bed, Potiphar's wife accuses him of having fondled or maybe 'harassed her sexually' and uses the same term (*ṣḥq*). In the episode of the golden calf in Exod. 32.6, the term describes a cultic, erotic dance in front of a deity. O. Keel has collected a series of iconographic data from Egypt where dance, including erotic types, were used in order to entertain the divinity.[159] Building on this

156. Langlamet, 'David, fils de Jessé', p. 44.

157. Schulte, *Die Entstehung*, p. 146 n. 43, and T. Veijola, *Die ewige Dynastie: David und die Entstehung seiner Dynastie nach der deuteronomistischen Darstellung* (Annales Academiae Scientiarum Fennicae B, 193; Helsinki: Suomalainen Tiedeakatemia, 1975), p. 67.

158. There is no apparent difference in meaning between *śḥq* and *ṣḥq*. It is comparable to another Hebrew root *ṣ'q* and *z'q* which both mean 'to cry'; cf. D. Bodi, *The Book of Ezekiel and the Poem of Erra* (OBO, 101; Freiburg: Universitätsverlag, 1991), p. 160, on Gen. 18.20 (*z'qh*), 'the outcry against Sodom and Gomorrah', and Gen. 19.13 (*ṣ'qh*), 'the outcry'.

159. See O. Keel, *Die Weisheit spielt vor Gott: Ein ikonographischer Beitrag zur Deutung des mesahäqät in Spr 8,30f* (Freiburg: Universitätsverlag, 1974), pp. 31-45,

evidence, U. Winter has suggested that David's dance during the transportation of the ark had some such erotic aspect to it.[160] Seen in this light, the objection which Michal makes concerning David's dance might reflect the view of Yahwistic circles which were uncomfortable with the religious syncretism introduced by the new king. We would suggest that this might be the reason why the Michal tradition has been preserved and inserted into the Davidic narrative cycle.

Apparently, David is not dancing alone. He plays the role of a dance leader in front of a group of dancers. Women participate together with the rest of the people in the general frenzy of a pagan fertility dance.[161] The terms 'leaping' (*mpzz*) and 'whirling' (*mkrkr*) describe the manner of the dance. The term *mkrkr* is extremely rare. It appears twice and exclusively in connection with David's dance before the ark (vv. 14 and 16). This feature of vocabulary would tend to confirm the antiquity of this fragment of the Michal tradition. The term was no longer understood in later periods. 1 Chronicles 15.29 replaces it with *rqd* ('to leap'), but retains the term *śḥq* ('dancing').[162] The term *rqd* suggests the skipping or leaping of rams, calves or bucks (Pss. 29.6; 114.4; Isa. 13.21) as well as the bouncing or jolting of chariots (Joel 2.5; Nah. 3.2). The Jerusalem Talmud (*Yom Ṭob* 5.63a) describes the action of *riqqud* in the following way, 'when dancing, one lifts one foot and then another', in opposition to *qippuṣ* where one jumps into the air with both feet together.

Following the LXX reading *orchoumenon* ('one dancing'), H. Orlinsky suggested reading *hā-rōqdîm* ('one of the dancers') instead of the Masoretic *hā-rēqîm* ('one of the vulgar fellows'). This reading reminds one of the pagan cultic dance known among the Phoenicians as reflected in the divine name *b'lmrqd* ('The dancing Ba'al'), known in Greek as *balmarkōdi* and *balmarkōs*.[163]

To explain the two rare Hebrew verbs used in this fragment, A. Caquot suggests that we relate *mkrkr* to the Arabic *takarkara* ('gyrate, to fly about, to

Figs. 1-19. In Jer. 31.3, however, the term *śḥq* has a neutral connotation: 'O virgin of Israel; again you shall adorn yourself with timbrels; and shall go forth in the dance of the merry-makers (*mḥl mśḥqym*)'.

160. Winter, *Frau und Göttin*, p. 522.

161. The Babylonian Talmud relates a rabbinic opinion hostile to such mixed dancing groups: 'If men sing and women respond, there is indecency; if women sing and men respond, it is like adding fuel to the flame' (*b. Soṭ.* 48a).

162. 'As the ark of the covenant of YHWH arrived at the City of David, Michal daughter of Saul looked out of the window and saw king David leaping (*mrqd*) and dancing (*mśḥq*), and she despised him in her heart'.

163. H.M. Orlinsky, '*Hā-rōqdīm* for *hā-rēqīm* in II Samuel 6.20', *JBL* 65 (1946), pp. 25-35.

flutter'), and *mpzz* to the Arabic *fazza* ('to bounce, to jump').[164] In this dance, probably of Canaanite origin, we imagine more some kind of disorderly gesticulation rather than harmonious graceful figures. Morever, David performs the dance in a state of ritual nudity for he is wearing a sort of loincloth which flies away in the whirl of the dance.[165] David's nudity in this ritual dance offends Michal who probably recognizes in it an element of the Canaanite fertility cult foreign to Yahwism. According to M. Weinfeld, one Hittite ritual attests to the practise of transporting sacred objects in a chariot supervised by two persons and accompanied by dancers, one of whom was naked.[166] Moreover, nudity was traditional in pilgrimages among pre-Islamic Arabs.[167] A. Caquot points out that 'such an appearance underlines the erotic character of the dance and the general meaning of the cult of which it was part'.[168] The injunction found in Exod. 28.42-43 'to make breeches for Aaron and his sons in order to cover their naked flesh' was probably a reaction to the ancient Canaanite and pagan practice of ritual nudity.

The term *krkr* appears three times in Ugaritic epic texts as a stereotypical description of someone showing joy. There is no agreement, however, as to its exact meaning. Should it be rendered 'to turn, to twiddle' or 'to snap (one's fingers)'?:

> When god El sees Athirat,
> he opens his jaws and laughs (*yprq lṣb wyṣḥq*);
> his feet upon the footstool he stamps (*p'nh lhdm yṯpd*)
> and snaps his fingers (*wykrkr uṣb'th*).[169]

2 Samuel 6.19 describes how David distributed among all the people, 'both men and women, to each a cake of bread (*ḥlt lḥm*), a meat portion (*'špr*), and a raisin cake (*'šyšh*)'. The term *'špr* only occurs twice in the Bible here and

164. A. Caquot, 'Les danses sacrées en Israël et à l'entour', in J. Cazeneuve *et al.* (eds.), *Les danses sacrées (Anthologie)* (Sources orientales, 6; Paris: Seuil, 1963), pp. 121-43 (140 n. 13).

165. McCarter, *II Samuel*, p. 171: 'In contrast to the ornate garment of the high priest (Exod. 28; 39), the ephod referred to here is a simple linen loincloth like that worn by the child Samuel (1 Sam. 2.18)'. See also A. Phillips, 'David's Linen Ephod', *VT* 19 (1969), pp. 485-87; N.L. Tidwell, 'The Linen Ephod', *VT* 24 (1974), pp. 505-507.

166. M. Weinfeld, 'Traces of Hittite Cult in Shiloh and Jerusalem', *Shnaton* 10 (1986–89), pp. 107-14 (Hebrew) + xvii-xviii (English abstract).

167. J. Wellhausen, *Reste arabischen Heidentums gesammelt und erläutert* (Berlin: W. de Gruyter, 3rd edn, 1961), p. 110.

168. Caquot, 'Les danses sacrées', p. 127.

169. *CTCA* 4 = II AB, IV.26-29 (quoted here); I AB III.14 and II D II.10. Y. Avishur, '*Krkr* in Biblical Hebrew and in Ugaritic', *VT* 26 (1976), pp. 257-61, who argues that *krkr* in Ugaritic means 'snapping (one's fingers)'. See also G.W. Ahlström, '*Krkr* and *ṯpd*', *VT* 28 (1978), pp. 100-101; A. Caquot, M. Sznycer and A. Herdner, *Textes ougaritiques*, I (LAPO, 7; Paris: Cerf, 1978), p. 204, translate it with 'fait tournoyer ses doigts'.

in the parallel passage in 1 Chron. 16.3.[170] The raisin cake (*'šyšh*) is mentioned by the eighth-century BCE prophet Hosea who connects it with idolatry associated with Canaanite fertility cults (*'šyš*, Hos. 3.1). It is mentioned in Isa. 16.7 (*'šyš*) in an oracle against Moab as being part of their typical practises. In Song 2.5 one of the lovers exclaims, 'sustain me with raisins (*'šyš*)... for I am sick with love'. They are thought to have had an aphrodisiac effect and are part of the ancient *hieros gamos* rite underlying the Song of Songs.[171] The *kwnym* that Jeremiah denounces in Jer. 7.18 and 44.19, offered to 'the Queen of Heaven', were also some kind of cakes. The Queen of Heaven stands for the great Mesopotamian goddess Ištar (Aštart), as it appears from the iconography of some jewels and seals found in archaeological excavations in Israel and dating from the time of Jeremiah.[172]

David seizes Michal's sarcastic 'honored' and turns it into a defiant, 'I will dishonor myself (*wnqlty*)' in v. 22. The two terms *kbd* and *qll* stand out against each other in two contrasting levels of meaning: their original sense is 'heavy' and 'light', while their derived sense is 'honor' and 'dishonor'. By the use of the same vocabulary (*qll*) the text is referring back to the beginning of David's relationship with the House of Saul where David asked whether it was a 'light or trifling thing' (*hnqlh*) in Saul's eyes to be the king's son-in-law, seeing that David was a 'poor man and lightly esteemed' (*nqlh*, 1 Sam. 18.23). Both David and Michal are aware that Michal represented an important rung in the ladder of David's rise to power. David picks up Michal's double entendre and adds *whyyty špl* ('and humiliate myself', v. 22), which may suggest pious modesty before YHWH.[173] David continues with an allusion to the honor from the maids which Michal already mentioned (*w'm-h'mhwt 'šr 'mrt 'mm 'kbdh*, 'but by the maids of whom you have spoken, by them I shall be held in honor', v. 22). What David calls 'honor' is perceived as 'dishonor' by Michal, a probable reference to some Canaanite *hieros gamos* rite.

As far as ancient Mesopotamia was concerned,

170. The meaning is uncertain. For a 'choice cut of meat', see the rabbinic tradition *b. Pesaḥ.* 36b, one sixth of a bullock (*šiššît hap-pār*) and Rabbinic Aramaic *šwpr'* ('beauty, best portion [of meat]'). This explanation fits the context, since according to 2 Sam. 6.13, 'when those who bore the ark had gone six paces, he sacrificed an ox and a fatling'. The rabbis suggest that David distributed the meat of the sacrifices to the people.

171. F.I. Andersen and D.N. Freedman, *Hosea* (AB, 24; Garden City, NY: Doubleday, 1983), p. 298; E. Jacob, C.A. Keller and S. Amsler, *Osée, Joël, Amos, Abdias, Jonas* (CAT, 11a; Geneva: Labor & Fides, 1985), p. 35.

172. T. Ornan, 'Ištar as Depicted on Finds from Israel', in B. Mazar (ed.), *Studies in the Archaeology of the Iron Age in Israel and Jordan* (JSOTSup, 331; Sheffield: Sheffield Academic Press, 2001), pp. 235-56.

173. So McCarter, *II Samuel*, p. 187, cf. Prov. 29.23: *wšpl-rwḥ ytmk kbwd* ('honor shall uphold the humble in spirit').

> One of the primary functions of the king...was to secure the fertility of the land by means of the annual performance of the sacred marriage ceremony. This ritual involved the king playing the role of Dumuzi-Ama'ušumgalanna, and consummating the marital union with a priestess representing the mother and fertility goddess. The successful union vouchsafed prosperity and fertility for the coming year.[174]

One Ugaritic text, dealing with 'The Birth of the Gods Šaḫar and Šalim', describes a fertility rite combining hierogamy and hydrophory (carrying and pouring water).[175] We know that the rite of hydrophory was practiced in the Jerusalem Temple during the feast of booths or *Sukkôt* (*Mishnah Sukkah* 5).[176] The two women mentioned in the Ugaritic text with whom El unites himself are representatives of the goddesses Athirat and Raḫmay. The hierogamy and the mimetic rite of copulation aimed at restoring and furthering the fertility of nature after a long period of drought and infertility.[177] Moreover, one of the etymologies of the name of Jerusalem is explained as a reference to the Canaanite god Šalim. The fact of Jerusalem's Canaanite origins was well known in ancient Israel. The prophet Ezekiel denounces the city's pagan past, 'Your origin and your birth are of the land of the Canaanites; your father was an Amorite, and your mother a Hittite' (Ezek. 16.3, 45). Ezekiel considers Jerusalem as part of the pagan world. For that reason he proclaims that the 'impure' (*ṭm'*) name of Jerusalem would one day be changed into a new name, 'And the name of the city henceforth shall be, YHWH is there' (Ezek. 48.35; cf. Isa. 62.2).[178]

As pointed out by A. Caquot, 'the punishment of Michal, her sterility, indicates a connection with fertility rites. Apparently, she despises all the religiousness that developed around the ark that came from Shiloh, maybe on account of a type of Yahwism, like that of her father, that was less permeated by Canaanite influences. This is why, in his reply, David feels obliged to insist that his celebration is Yahwistic, but in doing so he confirms Michal's implicit objection: the fertility (rites) come from Canaan, practiced by people whom a well brought-up Israelite woman can only despise'.[179]

174. D. Reisman, 'Iddin-Dagan's Sacred Marriage Hymn', *JCS* 25 (1973), pp. 185-202 (185).

175. T.H. Gaster, 'Ezekiel and the Mysteries', *JBL* 60 (1941), pp. 289-310.

176. I. Lévy, 'Cultes et rites syriens dans le Talmud', *REJ* 43 (1901), pp. 183-201 (194).

177. For a résumé of various hypotheses concerning the celebration of this liturgy in Ugarit, see Caquot, Sznycer and Herdner, *Textes ougaritiques*, I, p. 355. See also G. Barton, 'A Liturgy for the Celebration of the Spring Festival at Jerusalem in the Age of Abraham and Melchizedek', *JBL* 53 (1934), pp. 61-78, who makes a connection between the Ugaritic divine name *šlm* and the name of the city Jerusalem *yršlm*.

178. See M. Greenberg, 'Ezekiel', in M. Eliade (ed.), *The Encyclopedia of Religion* (New York: Macmillan, 1987), pp. 239-42 (242).

179. Caquot, 'Les danses sacrées', p. 127.

It has been suggested that in bringing the ark to his city, David was also acting as a king in a traditional Canaanite fertility cult, having taken over the position of the old Jebusite ruler.[180] From this perspective David was to consummate the sacred marriage rite with Michal. 'The expressions *bkwl-'z* (v. 14) and *mpzz* (v. 16) imply a wild and ecstatic dancing on David's part, and...there are good grounds for holding that it was also of a fertility and orgiastic character, and that it was a prelude to the sacred marriage'.[181] Michal as the 'woman at the window', a motif stemming from the religious field of the fertility goddess, was supposed to play her role in this rite by uniting herself with the king. In the exchange between the royal couple, Michal expresses her refusal to participate in this rite. In his reply David mentions the maids, suggesting that he would end the hierogamic ceremony with one of the female servants instead of Michal. W.W. Hallo[182] mentions that one purpose of the sacred marriage rite may have been to provide the king with a successor.

At first sight, this interpretation of our text might seem farfetched. However, the discovery of an elaborate liturgy of hierogamy in the texts from Emar confirms that, 180 years prior to David, the Syrian neighbors who were chronologically, geographically and maybe religiously the closest to ancient Israel, practiced such a ritual.[183] The 1020 texts from the private library of a family of diviners in Emar have the advantage of being dated with exceptional precision unusual for ancient texts: between 1320 and 1187 BCE. These texts are of paramount importance for the history of several aspects of ancient Semitic religion like divine pantheons, festivals, liturgies, rites, history of sacrifices, offerings, and cultic personnel. The long text on the 'enthronement of the *entu*-priestess' (Emar text 369), poses once again the issue of hierogamy in the ancient Northwest Semitic domain and calls for a new investigation of this field.[184]

180. C.L. Seow, *Myth, Drama, and the Politics of David's Dance* (HSM, 44; Atlanta: Scholars Press, 1989), sees in 2 Sam. 6 a celebration of the entry of a victorious divinity analogous to what was happening with the god Ba'al in Ugarit. The scene between Michal and David would have been inspired by Ugaritic dialogues between the god and goddess.

181. Porter, 'The Interpretation of 2 Samuel VI', p. 167.

182. W.W. Hallo, 'The Birth of Kings', in J.H. Marks and R.M. Good (eds.), *Love and Death in the Ancient Near East: Essays in Honor of Marvin H. Pope* (Guilford, CT: Four Quarters Publishing Company, 1987), pp. 45-52.

183. See D. Arnaud, *Recherches au pays d'Aštata. Emar VI: Textes sumériens et accadiens* (Paris: Editions Recherche sur les Civilisations, 1985–86); D. Fleming, *The Institution of Baal's High Priestess at Emar: A Window on Ancient Syrian Religion* (HSS, 42; Atlanta: Scholars Press, 1992).

184. M. Dietrich, 'Die Einsetzungsritual der *Entu* von Emar (Emar VI/3, 369)', *UF* 21 (1989), pp. 47-100. Our analysis of 2 Sam. 6 calls for modification of the conclusions reached by M. Nissinen, 'Akkadian Rituals and Poetry of Divine Love', in R.M. Whiting (ed.), *Mythology and Mythologies: Methodological Approaches to Intellectual Influences*

The episode ends with a significant statement in v. 23, that Michal, the daughter of Saul, had no child until the day of her death. That this information should be interpreted as a political statement is indicated by the way Michal is identified as *bt š'wl*.[185]

8. *David Exterminates the Last Members of Saul's Dynasty*

Fragment 6. The Massacre of Michal's Five Sons (2 Samuel 21.8-9):

> (8) The king (i.e. David) took the two sons of Rizpah the daughter of Aiah, whom she bore to Saul, Armoni and Mephibosheth; and the five sons of Michal the daughter of Saul, whom she bore to Adriel the son of Barzillai the Meholathite; (9) and he gave them into the hands of the Gibeonites, and they hanged them on the mountain before YHWH, and the seven of them perished together. They were put to death in the first days of harvest, at the beginning of the barley harvest.

In the present form of the Masoretic text, the last fragment of the Michal tradition appears among the appendices placed together at the end of the books of Samuel (2 Sam. 21–24). The disparate stories found in them are part of a Deuteronomistic critique or an attempt to deconstruct the Israelite royal ideology.[186] Although the last fragment does not deal with David's children, there are several elements that establish links to the previous one connecting it both to the Succession Narrative and to the Michal tradition. On the one hand, in order for Solomon to reign, the posterity of Saul has to be eliminated.

(Melammu Symposium, 2; Helsinki: The Neo-Assyrian Text Corpus Project, 2001), pp. 93-136.

185. J. Morgenstern ('*Beena* Marriage', p. 109) has seen here a reflection of the *beena* method of succession to the kingship, that is, where the kingship is transmitted through the woman: 'as long as [David] had Michal in his possession it was impossible for her to give birth to a son by any other husband, a son who might, as a descendant of Saul through his daughter, have had, according to the old *beena* method of succession to the kingship, a more valid, and to the northern tribes a more acceptable claim to the throne than David himself or any of his sons'. For a critique of Morgenstern's position, see W. Plautz, 'Zur Frage des Mutterrechts im Alten Testament', *ZAW* 74 (1962), pp. 9-30; *idem*, 'Die Form der Eheschliessung im Alten Testament', *ZAW* 76 (1964), pp. 298-318.

186. See Carlson, *David the Chosen King*, pp. 194-259. In the preceding verses (2 Sam. 21.1-7), one finds a narrative probably referring to the early times of David's reign (cf. 9.1 and 16.8). J.A. Flanagan, 'Court History or Succession Narrative? A Study of 2 Samuel 9–20 and 1 Kings 1–2', *JBL* 91 (1972), pp. 172-81 (176 n. 23), notes: '2 Samuel presupposes 2 Samuel 21, which has been relegated to an appendix because it casts a shadow on David's character'. Cf. *idem*, 'Succession and Genealogy in the Davidic Dynasty', in H.B. Huffmon, F.A. Spina and A.R.W. Green (eds.), *The Quest for the Kingdom of God: Studies in Honor of George E. Mendenhall* (Winona Lake, IN: Eisenbrauns, 1983), pp. 35-55.

On the other hand, the episode describing the breakup of the relationship between Michal and David ends with an affirmation of Michal's infertility. Apparently she refused to participate in the rite of hierogamy, which smacked of a Canaanite practise foreign to her understanding of Yahwism. In this last fragment (Fragment 6), the underlying issue is the conjuration of famine and infertility that had been already raging in the country for three years. Moreover, the execution of Saul's descendants has the appearance of a fertility ritual with the aim of bringing back the rain (2 Sam. 21.6, 9-10).[187] H. Cazelles, who also subscribes to the idea of David making a concession to a local Canaanite rite, offers some reasons why David decided to offer the Gibeonites the sons of Saul's concubine Rizpah.[188] It is connected with the importance of maternity and the role of the royal concubine in Canaanite beliefs about fertility. However, the action of Rizpah, of the House of Saul, testifies to her contempt for Canaanite rites, and her fidelity to her own, by preventing the birds from consuming the sacrifice.

David is extremely cautious in his elimination of Saul's descendants since he never officially admits his responsibility. According to the story, it is a matter of Gibeonite revenge which gives David a good pretext to execute the Saulides by another hand.[189] By attempting to annihilate the Gibeonites, Saul had violated the alliance which Joshua concluded with them (Josh. 9.15).

187. A.S. Kapelrud, 'King David and the Sons of Saul', in International Congress for the History of Religions, *The Sacral Kingship*, pp. 294-301 (299), suggests that by sacrificing the royal descendants David was making a concession to the Canaanite beliefs shared by certain strata of the Israelite population. Cf. also C. Dieterlé and M.V. Monsarrat, 'Famine, guerre et peste en 2 Samuel 21–24', in T. Römer (ed.), *Lectio difficilior probabilior? L'exégèse comme expérience de décloisonnement. Mélanges offerts à F. Smyth-Florentin* (Dielheimer Blätter zum AT, 12; Heidelberg: Diebner, 1991), pp. 207-20.

188. Note H. Cazelles, 'David's Monarchy and the Gibeonite Claim (II Sam. xxi, 1-14)', *PEQ* 87 (1955), pp. 165-75 (171): 'The monarchy of David aimed rather at assimilating the Canaanites and their sacred cities'. Also: 'The Ras Shamra texts attach considerable importance to maternity, whether that of Meshet Ḥory, Meshet Denty, Nikal, Anat or the heifer. In Jerusalem a special status was given to the *gebîrah*, the mother of the king. It is also apparent from the request of Abner (2 S 3,8) and that of Adonijah (1 K 2,11ff), and from the act of Absalom at Jerusalem (2 S 16,22), that the royal concubine had a special relation to the sacral character of the king in the eyes of the common people. It may be that the choice of David was inspired by these customs and by Canaanite mentality' (p. 173).

189. See J.C. VanderKam, 'David's Complicity in the Deaths of Abner and Esbaal: A Historical and Redactorial Study', *JBL* 99 (1980), pp. 521-39. The Samuel texts exculpate David from the murder of Abner and Eshbaal, as well as from the extermination of Michal's five sons. The Chronicler whitewashes David even further by omitting not only 2 Sam. 21, but also ch. 9, which tells of Meribaal, in order to have no reminiscences of the whole affair. Cf. D. Merli, 'L'immolazione dei Saulidi (2 Sam. 21,1-14)', *Bibbia e Oriente* 9 (1967), pp. 245-51.

A. Malamat has pointed out that the real context of this execution is the violation of a treaty oath and the curse connected with it. Natural disasters such as drought, famine and plague were often perceived as direct consequences of such a breach. For example, in the 'plague prayer' of Muršiliš II (fourteenth century BCE), the plague which broke out in the Hatti land was attributed to the violation of the peace treaty between Egypt and the Hittites.[190] Malamat's suggestion has been confirmed by F.C. Fensham who pointed out that in the treaty of Esarhaddon (680–669 BCE), drought is threatened as a result of breach of covenant, while the corpse of the transgressor is to be torn apart by wild animals. 'The Gibeonites left the corpses [of the Saulides] to be torn by birds and animals as part of the curse because their father had violated the treaty oath'.[191]

The Gibeonites required seven people from Saul's line, and in order to stop the curse of the famine David gave them the seven descendants of the man who breached the treaty. This sacred number corresponds to the sacred character of the treaty. Ancient Near Eastern treaties ended with an invocation of the divine Seven (in Akkadian *Sebetti*) whose role was to protect it. In the Sefire inscription (I A 11) containing a treaty between Barga'ya the king of KTK and Mati'el the king of Arpad (seventh century BCE), the two kings swore not to break the alliance by invoking several West-Semitic divinities, including El, Elyon 'and in the presence of the *Sebetti* (the divine Seven)'.[192] The idea of solidarity between generations was profoundly engrained in the mentality of the ancients. There is, however, a serious historical problem with this execution of Saul's descendants in the fact that the biblical texts do not mention the occasion when Saul broke the treaty with the Gibeonites.[193] When Shimei accuses David of 'the blood of the House of Saul' in 2 Sam.

190. See A. Malamat, 'Doctrines of Causality in Hittite and Biblical Historiography: A Parallel', *VT* 5 (1955), pp. 1-12; A. Goetze, 'Plague Prayer of Mursilis', in *ANET*, pp. 394-96.

191. F.C. Fensham, 'The Treaty between Israel and the Gibeonites', in E.F. Campbell and D.N. Freedman (eds.), *The Biblical Archaeologist Reader* (Garden City, NY: Doubleday, 1970), III, pp. 121-26 (126).

192. J. Fitzmyer, 'The Aramaic Inscriptions of Sefire I and II', *JAOS* 81 (1961), pp. 178-222 (192). See also Bodi, *The Book of Ezekiel*, pp. 164-71, for a bibliography on the divine seven *Sebetti*. In Ezek. 17.19-20, Zedekiah's breach of his vassal treaty with the Babylonian overlord is interpreted as a breach of the covenant with YHWH. Covenant violators were threatened with decapitation; see Sefire treaty I A 39-40 in J.A. Fitzmyer, *The Aramaic Inscriptions of Sefire* (BibOr, 19; Rome: Pontifical Biblical Institute, 1967), pp. 14-15, and the treaty between Ašurnirari VI and Mati'ilu of Bīt-Agusi. Cf. E.F. Weidner, 'Der Staatsvertrag Assurniraris VI von Assyrien mit Mati'ilu von Bît-Agusi', *AfO* 8 (1932), pp. 17-34 (18-19). On dismemberment of covenant violators see R. Polzin, '"HWQY" and Covenant Institutions in Early Israel', *HTR* 62 (1969), pp. 233-40.

193. See W. Brueggemann, '2 Samuel 21–24: An Appendix of Deconstruction', *CBQ* 50 (1988), pp. 382-97 (385).

16.8, it attests that there was a suspicion in Israel about David's disposal of Saul's family.

The account of the extermination of the last descendants of Saul's dynasty is also a prefiguration of the way David's descendants were going to end. In the last days of the Jerusalem monarchy, a similar curse will affect Zedekiah on account of his breach of the treaty with the Babylonians (Ezek. 17.19-20). Thus at the end of the Deuteronomistic historiography, the last descendants of David's dynasty, the sons of Zedekiah, will be slaughtered by the Babylonians in front of their father and he himself will be blinded (2 Kgs 25.7). Contrary to his action toward the dead bodies of Saul's descendants in 2 Sam. 21.12-14, David will not be there to gather the bones of the victims and bury them in the ancestral tomb. Zedekiah and Jehoiachin will die in Babylon. Thus the remains of the last members of the Davidic dynasty are scattered from Jerusalem to Babylon.

The name of Michal in the Masoretic text (MT and LXX^{B} Vaticanus) is generally emended to Merab following the LXX (Lucianic recension, two MT mss, LXX^{M} [Coisilianus], Syriac version and *Targum Jonathan*) because of the name of the father of the five sons (Adriel the son of Barzillai the Meholathite) and the apparent contradiction with the account of Michal's sterility. Michal's five sons could date from the time she lived with her second husband. Yet a difficulty still remains, since Adriel son of Barzillai the Meholathite was Merab's husband (1 Sam. 18.19). Therefore, one either emends 'Michal' to 'Merab' or 'Adriel' to 'Paltiel'. The traditional emendation of 'Michal' into 'Merab' appears to betray the influence of moral consideration for David. It seems gruesome that David should put to death his own wife's sons. Still, it must have been very urgent for David to eliminate Michal's sons since they had a double claim to the kingship of Israel, as Saul's grandsons and as the stepsons of David. Even Meribaal, who had no qualification for kingship owing to his bodily defects (2 Sam. 4.4), dreamt of the restoration of his House (2 Sam. 16.4). We may assume that Michal's sons had more than one prospect of becoming the nucleus of a movement to restore Saul's monarchy. Glück and Ishida[194] argue that from a dynastic-political point of view, there were stronger reasons for Michal's sons to be removed by David than Merab's. Therefore they prefer the emendation of 'Adriel' to 'Paltiel'. The confusion between these two names is also possible since in Aramaic Adriel means 'God has helped', while Paltiel means 'God has delivered' in Hebrew.[195]

A specialist in textual criticism, D. Barthélemy, points out that in this case the Masoretic text is superior to the Greek versions:

194. J.J. Glück, 'Merab or Michal', *ZAW* 77 (1965), pp. 72-81, and Ishida, *The Royal Dynasties in Ancient Israel*, p. 78.

195. Stoebe, 'David und Mikal', p. 232.

> The non-Masoretic forms testify to a rich literary creativity motivated most often by a preoccupation with the internal or external coherence of the text; we understand that the old version of LXX, in this case represented by the Palestinian one, preferred not to translate the episode concerning Merab in 1 Sam. 18.17-19. Moreover, it transcribes Michal in 2 Sam. 21.8 with *Michol* (Μιχολ) in order to avoid confusion with Michal the wife of David whose name is transcribed *Melchol* (Μελχολ).[196]

This invention of a new female name shows to what degree tradition has been embarrassed by implicating David in the massacre of Michal's children.

Without solving the problem completely we may offer a rhetorical-critical observation. It is significant that there is confusion between Merab and Michal at the beginning and at the end of the Michal tradition, building a sort of *inclusio*. In 1 Sam. 18.17 Saul offers David his older daughter Merab, hoping that David might fall by 'the hand of the Philistines'. However, when the marriage was to take place, 'Merab was given to Adriel the Meholathite for a wife' (1 Sam. 18.19). In the verses that follow Saul repeats the same scheme with David: 'So Saul said to David for the second time (*bštym*), "You will become my son-in-law today".'[197] The redactor clearly wanted the readers to connect this offer of the second daughter with the previous one. It might be another example of what G. Sheppard termed 'canon conscious redaction', that is, an indication within the text which tells us how to read and interpret it. 'For the second time' is an ironical comment about Saul. He is a 'shifty' person who does not keep his word or his promises. Hence, at the end of the Michal story in 2 Sam. 21.8-9, to find her married to Merab's husband does not come as a surprise. It points to the extent to which Saul's daughters were abused by their father. Saul has manipulated his family with the aim of bolstering his own position.

Moreover, as already noted in connection with the teraphim, there is a parallel with Jacob who was duped by his father-in-law Laban concerning the hand of his two daughters Leah and Rachel (Gen. 29.15-30). The relationship to the Jacob tradition may point out in a contrastive way what is missing in the relationship between David and Michal. While Jacob loves Rachel, the Samuel text says nothing about David's love toward Michal.[198]

This last fragment of the Michal tradition shows Michal and David's story ending in horror.

196. D. Barthélemy, 'La qualité du Texte Massorétique de Samuel', in E. Tov (ed.), *The Hebrew and Greek Texts of Samuel* (Proceedings IOSCS, Vienna, 22 August 1980; Jerusalem: Academon, 1980), pp. 1-44 (18-19, 43).

197. The phrase is usually understood as a redactional expansion since it does not occur in the LXX, and was added to facilitate the interpolation of 1 Sam. 18.17-19. *Bištayim* occurs in Job 33.14, where it means 'for the second time'.

198. See R.B. Lawton, 'I Samuel 18: David, Merob, and Michal', *CBQ* 51 (1989), pp. 423-25 (425).

9. *Conclusions*

According to G. von Rad, the story of Saul was Israel's ultimate achievement in writing tragedy: 'Israel never again gave birth to a poetic production which in certain of its features has such close affinity with the spirit of Greek tragedy'.[199] Likewise, for Northrop Frye, 'Saul is the one great tragic figure of the Bible'.[200] For some authors, David too is a tragic character being prey to a dramatic disintegration of his family after his affair with Bathsheba and the assassination of Uriah.[201] In my opinion, the story of Michal falls within the same category. In terms of the literary technique of dramatization, choice of vocabulary laden with tragic irony, use of puns and double entendres, setting, characterization and even 'plot', the Michal story is a masterpiece which stands on equal ground with Greek tragedies. Realizing the exceptional dramatic potential of the story of Saul's family, several playwrights have written tragedies based on the David–Saul power-struggle.[202] As pointed out by Schulte, Michal's tragedy consists in the fact that she became an object of political calculation.[203] As revealed in the analysis of the relevant passages, as far as David was concerned, the affair with Michal was clearly a diplomatic marriage contracted for its political advantages. Such marriages were not affairs of the heart, and here lies Michal's tragic fate. 'David, for his part, married Michal not for love but because "it pleased David well to be the king's son-in-law" (18.26). His relationship to her is always colored by practical considerations.'[204] In her tragic condition she is among thousands of

199. G. von Rad, *Old Testament Theology* (trans. D.M.G. Stalker; New York: Harper & Row, 1962), I, p. 325.

200. N. Frye, *The Great Code: The Bible and Literature* (New York: Jovanovich, 1981), p. 181.

201. See J.W. Whedbee, 'On Divine and Human Bonds: The Tragedy of the House of David', in G.M. Tucker *et al.* (eds.), *Canon, Theology and Old Testament Literature* (Festschrift B.S. Childs; Philadelphia: Fortress Press, 1990), pp. 147-65; J.C. Exum, *Tragedy and Biblical Narrative: Arrows of the Almighty* (Cambridge: Cambridge University Press, 1992).

202. See Gide, *Saül*; D.H. Lawrence, *David*, in *The Complete Plays of D.H. Lawrence* (New York: The Viking Press, 1966), pp. 63-151. See also O. Millet and Ph. de Robert, 'David et Batshéba dans la littérature française', in W. Dietrich and H. Herkommer (eds.), *König David—biblische Schlüsselfigur und europäische Leitgestalt* (Stuttgart: W. Kohlhammer, 2002), pp. 777-93 (with bibliography). Some years ago, the theologian Walter Hollenwegger wrote a theater piece on Michal's tragedy for the stage in Zurich. For Michal in the movies, see J.C. Exum, 'Michal at the Window, Michal in the Movies', in *eadem*, *Plotted, Shot, and Painted: Cultural Representations of Biblical Women* (JSOTSup, 215; Sheffield: Sheffield Academic Press, 1996), pp. 54-78 (with bibliography).

203. Schulte, *Die Entstehung*, p. 146.

204. So Berlin, 'Characterization in Biblical Narrative', pp. 70-71.

other ancient Near Eastern 'diplomatic brides' exchanged between rulers in order to seal political transactions. Thus a Babylonian king writes to Amenophis III of Egypt, 'You want my daughter for your wife, yet my sister, whom my father gave you, is there with you and no one has seen her of late whether she is alive or dead'.[205] The subject is as contemporary as ever: the dark side of political power-struggle, of unscrupulousness and opportunism. Michal's suffering was not in vain. It remained recorded in the Scripture as a powerful critique of unjust human structures. The Michal tradition contains a redeeming theological quality, as an expression of Yahwism which criticizes and transcends the will for power and domination. The Michal tradition may be taken as a first attempt at deconstructing royal ideology in ancient Israel and as a critique of religious syncretism. Deconstruction contains political strategy. It shifts the perspective and re-elaborates what has always been oppressed, minimized, marginalized and despised, and attempts to show that what has been dominated overflows and represents a constitutive part of the dominating structure. Deconstruction is therefore always deconstruction of the dominating power and of its principles.[206]

Michal falls into the category of abused women of the Bible. Her story could well be part of what Phyllis Trible aptly termed the 'Texts of Terror', Michal being another victim of patriarchy.[207] In these biblical records of the victims of oppression, the reader hears the prophetic voice reaffirming YHWH's act of liberation. The history of patriarchal societies shows that it is always women and not men that call into question the reigning political structures and societal arrangements. This is due to the fact that men enjoy a privileged status in this type of society:[208]

> It is not the establishment representative of an exploitative society which finally exposes the revolutionary liberating dynamic inherent within a religious tradition, or which discovers fresh metaphors capable of infusing individuals with vitality to become actors in the drama of new creation; that

205. Quoted in D.R. Hillers, *Covenant: The History of a Biblical Idea* (Baltimore: The Johns Hopkins University Press, 1969), p. 27.

206. See M. Goldschmit, *Jacques Derrida: une introduction* (Paris: Pocket, 2003), p. 22.

207. P. Trible, *Texts of Terror: Literary-Feminist Readings of Biblical Narratives* (Philadelphia: Fortress Press, 1984). J. Moltmann ('Die Bibel und das Patriarchat', *EvTh* 42 [1982], pp. 480-84) reminds us that the struggle for freedom and equality for women is very ancient indeed: 'Die unter dem Namen "Feminismus" bekannte Bewegung ist zwar eine moderne, aber die mit "Matriarchat" und "Patriarchat" bezeichneten Kultur- und Herrschafts-kämpfe um Freiheit, Besitz und Eigentum reichen bis in vorhistorische Zeit zurück, wie Bachofen, Bornemann, Ranke-Graves, Sir Galahad, Göttner-Abenrodth, Fester, König, Downing, Stone und die Fülle der neueren, religionsgeschichtlichen Forschungen beweisen'.

208. E. Badinter, *XY: De l'identité masculine* (Paris: O. Jacob, 1992), p. 24.

> exposure and discovery comes rather from the groups discriminated against and exploited by the establishment, it comes from the very passion of their liberation struggle.[209]

Michal looked through the window, watched David dancing around the ark and saw through the scheme of David, the 'master gamesman'.[210] She 'despised him in her heart' (2 Sam. 6.16) because she realized David's infidelity to the covenant and condemned the concessions he was making to Canaanite fertility rites. David's justification that he was 'dancing before YHWH' is unconvincing. The text itself indicates that David is pushing YHWH's hand. David himself is 'blessing his household' (6.20a) because YHWH is not blessing all of David's plans. The most opportune royal descendant through Michal uniting the House of Saul and the House of David will never be born. The Michal tradition is a trenchant critique of David's opportunism. She felt revulsion upon seeing the cavortings of the sheepherder-become-king who felt his kingship would be secured if he attached new numbers to his harem and spawned new sons. The Babylonian Talmud (*b. Sanh.* 21a) says that 'David had four hundred children, and all born of captive women taken as concubines by the king because of their beauty'.

With regard to our methodological guidelines we should draw some further conclusions concerning David's character as revealed in his relationship with Michal and her father Saul. The overall impression is that both David and Saul are unscrupulous individuals. In 1 Sam. 18.20-28, Saul attempted to kill David by proxy, using the Philistines as agents and his daughter as bait. Saul failed in his attempt. That Saul and David are not radically different in character is manifest in the fact that later David uses a proxy in order to kill Uriah (2 Sam. 11).[211] The difference is that David has more success in the execution of his plans. The first two rulers of Israel were not just what Aristotle defined in a positive way, 'man as a political animal'.[212] Rather, they illustrate the paradox of political power and the negative assessment made of it by Voltaire who thought that politics had its source more in human perversity than in the grandeur of the human spirit (*Le sottisier*).

We have noted the irony in the use of the term *yšr* in the murderous deal between Saul and David. Saul and David have banalized the meaning of the concept *yšr* by using their office for private ends. They both use religion for personal gains.

209. P.D. Hanson, 'Masculine Metaphors for God and Sex-Discrimination in the Old Testament', *The Ecumenical Review* 27 (1975), pp. 316-24 (324).

210. The expression comes from E.W. Jorgensen and H.I. Jorgensen, *Eric Berne: Master Gamesman—A Transactional Biography* (New York: Grove Press, 1984).

211. So Gunn, *The Fate of King Saul*, p. 81.

212. So Alter, *The Art of Biblical Narrative*, p. 119.

The present analysis of Michal's and David's relationship has revealed some gruesome details. One is struck by David's insensitivity, unscrupulousness and abusiveness toward his wife Michal. Absorbed in his rise to power, he left Michal's love to die. In the light of the above analysis it is hard to accept the biblical statement about David being 'a man according to YHWH's heart'. It may express the idea that no matter how base a person may be, God does not shrink from loving the wretched creature. In that case it refers to YHWH's approval of David's readiness and capacity to repent. It seems more probable, however, to read it as a piece of Davidic political propaganda. It would represent an effort to legitimize royal power, a well-known genre in ancient Near Eastern literatures.[213] It is found in ancient Egypt in the prophecy of Neferty, a priest of the twelfth Dynasty, c. 2000 BCE. Under the guise of a prophecy, the text praises the merits of the Pharaoh on the throne, Amenemhet I, in opposition to the calamitous reign of his predecessor.[214]

In Mesopotamia, the Assyrian Annals praise the merits of the reigning sovereigns. Hittite texts known as the 'Apology of Hattušiliš'[215] offer the closest parallels to the biblical narrative. Several texts were written in order to justify the reign of Hattušiliš III, who reigned in the thirteenth century BCE, and who usurped or forced his way to the throne. In his apology, Hattušiliš describes his youth as a priest in the service of the goddess Ištar. As the youngest and weakest child of Muršiliš II, he was not expected to live and was assigned to the service of Ištar. He relates the death of his father and the accession of his brother Muwattališ to the throne while Hattušiliš is appointed governor of a province of the northern country, the northern part of the Hittite homeland. In spite of the jealousy of the new king, with the support of his goddess, Hattušiliš goes from success to success. He is appointed chief of the army. His brother Muwattališ dies with no legitimate son. Urhi-Tešub, the son of one of Muwattališ's concubines, takes the throne. While Hattušiliš remains loyal to the new king for seven years, the latter nevertheless progressively relieves him of most of his offices, seeking to destroy him, which prompts Hattušiliš to declare war on his nephew. Owing to help received from Ištar, who promised him kingship from the beginning, he takes the throne from Urhi-Tešub.[216] The redactor of the biblical narrative seems to

213. See H. Tadmor, 'Autobiographical Apology in the Royal Assyrian Literature', in H. Tadmor and M. Weinfeld (eds.), *History, Historiography, and Interpretation: Studies in Biblical and Cuneiform Literatures* (Jerusalem; Magnes Press, 1983), pp. 38-41; A. Weiser, 'Die Legitimation des Königs David', *VT* 16 (1966), pp. 325-54.

214. Vermeylen, 'La Maison de Saül', pp. 58-59.

215. H.A. Hoffner, Jr, 'Propaganda and Political Justification in Hittite Historiography', in H. Goedicke and J.J.M. Roberts (eds.), *Unity and Diversity: Essays in the History, Literature, and Religion of the Ancient Near East* (Baltimore: The Johns Hopkins University Press, 1975), pp. 49-62.

216. P.K. McCarter, 'The Apology of David', *JBL* 99 (1980), pp. 489-504 (495-99).

have written with a similar goal: to convince the readers of the legitimacy of the House of David as over against that of Saul.

It is significant that YHWH refused to have a temple built by such a man. YHWH did not approve all of David's plans. The fact that the Messiah was promised to come from the Davidic line does not invalidate our conclusion. The Messianic predictions do not fail to point out that the Messiah will fully manifest the characteristics which David lacked, 'There shall come forth a shoot from the stump of Jesse...but with righteousness he shall judge the poor (*wšpṭ bṣdq*), and decide with equity (*bmyšwr*) for the meek of the earth' (Isa. 11.1-4).[217]

There is a world of difference between the rule of David which lacks the features of *ṣdq* and *mšr* and the Messianic rule. Only the latter displays what in the ancient Near East was considered to be the main characteristics of an ideal rule.[218] Furthermore, the promises attached to the covenant between YHWH and David and his descendants are *conditional*. This has rightly been pointed out by Mowinckel: 'If the king truly adheres to Yahweh and obeys his commandments and rules the people according to Yahweh's "right" and "justice", then Yahweh will uphold the eternal kingdom of David, endow his sons with all blessings and through him let them flow to the people (Ps. 89.21ff)'.[219]

The tragedy of Michal is a powerful reminder that the biblical God does not condone opportunism and abuse of human beings. The story of Michal might have been preserved and recorded in Scripture for at least two reasons. On the one hand, it represents a critique of the monarchy and deconstruction of the royal ideology. It exposes the abuses and the merciless power-struggle which the monarchy generated in Israelite society. On the other hand, it

217. The same pair *ṣdq* and *mšr* occurs in Ps. 98.9: '[YHWH] will judge the world with righteousness (*ṣdq*) and the peoples with equity (*mšr*)'. Cf. also Ps. 96.10: '[YHWH] will judge the peoples with equity (*mšr*)' and v. 13 '[YHWH] will judge the world with righteousness (*ṣdq*)'. In the 'Song of Moses' in Deut. 32.4, YHWH is designated as 'just and right' (*ṣdyq wyšr*).

218. Traditionally it is believed that the Chronicles indulge in a one-sided glorification of David and systematically omit any reference to David's misdeeds like the story of Bathsheba. It is possible, however, to view the situation differently. A.G. Auld, *Kings without Privilege: David and Moses in the Story of the Bible's Kings* (Edinburgh: T. & T. Clark, 1994), argues that Samuel–Kings and Chronicles rest on a common foundation-document, into which the editors of Samuel–Kings have inserted the story of Bathsheba, which was unknown to the editors of Chronicles. This makes it possible to view the Bathsheba episode as an anti-monarchic addition which might have been made at quite a late stage in the development of Samuel–Kings.

219. S. Mowinckel, 'General Oriental and Specific Israelite Elements in the Israelite Conception of the Sacral Kingdom', in International Congress for the History of Religions, *The Sacral Kingship*, pp. 283-93 (292).

represents the views of Yahwistic circles which felt uneasy with the Canaanite features which David introduced into the official cult.[220] As pointed out by Porter,

> The reasons for Michal's action can only be conjectured: but possibly, coming as she did from the north where traditional Yahwism was strongest and belonging to the tribe and royal house which most firmly supported it, she represented what seems to have been the invariable reaction of that Yahwism to the fertility aspect of Canaanite religion.[221]

220. J.A. Soggin, 'Der offiziel gefördete Synkretismus in Israel während des 10. Jahrhunderts', *ZAW* 78 (1966), pp. 179-204.

221. Porter, 'The Interpretation of 2 Samuel', p. 165.

2

The Daughters of Saul and the Daughters of Zimri-Lim

1. *The Historical Problem: Saul Offers his Two Daughters to David*

Historical-critical scholarship considers it improbable that Saul could have offered his two daughters Merab and Michal to David as wives. This double offer is perceived as being a legendary amplification in the Samuel narratives rooted in traditional folk tale motifs and therefore unrelated to history. This is partially due to the fact that Saul's offer of his elder daughter Merab occurs in the context of the David and Goliath story, itself burdened with folk tale amplifications.[1] The latter has been analyzed from an ethnopoetic perspective, in the light of V.J. Propp's formal analysis of Russian fairy tales and A. Skaftymov's study of Russian epic songs.[2] Indeed, in folk tales one often finds the motif of the king offering his daughter to the valorous warrior as a reward for his exploit. Before David fought with Goliath in 1 Sam. 17.25, 'the men of Israel said..."[T]he man who kills him [Goliath], the king will enrich with great riches, and will give him his daughter, and make his father's house free in Israel"'.

After David's victory over Goliath in 1 Sam. 18.17-19, we read how Saul is about to give his elder daughter Merab to David. At the last minute, however, he gives her away to another man:

> (17) Then Saul said to David, 'Here is my elder daughter Merab; I will give her to you for a wife; only be valiant for me and fight YHWH's battles'. For

1. D. Barthélemy, D.W. Gooding, J. Lust and E. Tov (eds.), *The Story of David and Goliath: Textual and Literary Criticism* (OBO, 73; Freiburg: Universitätsverlag, 1986). The four contributors to this volume reached something of an impasse in their conclusions. The LXX text of this story represents only some 55 per cent of the MT. A.G. Auld and C.Y.S. Ho, 'The Making of David and Goliath', *JSOT* 56 (1992), pp. 19-39 (24), tend to side with Tov and Lust in seeing the LXX's story as more original.
2. H. Jason, 'The Story of David and Goliath: A Folk Epic?', *Bib* 60 (1978), pp. 36-70 (61), finds that 'the text can be measured with all the folkloristic tools, and fits its models'.

> Saul thought, 'Let not my hand be upon him, but let the hand of the Philistines be upon him'. (18) And David said to Saul, 'Who am I, and who are my kinsfolk, my father's family in Israel, that I should be son-in-law to the king?' (19) But at the time when Merab, Saul's daughter, should have been given to David, she was given to Adriel the Meholathite for a wife.

The historical existence of Merab, Saul's supposed elder daughter, and the episode of her missed marriage to David are systematically questioned by biblical scholars. Moreover, the fact that the above verses of the Masoretic text of 1 Sam. 18.17-19 do not appear in the Greek version casts further doubt on their authenticity. They are usually taken as a doublet, that is, a repetition of the Michal episode that begins in the following v. 20, which means that they would therefore be chronologically posterior to it.[3]

Michal's marriage to David suffers as well from its too close connection to the David and Goliath episode, a connection which makes its historicity doubtful. Historians place the moment when Michal became David's wife at a later point in time in an attempt to dissociate it completely from the troubling David and Goliath story. According to H.J. Stoebe, the marriage between Michal and David only occurs after the marriage of David and Abigail in 1 Samuel 25.[4] While the entire Merab incident would be a later addition totally lacking any originality, he nevertheless considers the marriage of Michal and David as a genuine historical fact. In M. Noth's opinion, the marriage of Michal and David only occurred after Saul's death, at the moment when the civil war broke out between the House of Saul and the House of David in 2 Sam. 3.6. David says that he is ready to negotiate with Abner, commander of Ishbosheth's army, on one condition: Abner should bring Michal back to him, the daughter of Saul 'whom he had betrothed at the price of a hundred foreskins of the Philistines' (2 Sam. 3.14). David's motivation in making this request would have been political. Having obtained supremacy over Judah he strived to ensure control over the northern tribes that were traditionally faithful to the House of Saul. F. Langlamet combines both Stoebe's and Noth's positions when he affirms that one can maintain the historicity of Michal's marriage to David, saying, however, that historically it is most probable that this marriage occurred only after Saul's death.[5]

Noth's argument is as follows:

3. J. Briand, 'Les figures de David en 1 S 16,1–2 S 5,3. Rapports entre littérature et histoire', in Desrousseaux and Vermeylen (eds.), *Figures de David à travers la Bible*, pp. 9-34 (19).

4. Stoebe, 'David und Mikal', p. 228.

5. F. Langlamet, 'De "David, fils de Jessé" au "Livre de Jonathan" ', *RB* 100 (1993), pp. 321-57 (332 n. 13), states: 'Quant à l'historicité du mariage de David avec Mikal, on peut la maintenir, mais l'opinion selon laquelle ce mariage n'aurait eu lieu qu'après la mort de Saül reste la plus probable'.

> The later tradition made Michal become David's wife during Saul's lifetime, in the context of David's victory over Goliath (1 Sam. xviii, 27). This is historically incorrect and the reference to this tradition in 2 Sam. iii, 14 is shown by the context to be secondary. In 2 Sam. iii, 15 the context requires 'Abner' (instead of 'Ishbosheth') as the subject of the sentence.[6]

In my opinion, the mention of Ishbosheth seems justified, and should be maintained. David is involved in a major political transaction and the demand for Michal must have been addressed to Ishbosheth, the heir of the House of Saul. According to J.H. Grønbaek,[7] it was essential to implicate the official successor of the House of Saul in this transaction in order to legitimize this remarriage and to confirm the rights of David in Saul's heritage. Obtaining the authorization of a subordinate like Abner, the chief of Ishbosheth's army, would not have sufficed.

For some, the insertion of the Merab episode might have been prompted by the redactor's goal of making David's story resemble that of the patriarch Jacob. He too was offered two sisters—the two daughters of Laban. According to Gen. 29.26-28, Jacob had to serve his father-in-law Laban seven years in order to marry his younger daughter Rachel. He had already served the same number of years in order to marry the elder daughter Leah.

In their Samuel commentary, A. Caquot and Ph. de Robert suggest an additional reason for the so-called 'Merab amplification'. They suppose that the redactor wanted to respect a non-written law attested in different ancient and modern societies according to which it is not permitted to marry the younger daughter before the elder one.[8]

The above explanations show the embarrassment of the commentators when faced with this unusual sequence in the Samuel narrative where Saul offers his two daughters, one after the other, to the same man.

In the study of ancient texts, historical criticism applies the methodological principle of analogy. Since E. Troeltsch, it has become a standard procedure of historical investigation to try to establish analogies between historically similar events or texts.[9] The observation of analogies between similar events in the past gives the historian the possibility of ascribing to them a certain degree of probability. Furthermore, it allows one to explain what is unknown

6. Noth, *The History of Israel*, p. 184 n. 1.

7. Grønbaek, *Die Geschichte vom Aufstieg Davids*, p. 238.

8. A. Caquot and Ph. de Robert, *Les Livres de Samuel* (Geneva: Labor & Fides, 1994), p. 224.

9. E. Troeltsch, 'Ueber historische und dogmatische Methode in der Theologie', in *idem*, *Gesammelte Schriften* (Tübingen: J.C.B. Mohr, 1913–22), II, pp. 729-53 (733), states: 'Die Beobachtungen von Analogien zwischen gleichartigen Vorgängen der Vergangenheit gibt die Möglichkeit, ihnen Wahrscheinlichkeit zuzuschreiben und das Unbekannte des einen aus dem Bekannten des anderen zu deuten'.

from that which is better known. Analogy is considered one of the principal tools of the historian's trade. A recent example of the application of this principle is the analogy drawn between the House of Mopsos (*byt mpš*), which reigned in Cilicia (Que) in Asia Minor from 1184 to 696 BCE, and the House of David, whose reign was somewhat shorter.[10] Moreover, there seems to have been contacts between the two houses. As far as the study of ancient texts is concerned, M. Liverani points out the benefit of establishing, whenever possible, a 'homologous series':

> The most productive type of study of the single document towards its total comprehension derives...from the setting of the text in a homologous series, chosen so as to enlighten the particular structure under study, and to set apart the paradigmatic variants and the syntagmatic successions.[11]

The skepticism of historians concerning biblical narratives dealing with the beginning of Israel's tribal chiefdom is related to the now abandoned consensus that existed since J. Wellhausen. In his time, the narrative in the books of Samuel was considered to be 'a good historical source'.[12] This initial point of view was first modified by redaction-critical analysis,[13] and is nowadays largely supplanted by literary, stylistic and rhetorical studies belonging

10. The House of Mopsos is mentioned in eighth-century BCE Phoenician inscriptions of Karatepe (A 1.16; II.15; III.11; C IV.12), as well as in a recently discovered Luwian-Phoenician inscription, on which see A. Lemaire, '"Maison de David", "Maison de Mopsos", et les Hivvites', in C. Cohen, A. Hurvitz and S.M. Paul (eds.), *Sefer Moshe: The Moshe Weinfeld Jubilee Volume* (Winona Lake, IN: Eisenbrauns, 2004), pp. 303-12 (with bibliography). For a recent edition of the Phoenician Karatepe inscriptions, see H. Çambel, with a contribution from W. Röllig and J.D. Hawkins, *Corpus of Hieroglyphic Luwian Inscriptions*. II. *Karatepe-Aslantaş* (UISK, 8.2; Berlin: W. de Gruyter, 1999), 'House of Mopsos' on pp. 51, 53, 67; J. Vanschoonwinkel, 'Mopsos: légendes et réalité', *Hethitica* 10 (1990), pp. 185-211.

11. M. Liverani, 'Memorandum on the Approach to Historiographic Texts', *Or* 42 (1973), pp. 178-94 (181). Together with his research team, he applied this principle in the study of ancient Near Eastern battle reports; see E. Badalì, M.G. Biga, O. Carena, G. di Bernardo, S. di Rienzo, M. Liverani and P. Vitali, 'Studies on the Annals of Aššurnasirpal II. I. Morphological Analysis', *Vicino Oriente* 5 (1982), pp. 13-73.

12. For example, for J. Wellhausen (*Einleitung in das Alte Testament* [Berlin: F. Bleek, 4th edn, 1878], p. 277) the story of the succession to the throne of David (2 Sam. 9–20; 1 Kgs 1–2), was a 'good historical source'. Likewise, Rost, *Die Überlieferung von der Thronnachfolge Davids*, and G. von Rad, 'The Beginnings of Historical Writing in Ancient Israel', in *idem*, *The Problem of the Hexateuch and Other Essays* (Edinburgh: Oliver & Boyd, 1966), pp. 166-204, attributed to this narrative considerable historical value.

13. This consensus was shattered by Whybray, *The Succession Narrative*. See also Veijola, *Die ewige Dynastie*, p. 130. Langlamet, 'Pour ou contre Salomon?', identifies several redactional standpoints in the narrative as he analyzed first a pro-Solomonic point of view and then potentially multiple pro-Davidic ones.

to the field of 'narratology' that tend to focus on the final form of the text. In our time, the prevalent opinion holds that the narratives of Saul's and David's beginnings belong more to the genre of 'serious entertainment'[14] than to historical narrative.

Without denying the pertinence of these various modern approaches, it seems, nevertheless, that critics have failed to recognize the possible historical value of the sources that have been used in the composition of the biblical text. Therefore, before relegating Merab to a detail of a traditional folk tale, as is generally done, it might be useful to review ancient Near Eastern marriage practices. The data from Mari, a site in northern Syria, a region that is geographically, linguistically, socially and culturally close to ancient Israel, offer a remarkable analogy to Saul's marriage transactions involving his two daughters Merab and Michal offered to David.

2. *The Daughters of Zimri-Lim: A Mari Analogy*[15]

The Mari Royal Archives dating from the eighteenth century BCE have revealed a considerable number of letters that were sent by women, some of which were written by female scribes.[16] This collection of letters, unique in its genre and of exceptional importance for the study of the role of women in the ancient Near East, has been collected in a special volume aptly entitled by modern translators 'Feminine Correspondence'.[17] By analyzing these letters and comparing them to other documents from the Mari archives, several Assyriologists established the identity of the royal harem of the last

14. Gunn, *The Story of King David*, p. 38, states: 'the primary generic classification of the narrative should be as a story in the sense of a work of art and entertainment'. See also Fokkelman, *Narrative Art and Poetry*; H. Hagan, 'Deception as Motif and Theme in 2 Sam. 9–20; 1 Kgs 1–2', *Bib* 60 (1979), pp. 301-26.

15. For bibliography on Mari and the biblical literature see, among others, A. Lemaire, 'Mari, la Bible et le monde Nord-Ouest sémitique', *MARI* 4 (1985), pp. 549-58; *idem*, 'Traditions amorrites et Bible: le prophétisme', *RA* 93 (1999), pp. 49-56; A. Malamat, *Mari and the Early Israelite Experience* (Oxford: Oxford University Press, 1989), pp. 125-44; *idem, Mari and the Bible* (Studies in the History and Culture of the Ancient Near East, 12; Leiden: E.J. Brill, 1998), and the critical review of it by D. Charpin (*RA* 93 [1999], pp. 91-93).

16. See N. Ziegler, *Le harem de Zimrî-Lîm: La population féminine des palais d'après les archives royales de Mari* (Mémoires de NABU, 5; Florilegium marianum, 4; Paris: Société pour l'étude du Proche-Orient ancien, 1999), pp. 91-92, 'Les femmes scribes'; S.A. Meier, 'Women and Communication in the Ancient Near East', *JAOS* 111 (1991), pp. 540-47.

17. G. Dossin and A. Finet, *Correspondance féminine* (ARM, 10: Paris: Geuthner, 1978).

Bedouin king Zimri-Lim.[18] Moreover, they were able to elucidate his marriage transactions implying the practise of providing one's daughter with a dowry (*nidittum*) and obtaining a 'counter-gift' (*terḫatum*) from the family of the bridegroom. This correspondence reveals Zimri-Lim's highly elaborate matrimonial policy which used his daughters as bargaining chips in the accomplishment of his political ambitions. Zimri-Lim had at least ten daughters, all expressly named in the documents—a fact that enables us to identify them precisely. In the palace catalogue, the royal princesses are listed in Zimri-Lim's harem, which means that they lived in the quarters reserved for women.

Among the daughters of Zimri-Lim, the tragic story of Kirûm and her sister Šimātum has attracted the attention of several scholars who establish a very precise historical analysis of the chronological sequence of their marriages to the same man, Ḫāya-Sūmû.[19]

Kirûm was the younger daughter and her name means 'garden, orchard'.[20] Šimātum was the elder one. The meaning of her name has not yet been explained in a satisfactory manner, though it might be possible to elucidate her name as a combination of *šīmum* meaning 'price' and the ending *-atum* derived from -(*i*)*atum*, found in Old Babylonian personal names where it serves to make diminutives.[21] Her name would therefore mean something like 'precious one', or 'little precious one'.[22]

Zimri-Lim's matrimonial transactions turned the lives of Kirûm and Šimātum into a nightmare, first straining and eventually breaking up the friendship and complicity they probably enjoyed in their youth. Their difficulties emerged when their father Zimri-Lim decided to marry them off, one after another, to the same man. Ḫāya-Sūmû was Zimri-Lim's vassal from the city of Ilānṣurā in a region north of Mari, near one of the sources of the Ḫabur river, near Šagar Bazar and east of Ḫarran. He was one of Zimri-Lim's principal military allies. In the eleventh and twelfth year of Zimri-Lim's reign, in the course of the latter's major campaigns against Idamaraṣ and Eluḫut,

18. See B. Lafont, 'Les filles du roi de Mari', in J.-M. Durand (ed.), *La femme dans le Proche-Orient antique* (RAI, 33; Paris: Editions Recherche sur les Civilisations, 1987), pp. 113-21 (114); Ziegler, *Le harem de Zimrî-Lîm*, p. 64, on Kirûm.

19. Sasson, 'Biographical Notices', pp. 68-70; J.-M. Durand, 'Trois études sur Mari', *MARI* 3 (1984), pp. 127-80, especially 162-80, Section III, 'Les femmes de Ḫāyā-Sūmû', Annexes I et II. Durand established a complete dossier with additional documents. The present study follows this new interpretation of the pertinent documents.

20. A comparison with the Hebrew *kerem* ('orchard, vine') is sometimes suggested.

21. J. Lewy, 'Studies in Akkadian Grammar and Onomatology', *Or* 15 (1946), pp. 361-415 (366-67): 'On Some Old Babylonian Names in *-ia*, *-tum*, *iatum* and *-iatum*'.

22. Cf. the English terms 'precious' and 'pretty', which derive from the Latin *pretiosus* ('valuable') and *pretium* ('price').

Ḫāya-Sūmû provided military backing and furnished his suzerain with troops.

In a region that was troubled with chronic unrest and shifting alliances,[23] the role of the Mari princesses married and living at foreign courts seems to have been quite obvious. Zimri-Lim was using his daughters as spies in order to obtain precious information. Benefiting from their rank and pre-eminent position at the court of his vassals, Zimri-Lim's daughters were expressly solicited by their father to provide him with first-hand intelligence concerning the political activities of their royal husbands.[24]

The elder daughter Šimātum was the first to become Ḫāya-Sūmû's wife, in the year when Zimri-Lim, who belonged to the northern or Sim'alite Bedouin tribes, acceded to the throne of Mari.[25] While formally recognizing the sovereignty of his suzerain and father-in-law Zimri-Lim, Ḫāya-Sūmû had, nevertheless, a freedom of military action and conducted independent political negotiations.[26] It was probably because his independence was considered too great that Zimri-Lim decided to use this particular subterfuge: he offered his younger daughter Kirûm to Ḫāya-Sūmû in the hope of obtaining intelligence through her concerning his alliances, to hamper or to control his independence and thus succeed in making him more cooperative.

The younger daughter Kirûm was given in marriage to Ḫāya-Sūmû, two years after her elder sister Šimātum, in the second year of Zimri-Lim's reign. The vassal, being no dupe, quickly realized the indelicate maneuver of his father-in-law. Ḫāya-Sūmû then threatened to kill his newly wed bride Kirûm and decided to isolate her from his palace, barring her access to his political friends and allies. By contrast, Šimātum had succeeded in convincing her husband of her undivided fidelity to his cause. Moreover, even in her letters to her father, she tried to convince Zimri-Lim of the political loyalty of her husband. Should this be taken as her making a sly maneuver, seeing the predicament that befell her younger sister? Or was she genuinely in love with

23. On the political history of Mari and its region, see D. Charpin and N. Ziegler, *Mari et le Proche-Orient à l'époque amorrite: essai d'histoire politique* (Paris: Société pour l'étude du Proche-Orient ancien, 2002); D. Charpin, D.O. Edzard and M. Stol, *Mesopotamien: Die altbabylonische Zeit* (OBO, 160; Freiburg: Freiburg Academic Press, 2004), Chapter 1, 'Histoire politique du Proche-Orient amorrite (2002–1595)'.

24. D. Charpin and J.-M. Durand, 'La prise du pouvoir par Zimri-Lim', *MARI* 4 (1985), pp. 293-343 (335): '§ 5. La politique matrimoniale de Zimri-Lim'. Cf. also Lafont, 'Les filles du roi de Mari', p. 121.

25. Durand, 'Trois études sur Mari', p. 162. The listing of Šimātum's dowry in *ARMT*, 12, 322, uses the local Mari terminology in order to designate the gifts (*nidintum, nidittum* from the verb *nadānum* ('to give); the term dowry comes from Latin *dos*, *dotis* ('gift').

26. According to M.C. Astour, 'The North Mesopotamian Kingdom of Ilānṣurā', in G.D. Young (ed.), *Mari in Retrospect* (Winona Lake, IN: Eisenbrauns, 1992), pp. 1-35, in *ARMT*, 2, 62, Ḫāya-Sūmû is obsequious toward his father-in-law Zimri-Lim by calling himself 'your son', and by declaring 'these cities are your cities'.

Ḫāya-Sūmû and convinced of her husband's innocence? Šimātum was behaving like Michal in 1 Sam. 19.10-18 (Fragment 2) who sided with her husband David against her father Saul.

Yamṣûm, a military man,[27] and chief of the Mari garrison stationed in Ilānṣurā, Ḫāya-Sūmû's capital, sent letters to Zimri-Lim. These offer precious details on the court intrigues and the life that the two sisters Kirûm and Šimātum experienced there. Yamṣûm points out something unusual in that a vassal should be given two daughters by his suzerain, and presents this favor as a significant political gesture. He underlines the trust that Zimri-Lim places in Ḫāya-Sūmû saying, 'Since Šamšī-Addu died, there were four powerful kings. But they had not married two daughters of Yaḫdun-Lim's (stock). Now, you have married two daughters of my lord. You have, however, uttered disparaging words in respect to my lord.'[28]

The reconstruction of the story of Kirûm and Šimātum was gradual, necessitating the dovetailing of wrongly separated tablet fragments and combining what at first seemed to be unrelated details. Initially, it was suggested that the absence of a male heir prompted Ḫāya-Sūmû to contract successive marriages with Zimri-Lim's two daughters. Šimātum's supposed infertility was also adduced as a possibility of his second marriage to her younger sister Kirûm.[29] In the course of research, however, the hypothesis of the supposed sterility of the successive wives had to be abandoned. The attentive study of additional letters revealed that Šimātum gave birth to twins and that Kirûm too gave birth to a son. Therefore, the probability that Zimri-Lim used his daughters as a means of achieving his goals and increasing the political stability of his reign and of his region remains the most plausible explanation of his daughters' successive marriages to the same man.

Throughout Zimri-Lim's reign the region of Mari did not enjoy political stability. In order to pacify the local population, Zimri-Lim used other devices as well, such as the redistribution of lands and domains. He granted lands and possessions that belonged to those who died or were missing to his subjects.[30]

27. Yamṣûm defines himself in the following manner: 'Since my early childhood, I have not ceased to practice military service and I understand nothing of agriculture' (D. Charpin, *Archives épistolaires de Mari*, I/2 [ed. D. Charpin, F. Joannès, S. Lackenbacher and B. Lafont; ARM, 26; Paris: Editions Recherche sur les Civilisations, 1988], p. 46, text 333 [M.5468]).

28. Charpin, *Archives épistolaires de Mari*, I/2, p. 57, text 303 [A.1168], ll. 20′-25′: *iš-tu* ᵈutu-*ši*-ᵈIM *i-mu-tù* 4 lugal-meš *i-ba-šu-ú dan-nu-tù-um ù* dumu-mí *ia-aḫ-du-li-im* 2 ⌜mí *ú-ul*⌝ *i-ḫu-zu-ú* [*i-n*]*a-an-na* dumu-mí *be-lí-ya ta-aq-bi* 2 mí *ta-ḫu-uz* [*ù ṭ*]*ú-pu-ul-ta*$_8$ *be-lí-ya ta-aq-bi.*

29. Durand, 'Trois études sur Mari', pp. 164-67. Since the Mari letters do not speak of infertility and the reference in *ARMT*, 10, 26 does not give the name of the twins' mother, this explanation remains hypothetical.

30. B.F. Batto, 'Land Tenure and Women at Mari', *JESHO* 23 (1980), pp. 209-39 (217).

It seems therefore that Zimri-Lim gave his second daughter to the same vassal in order to get a better grip on his politically volatile son-in-law. While Šimātum succeeds in preserving the trust of her husband and her privileged position at court, Kirûm falls from grace. A bitter strife erupts between the two sisters, heightened by political rivalry. Kirûm, faithful to the injunctions of her father, keeps sending letters providing him with political intelligence. Šimātum does the opposite. She never fails to reassure her father of the supposed loyalty of her husband. Aware of treason in his own backyard, Ḫāya-Sūmû ostracizes Kirûm, treating his daughter harshly. Kirûm's position at Ḫāya-Sūmû's court is so jeopardized that she prefers to leave him and return to her father's court.

Their behavior and the content of their letters indicate that Zimri-Lim uses his daughters as political informants. After her marriage to Ḫāya-Sūmû, and having reached her husband's capital Ilānṣurā, Šimātum sends a letter to her father (*ARMT*, 10, 94), saying that she has visited Ilānṣurā where her husband resides, as well as the cities of their allies (ll. 3-7). 'Since the day I left Mari, I have not stopped traveling. I have seen all the cities, those that serve as dwellings to my lord, and the officers of my lord have seen me.'[31] These lines indicate that she is assuming her role as a new queen. She is presented to the subjects of her kingdom and is becoming acquainted with its extent and with its main alliances. Her husband introduces her as his new queen, daughter of the powerful tribal chief from Mari, among the most prestigious cities in Syria. Another letter (*ARMT*, 10, 5) reads like a memento written by the secret service. Šimātum[32] provides her father with the information that he requests: 'concerning the report about which my lord had wr[itt]en me' (*aššum tēmim ša bēlī i*[*špur*]*am*, l. 3). She tells him that another spy named Maṣi-El, whom the king had ordered to watch the hostile city of Šubat-Enlil and to enter it, has not come out of it yet. Her husband Ḫāya-Sūmû had concluded an official military alliance with another vassal named Turum-natki following the order of their common suzerain Zimri-Lim, 'between them, they have pronounced the oath of the gods' (*ina birīšunu nīš ilāni izkurū-ma*, l. 10). Together they launched an attack against the city of Šubat-Enlil. If one may judge from this letter, Šimātum seems to fulfill completely her mission of informing her father of her husband's political transactions and military operations.

31. *ARMT*, 10, 94.3-7: *iš-tu* u_4*-mi-im ša iš-*[*tu Ma-ri*^{ki} *ú-ṣú*] *ma-di-iš al-ta-*[*am*?-*ma*?-*ad*?] *ù a-la-ni ka-la-šu-nu a-*[*mu*?-*ur*?] *ša ki-ma šu-ba-at be-lí-ya-*[*ma*] *ù ša ki-ma* <*it*?-*ti*?> *be-lí-ya i-*[*la*?-*ku*?], following a new collation and translation by J.-M. Durand, *Documents épistolaires du palais de Mari* (LAPO, 18, Paris: Cerf, 2000), III, p. 430; in *al-ta-*[*am*?-*ma*?-*ad*?] Durand reads the verb *lasāmum* in the Gtn conjugation with an iterative meaning: 'to travel to and fro'.

32. See Durand, *Documents épistolaires*, III, p. 433 n. a. The text reads ^{f}*ši-tum*, which Durand emends to *ši-*<*ma*>*-tum*.

The younger daughter Kirûm is mentioned among the women of the royal harem in Mari in the first and second years of Zimri-Lim's reign. It is only at the end of the third year of Zimri-Lim that Kirûm is mentioned as Ḫāya-Sūmû's wife. It can be inferred that two or three years have elapsed between the marriages of the two sisters to the same vassal. Kirûm's determined character has been noted, as well as her manner of asking pertinent questions pertaining to political issues. Moreover she is giving her father her opinion concerning the appropriate actions to be taken in order to subdue the revolt in the region (*ARMT*, 10, 31). This indicates that Kirûm is an adult woman. Her opinion on political affairs matters to her father. She says, 'You are going away, yet you have done nothing to settle the situation in the land (lit. "to set things right"); after your departure, the land will become hostile. Here is what I said to my father and lord and he did not listen to me!' (*ARMT*, 10, 31.7-11).[33] Later in the same letter (ll. 7′-13′) she continues, saying, 'Now, even if I am just a woman, let my father and lord pay attention to my words: These are always the words of the gods (*awāt ilāni*) that I send to my father. Go to the Upper-Country, reside in Naḫur and do everything that the gods will show you!'[34]

This passage shows how Kirûm skilfully circumvents the problem of the exclusion of women from active political life. Having difficulties in making her father accept her advice concerning political action, she refers to her message as being the 'word of the gods' (*awāt ilāni*). She is either referring to some divinatory technique like hepatoscopy, or she is conveying her premonitory dreams (oniromancy) which she interprets as messages from the gods.[35] In order to give her words greater weight in the eyes of her father, she claims that she has obtained her information through divine revelation, an argument that bridges the male–female social and political division.

From the beginning of her relationship with her husband, Kirûm seems to have been hampered in her travels, as is indicated in two fragments of the same letter (*ARMT*, 10, 34 and 113).[36] She sends a message concerning her resolve to return to Mari (*ARMT*, 10, 34). Her father had promised 'once, twice', to take her back, but he had not carried out his promise. On the back of the same tablet, Kirûm requests that her father secure her a 'throne for a

33. *ARMT*, 10, 31.7-10: *ta-at-ta-la-ak* [*ù mi-i*]*m-ma ma-a-tam ù-ul tu-uš-te-še-er* [*wa*]-*ar-ki-ka-a-ma ma-a-tum* [*i-n*]*a-ak-ki-ir an-ni-tam a-na a-bi-ya ù be-lí-ya aq-bi-ma ú-ul eš-me-en-ni.*

34. *ARMT*, 10, 31.7′-13′: [*i-n*]*a-an-na ù šum-ma a-na-ku sì-ni-ša-ku* [*a-b*]*i ù be-lí a-na a-wa-ti-ya* [*l*]*i-qú-ul a-wa-at ilāni*^{meš} *a-na ṣe-er a-bi-ya aš-ta-na-ap-pa-ar e-el-em-ma i-na Na-aḫ-ur*^{ki} *ši-ib-ma ù ma-li ilāni*^{meš} *ú-ka-la-mu-ka e-pu-úš.*

35. Durand, *Documents épistolaires*, III, p. 436 n. g.

36. Durand, 'Trois études sur Mari', p. 164, was able to make a join between *ARMT*, 34 and 113, showing that letter 113 comes from Kirûm.

queen'. In him alone does she trust, because in her husband's town, Ilānṣurā, she is not treated as a queen: 'My father and lord should install me on a throne (worthy) of a queen: Let him do what is needed so that my heart may no longer be grieved' (*ARMT*, 10, 34.8′-13′).[37]

Four years elapse before Kirûm gives birth to a son. This event took place in the sixth year of Zimri-Lim. Šaknum, one of Zimri-Lim's servants, informed the sovereign in a letter, 'Something else: Kirûm has given birth to a boy, may my lord rejoice!'[38]

In another letter, Kirûm indicates that her husband Ḫāya-Sūmû, who was supposed to go to Mari, is opposed to her leaving the city: 'If you and I leave together, to whom shall we leave the city? Until I return from Mari, you should remain here!' (*ARMT*, 10, 113.6-11). 'In fact, the day that Ḫāya-Sūmû comes back to the land of Ida-Maraṣ, let my lord send a cart or a litter with him, so that I may go to my father and lord, and that I may sacrifice to the gods of my father (*a-na ilāni*^meš *ša a-bi-ya ni-*[*q*]*í-im lu-uq-qí*). May I know prosperity there (*lu-úš-li-im*, root *šlm*)! Moreover, I am all set to leave' (ll. 13-23).[39] Kirûm refers to a custom for princesses who married abroad to return to their father's house in order to perform the rites of ancestor worship.

Another one of Kirûm letters indicates that her situation at her husband's court is steadily deteriorating. Ḫāya-Sūmû and his first wife Šimātum, Kirûm's sister, have become overtly hostile to her and have deprived her of her female servants: 'Moreover, even the last female servants, she (i.e. Šimātum) had taken them away, saying, "My lord has decided so!"' (*ARMT*, 10, 32.15′).

In her letter to her father, Zimri-Lim, Kirûm complains: 'Ḫāya-Sūmû tells me to my face, "You occupy here the office of *ḫazannūtum* (political representative or official resident). Once I kill you, may your 'Star' (Zimri-Lim) come and take you back!"' (ll. 11′-14′).[40]

Now, even her sister Šimātum threatens her and treats her with hostility: 'Šimātum tells me to my face, "May my Star do to me as he wishes! I, however, will do with you as I wish!" If my lord should leave me here and not take me back, I will die, I will not survive (*a-ma-at ú-ul a-ba-lu-uṭ*)!' (ll. 20′-28′).

The term *ḫazannūtum* is important in that it reveals the position that Kirûm occupied in her husband's city. It stands for a precise political office. When establishing an alliance, the suzerain would send a *ḫazannum*, an

37. *ARMT*, 10, 34.8′-10′: *a-bi ù be-lí a-na* ^iš*kussi šar-ra-tim* [*li*]*-še-ši-ba-an-ni ša la-a ma-ra-aṣ li-ib-bi-ya*.

38. Charpin, *Archives épistolaires de Mari*, I/2, p. 125, text 351 [M.8467], l. 24: *ša-ni-tam* ^f*ki-ru-ú* dumu-nita$_2$ *iš-li-im be-lí ḫa-di*); cf. the verb *išlim* from the root *šlm* with a transitive sense expressing the idea that the birth had a successful outcome.

39. Durand, *Documents épistolaires*, III, p. 437.

40. In their correspondence, the daughters of Zimri-Lim call their father 'Star'.

official political representative as a guarantee of his authority and control over the vassal.[41] This role is described in *ARMT*, 2, 109.9-10, where Šukru-Tešub the king of Eluḫḫut writes to Šub-Rām the king of Šubat-Enlil and of nearby Susā: *kīma* [lú]*ḫazannī ina ālim*[ki] [*še-t*]*u wāšib u ālum*[ki] *Amaz*[ki] *iyaum a*[*t-ta*] *tīde* ('as you know my political representative *ḫazannum* dwells in that city and the city of Amaz is mine').[42] According to other texts, this function corresponds to the magistrate of the city or to the mayor as in Ugarit.[43] The political office of *ḫazannūtum* that was incumbent on Kirûm explains her outrage when her husband decides to exclude her from his political meetings, preventing her from supervising his dealings and from providing the required report to her father.

In the conflict which opposed Ḫāya-Sūmû and Kirûm, Yamṣûm, the chief of the Mari garrison stationed in Ilānṣurā, sided with the latter and reproached the former for his submission to the Elamites, Zimri-Lim's political enemies. Apparently, the court in Ilānṣurā was divided into two opposing political factions. On the one side there was the pro-Elamite party with Šimātum, Aqba-abum and Luria, while on the other side was the anti-Elamite party with Kirûm, Yamṣûm and Ulluri. One important feature of these documents is to show the political role that the wives of the vassal played and the part they adopted in the factions and quarrels that divided the local court.[44]

The tensions at Ḫāya-Sūmû's court came to a head. The letters reveal a desperate Kirûm sequestered by her husband who is threatening to kill her. She is undergoing severe 'moral harassment'.

In *ARMT*, 10, 33.5,18, Kirûm twice says that her life is endangered (*iktaru na-pá-aš-ti*, lit. 'my life is in desperate straits').[45] She feels so outraged and scorned by her husband that she threatens to commit suicide: 'I am tired of living from hearing Šimātum's words! If my lord does not take me back to Mari, I will run and immediately (*a-ṣa-ba-at ap-pi*) throw myself from a roof ([*i*]*š-tu ú-ri-im a-ma-qú-ut*)' (ll. 5-9).[46] She desperately wants to leave her

41. A. Finet, 'Iawi-Ilâ, roi de Talḫayûm', *Syria* 41 (1964), pp. 117-42 (130-34).

42. J.-M. Durand, *Documents épistolaires du palais de Mari* (LAPO, 16, Paris: Cerf, 1997), I, p. 516, who transcribes the title as *ḫaṣṣiānum* and defines it as 'a local representative of the suzerain's interests'. On Šūb-Rām and *ḫaṣṣiānum* see 517 nn. b and c.

43. Cf. the translation of the term in *CAD*, Ḫ, 1956, p. 163: *ḫazannu* is 'chief magistrate of a town, of a quarter of a larger city, a village or large estate-mayor, burgomaster, headman'. So too *AHw*, 338, 'Bürgermeister'; cf. in Ugarit [lú]*ḫazannu āli*, 'mayor of the city' (*PRU*, III, 135a 15).

44. Charpin, *Archives épistolaires de Mari*, I/2, p. 45.

45. The form *iktaru* comes from the verb *karû*; cf. *CAD*, K, 1971, p. 230, section 3 *karû* B: 'with *napištu*, to bring into deathly danger'.

46. Durand, *Documents épistolaires*, III, p. 444 n. a. The expression *appam ṣabātum*, corresponds to *ṣibit appim*, literally 'in a sneeze', meaning an action performed rapidly, 'in a twinkle of an eye'.

husband Ḫāya-Sūmû and his court. In fact, she wants to get out of this arranged marriage.

Her unhappy marriage ends in divorce. By insisting and claiming her profound unhappiness with the way she is treated, Kirûm succeeds in obtaining divorce:

> He cut (*ibtuq*) my cord (*biqtī-ni*), in front of the kings (*maḫar šarrāni*), saying, 'Go away to you father's house! (*atlaki ana bīt abīki*, ll. 25-29). I have turned my eyes away from the face of my wife!' Moreover, the female servant I spoke about to my lord, he took her away from me and gave her to Šimātum.[47]

The letter enumerates a series of symbolic actions revealing the divorce procedure in northern Syria in the eighteenth century BCE. First, the expression 'to cut the cord' (*bitqam batāqum*) describes a gesture with an opposite meaning to the one which consists in tying or binding (*rakāsum*) a cord in a symbolic act of making an alliance. Old Babylonian texts have a similar expression, *sissiktam batāqum* ('to cut the hem [of a garment]'), as a symbolic action of divorce.[48] Secondly, the kings or rather sheikhs in front of whom Ḫāya-Sūmû's gesture takes place represent Ilānṣūrā's vassals who are witnessing this legal procedure. Thirdly, the turning of the husband's eyes away from his wife is also a symbolic gesture. To see a person is to 'possess' that person. To turn the eyes away from one's wife means that she no longer belongs to her husband. He no longer owns her and she is free to go back to her father's home. Fourthly, her husband Ḫāya-Sūmû takes a female servant away from Kirûm and gives her to his other spouse Šimātum. He was probably taking back a gift which he had previously given her.

The right of a wife to divorce her husband in Old Babylonian law has been the subject of considerable discussion. Some scholars deny that the wife had the legal right to divorce her husband at all.[49] Propounding a radically opposite view, A. van Praag considers that the wife had rights virtually equal to the husband in this respect.[50] A third opinion is to regard the cuneiform

47. Durand, *Documents épistolaires*, III, p. 444, n. e; *CDA*, p. 46: *bitqu*(*m*) ('cutting [of umbilical cord]').

48. See S. Greengus, 'The Old Babylonian Marriage Contract', *JAOS* 89 (1969), pp. 505-32 (515 n. 44); A. Draffkorn Kilmer, 'Symbolic Gestures in Akkadian Contracts from Alalakh and Ugarit', *JAOS* 94 (1974), pp. 177-83 (182 n. 24, with bibliography); P.A. Kruger, 'The Hem of the Garment in Marriage: The Meaning of the Symbolic Gesture in Ruth 3.9 and Ezek 16.8', *JNWSL* 12 (1984), pp. 79-86.

49. G.R. Driver and J. Miles, *The Babylonian Laws* (Oxford: Clarendon Press, 1952–55), II, p. 223, commenting on CH 142.60. *izîr* from the root *zâru* ('to hate') connotes sexual aversion and refusal of conjugal rights. It is paralleled by Hebrew *śn'* ('to hate', Deut. 22.13; 24.3; Judg. 14.16; 15.2).

50. A. van Praag, *Droit matrimonial assyro-babylonien* (Archaeologisch-historische Bijdragen, 12; Amsterdam: N.V. Noord-Hollandsche Uitgevers Maatschappij, 1945), pp. 193-204, Chapter 8, 'Les divorces', especially pp. 199-200.

sources as conflicting and to explain the wife's rights in terms of the different laws applied. Thus P. Koschaker distinguishes between *Muntehe* or *Kaufehe* (marriage by purchase through the practice of *terḫatum*), where the wife has no right to divorce, and *muntfreie Ehe*, in which each partner was equally entitled to initiate divorce proceedings.[51] R. Westbrook reviews the various texts and arguments for each of these positions.[52] He concludes that the sources give the impression that a more liberal attitude to divorce by the wife prevailed in the old Sumerian-speaking cities of the south over against the Akkadian-speaking populations in the north:

> The marriage contract is generally between the husband and the bride's father. Its principal terms are performed by the completion of marriage itself, but some survive into marriage, and the benefit and burden of such terms will then pass to the wife. The divorce-clauses are of this nature. They survive as contingency clauses—to regulate the effects of a situation that could arise through the exercise of rights derived from the status of marriage. In the case of the husband, they basically provide compensation upon this contingency, although the penalty does contain an element of deterrent. In the case of the wife, however, the purpose of the clause has often been transformed by raising the deterrent element of the penalty to a point where it renders the contingency itself virtually impossible. The OB law of divorce thus frequently presents a dichotomy which has been a source of much confusion, but which in our view is not the expression of a conflict within the legal system or even between two legal systems; it is the difference between theory and practice.[53]

According to R. Westbrook, in Old Babylonian times the woman had a theoretical right to ask for a divorce. In practise, however, that right was rarely exercised by a woman. There were too many hindrances for the woman to have recourse to this possibility.

The Old Babylonian Code of Hammurabi states:

> If a woman has despised (*izēr-ma*) her husband and has said, 'You shall not take me', her situation shall be assessed by her community. If she has been looked after and there is no blame, but her husband has erred and greatly disparaged her, that woman has no guilt. She shall take away her marriage gift (*šeriktum*) and go to her father's house. (CH 142)

Westbrook interprets this law as relating to refusal to complete an inchoate marriage and does not deal with divorce.[54]

51. See P. Koschaker, 'Eheschliessung und Kauf nach altem Recht, mit besonderer Berücksichtigung der ältesten Keilschriftrechte', *Archiv Orientální* 18 (1950), pp. 210-96; *idem*, 'Zur Interpretation des Art. 59 des Codex Bilalama', *JCS* 5 (1951), pp. 104-22 (116-18).

52. R. Westbrook, 'Old Babylonian Marriage Law' (unpublished PhD dissertation, Yale University, 1982, UMI Microfilms, Ann Arbor no. 8221763), II, pp. 224-38.

53. Westbrook, 'Old Babylonian Marriage Law', II, pp. 239-40.

54. See Richardson, *Hammurabi's Laws*, p. 87: 'unwilling to marry'; cf. Westbrook, 'Old Babylonian Marriage Law', II, p. 66.

Kirûm, being a royal princess, daughter of the most powerful local king in the region, took full advantage of the possibility that existed in Old Babylonian times of obtaining a divorce. She continued to claim her right until she obtained the official divorce ceremony from her husband. It seems that the divorce between Ḫāya-Sūmû and Kirûm took place at the end of the first half of the ninth year of Zimri-Lim. After that date, it is supposed that Kirûm was free to go back to her father's house in Mari. This fact cannot be verified, though, since the ration lists from the end of Zimri-Lim's reign are missing.[55]

In the context of ancient Israel, Michal did not have the possibility of obtaining a divorce from her royal husband. Biblical texts are silent concerning the woman as plaintiff in a divorce proceeding. Deuteronomy 24.1 mentions a *spr krytt* ('bill of divorce'). Deuteronomy 24.3 uses the verb *śn'* ('to hate') as an expression of a will to divorce. The verb, *grš* ('to divorce', in Deut. 22.19 and Num. 30.10) and *trk* ('to repudiate', in Lev. 21.7), attested in biblical texts, are linked exclusively to the male's power, authority and decision (Deut. 22.13-19; 24.1-4).[56] The rabbis in the Talmud project the existence of a *gṭ* ('divorce letter') in the time of David (see below, Chapter 3). The earliest extra-biblical evidence for the right of divorce given to a Jewish woman stems from the fifth-century BCE Aramaic Elephantine marriage contracts. Only three marriage contracts have survived to the present day in a good state of preservation.[57] These marriage contracts contain a divorce clause. In l. 23 of B2.6 the words that the woman named Mipṭaḥyah will have to state in case of divorce are the following: 'I hate (*śn'*) Esḥor, my husband'. The documents adds that she will have to pay 'the silver of hate' (*ksp śn'*).[58]

3. *The Suicide Motif in Mari and in One Greek Tragedy*

The threat made by Kirûm to throw herself from the roof if she is not freed from her husband and taken back home to Mari allows us to continue the search for analogies and to trace the motif of suicide by oppressed women to a piece of Classical Greek literature. The motif reappears some thirteen centuries after the Mari 'Feminine Correspondence'. In Greek literature, however, we are dealing with a different genre. It is not a piece of correspondence but a myth used in the context of a fictional play.

55. Ziegler, *Le harem de Zimrî-Lîm*, p. 64.

56. E. Lipiński, 'The Wife's Right to Divorce in the Light of Ancient Near Eastern Tradition', *The Jewish Law Annual* 4 (1981), pp. 9-28.

57. B. Porten and A. Yardeni, *Textbook of Aramaic Documents from Ancient Egypt*. II. *Contracts* (Winona Lake, IN: Eisenbrauns, 1989). The documents are referred to as B2. 6 (458 or 445 BCE); B3. 3 (449 BCE); B3. 8 (420 BCE).

58. The evidence has been analyzed by H. Nutkowicz, 'Concerning the Verb (*śn'*) in Judean-Aramaic Contracts from Elephantine' (forthcoming).

In the tragedy *Supplices*, dating from about 466 BCE,[59] Aischylus elaborates his intrigue starting from the Greek myth of two brothers Danaos and Aigyptos. They are the two sons of Io, a priestess of the goddess Hera on the island of Argos. The god Zeus, an inveterate womanizer, seduces the young priestess Io and she becomes pregnant. In order to hide his misdeed from his wife Hera, he transforms Io into a cow. Hera, jealous and furious, expels the young woman-cow, forcing her to wander across the Bosporus (thus revealing the etiology of that geographical name which means 'the passage of the cow') and across the Mediterranean. The young priestess ends her peregrinations in Egypt. Her two sons Danaos and Aigyptos beget fifty sons each. The numerous sons of Aigyptos want to marry their cousins, the daughters of Danaos, and are ready to use violence in order to obtain what they want. The young females decline this forced marriage, which amounts to becoming the slaves of the sons of Aigyptos. Perhaps they are refusing an incestuous relationship with their cousins? The tragedy describes the daughters of Danaos, imploring, weeping and defenseless, pursued by their powerful male cousins. They flee to the island of Argos, the homeland of their illustrious grandmother, and ask the local king for asylum and protection. In one song, they implore the god Zeus, once the lover of their ancestress, to protect them as defenseless women against their pursuing enemies, 'a hive of insolent males' (*arseno-plēthē d'hesmon hubristēn*, ll. 29-30). They describe their fear of their male cousins, powerful men inflamed with hubris and with no respect for women (l. 81). In this context, the Greek term *hubris* is synonymous with 'oppression'.[60] They ask the king of Argos to realize 'the extent of the hubris (*hubrin*) of the males' (l. 426). The king, however, desirous to avoid a war with the Egyptians, refuses to help them. Desperate, the young women point to their belts with which they keep their robes tight around their waist. These belts are their *mēchanē kalē* ('marvelous expedient'). If the king refuses to take them back to their ancestral island and offer them his protection, they too will commit an act of hubris: by transgressing the imposed limits and committing

59. See A.F. Garvie, *Aeschylus' Supplices: Play and Trilogy* (London: Cambridge University Press, 1969), p. 11; A.J. Podlecky, 'Quelques aspects de l'affrontement entre les hommes et les femmes chez Eschyle', in E. Lévy (ed.), *La femme dans les sociétés antiques*, pp. 59-71.

60. Cf. Bodi, *The Book of Ezekiel*, pp. 117-61, on the Akkadian term *ḫubūru* in the Atraḫasīs Epic where it can stand for 'excess and immoderation', and might come close to the Greek *hubris*, defined in Classical Greek literature as the human tendency to overstep the natural limits set by the gods (pp. 125-28). Note W. von Soden, 'Der Mensch bescheidet sich nicht: Überlegungen zur Schöpfungs-erzählungen in Babylonien und Israel', in M.A. Beek *et al.* (eds.), *Symbolae biblicae et Mesopotamicae F.M.T. de Liagre Böhl dedicatae* (Leiden: E.J. Brill, 1973), pp. 349-58, who describes human beings in Atraḫasīs refusing to accept limits to their liberty.

a sacrilege against the gods of the land they will hang themselves with their belts from the divine statues of the gods.

The main theme of this tragedy is the relationship between women and those holding power and authority which makes this play an exceptional testimony of Classical Greek literature. The role of women in Greek society is depicted from the point of view of those who wield social and political authority and who control female sexuality. The myth at the basis of this tragedy reveals the rather dismal condition of women in Classical Greek society.

4. *The Marriage Gift or Counter-Gift in Israel and Mari*

Going back to the Mari 'Feminine Correspondence', stemming from the Northwest Semitic world to which the ancient Hebrews also belonged, we can see one additional aspect that connects these two cultures. The Mari marriage practice of the *terḫatum*[61] or 'counter-gift' corresponds to the Israelite *mōhar*. In 1 Sam. 18.25, for his marriage with his daughter Michal, Saul asks that as a counter-gift or *mōhar* David should bring 'one hundred Philistine foreskins'.

The Israelite *mhr* is a sum of money which the bridegroom had to give to the father or to the family of the bride. It is not really a 'bride-price', since the bride was not bought. Rather, it is compensation or indemnity for the economic services which the young women would no longer perform for her father's household.[62]

Both the Mari *terḫatum* and the Israelite *mōhar* represent the counter-gift which the bridegroom or the family of the bridegroom should give to the bride's father or family (cf. Gen. 34.12; Exod. 22.15).The Hebrew *mhr* has been compared to a similar phenomenon mentioned in the Codex Hammurabi §151-61, 163-64, 166, where the bridegroom, or frequently his father, had to

61. The *terḫatum* represents a counter-gift or a present that the bridegroom or the bridegroom's father offers to the bride's father; for further discussion, cf. J. Klíma, 'La vie sociale et économique à Mari', in J.-R. Kupper (ed.), *La civilisation de Mari* (RAI, 15; Paris: Les Belles Lettres, 1967), pp. 39-50 (44); *idem*, 'Le règlement du mariage dans les lois babyloniennes anciennes', in W. Meid and H. Trenkwalder (eds.), *Im Bannkreis des Alten Orients* (Festschrift Karl Oberhuber; IBK, 24; Innsbruck: Institut für Sprachwissenschaft der Universität, 1986), pp. 109-21. Cf. CH R VII: 28 § 139: *šumma terḫatum lā ibašši 1 mana kaspam ana uzzubîm inaddiššim* ('If there is no counter-gift, he shall give one *mana* of silver as "repudiation indemnity"'); so Finet, *Le Code d'Hammurapi*, p. 88; cf. also CH R VII: 28 § 141.49-51. This indemnity could have been paid in goods or in money.

62. According to R. de Vaux, *Ancient Israel* (New York: McGraw–Hill, 1965), I, p. 27, a similar custom with the same name (*mahr*), is found among modern Palestinian Arabs. The *mahr* is a sum of money paid by the fiancé to the girl's parents.

give a sum of money or its equivalent (the *terḫatu*) to the father of the girl along with other gifts (cf. Deut. 22.29; Gen. 24.22, 53).[63]

The 'dowry' (*nidittum*[64]) given by the father to his daughter, and the *terḫatum* represent the two essential aspects of the Mari marriage practises. In Mari one finds a long catalogue (*ARMT*, 12, 322) representing a list of goods or gifts that Šimātum brought with her on the occasion of her marriage to Ḫāya-Sūmû. The corresponding Old Babylonian term for Mari's *nidittum* is *šeriktum*.[65]

One finds an additional example of *nidittum* in the context of the princess Narāmtum, in *ARMT*, 22, 232.5'. The same term appears in order to describe the dowry of a priestess (*ARMT*, 22, 154.5).

Biblical Hebrew uses a cognate of the Akkadian *nidittum* in Ezek. 16.3, where the *hapax nēdeh*[66] occurs, designating a gift offered to Jerusalem personified as a loose woman. In his invective against the prostitution of Jerusalem, the prophet Ezekiel says that all prostitutes receive a *nēdeh*. In the case of Jerusalem as an unfaithful wife, however, she is making a gift (**nādān*) to all her lovers. Greenfield explained the Hebrew **nādān* etymologically as deriving from the Akkadian *nidnu* ('gift') which can also mean a 'marriage gift'.[67]

Beyond this Akkadian etymology of a Hebrew term, there is one more important link between the Mari and Israelite marriage customs. It is the practice of a 'counter-gift'. The Mari *terḫatum* seems to correspond to the Hebrew *mōhar* and to the Arabic *mahr*.[68] Thus in *ARMT*, 2, 40, Yasim-El, a

63. On this point see E.M. MacDonald, *The Position of Women as Reflected in Semitic Codes of Law* (Toronto University Oriental Series, 1; Toronto: University of Toronto Press, 1931), pp. 12-13; and Driver and Miles, *The Babylonian Laws*, I, pp. 259-60. In Asia Minor one finds the same phenomenon called *kušata*; cf. A. Goetze, *Kleinasien: Handbuch der Altertumwissenschaft* (Munich: Beck, 1933), p. 104.

64. Cf. YOS 2, 25,10-14 OB letter: *mimma nudunnâm ša* PN *ana mārtīša iddunūma ana bīt* NP_2 *ušēribu*[*ši*] ('the whole dowry that PN gave to his daughter and which made her enter the house of PN_2'), quoted in *CAD*, N/II, 1980, p. 310.

65. Cf. CH R XII, § 171.78-85: *ḫīrtum šeriktaša u nudunnâm ša mussa iddinūšim ina ṭuppim išturūšim ileqqe* ('The initial wife shall take the dowry and the wedding gift which her husband presented to her and wrote on a document for her').

66. M. Greenberg, *Ezekiel 1–20* (AB, 22; Garden City, NY: Doubleday, 1983), p. 285: 'The hapaxes *nede* and *nadan* "gift" (G S T V render as *'etna(n)* in vss. 31, 34) appear to be morphological variants like *'etna* and *'etnan* (Hosea 2.14; 9.1), "harlot's hire"'.

67. See J.C. Greenfield, 'Two Biblical Passages in the Light of their Eastern Background—Ezekiel 16.30 and Malachi 3.17', *IEJ* 16 (1982), pp. 56-61; *CAD*, N/II, pp. 108a-109; *AHw*, 786a.

68. In the Nuzi documents dating from the fifteenth–fourteenth centuries BCE, the *terḫatum* ('counter-gift') consists of forty sheqels of silver (*kaspu*); see C.H. Gordon, 'The Status of Woman Reflected in the Nuzi Tablets', *ZA* 43 (1936), pp. 146-69 (157).

high official of Zimri-Lim, informs his sovereign of a political marriage: 'Išmê-Dagān concluded a peace with the Turrukeans. He takes the daughter of Zaziya (as wife) for his son Mût-asqur. Išmê-Dagan had brought silver and gold to Zaziya, as a *terḫatum*' (ll. 5-9).

In *ARMT*, 1, 77.8-13 Šamši-Addu writes to Yasmaḫ-Addu and mentions the sum of five talents of silver representing the *terḫatum*: 'I will take the young girl, daughter of Išḫī-Addu. The House of Mari is of great nobility just like the House of Qaṭna. The counter-gift (*terḫatum*) is mediocre, so much so that it is shameful to offer it. There are (just) five talents of silver as a *terḫatum* to offer to Qaṭna.'[69] The letter indicates that the sum is not enough. It is again a matter of political marriage with a high-ranking princess, the daughter of the king of Qaṭna, and a more significant sum should have been given as a counter-gift.

Šimātum's dowry (*nidittum*) is listed in a detailed catalogue (*ARMT*, 22, 322 and 25, 603). These two lists give an overview of what constituted the dowry of a Mari royal princess in the eighteenth century BCE. One finds here jewelry, gold, silver, bronze tools, clothing, luxury vestments, furniture made out of precious wood, a dozen female servants and a personal scribe. Zimri-Lim was expecting precious political intelligence from the court at Ilanṣurā where his daughter was getting married to his vassal Ḫāya-Sūmû. The particular interest of this list of Šimātum's dowry is the express mention of a female scribe placed at her service (*ARMT*, 22, 322.58). This indicates that even at such an early time in northern Syria one could find educated females trained in scribal art and placed at the disposal of a royal princess. The advantage of having a female scribe is obvious—she could have easy and immediate access to the female quarters where the princess lived. Moreover, the presence of a scribe, in this case a female one, was essential for Zimri-Lim's purposes of rapidly obtaining information concerning the political transactions at his vassal's court. Zimri-Lim was using his daughters as spies.

When comparing the Mari system of dowry (*nidittum*) and counter-gift (*terḫatum*) with the ancient Israelite marriage transactions between Saul and David, one can suppose that Michal, being a royal princess, had also received an important dowry from her father. This can be deduced indirectly from the biblical text. In 1 Sam. 17.54, before his marriage with Saul's daughter, it is stated that David owned only a tent. David repeatedly protests that neither he nor his father's house possesses riches. In 1 Sam. 19.11, however, David has a house (*byt-dwd*). The house was probably part of Michal's dowry. A large number of female servants also came with it. When, for example, in 1 Sam. 25.42, David marries Abigail, a rich widow of a farmer from the region of

69. Durand, 'Les dames du palais', p. 403, and *idem*, *Documents épistolaires*, III, p. 170.

Carmel, south of Jerusalem, she rides on a donkey (a royal symbol both in Mari and in ancient Israel and distinct from the Mesopotamian tradition[70]) to meet David. Moreover, she is escorted by five female servants (*n'rwtyh*). *A fortiori*, a royal princess like Michal must have had an even greater number of female servants.

In light of the Mari counter-gift (*terḫatum*), often representing something valuable and substantial, Saul's request that David give just one hundred Philistine foreskins as a *mōhar* is surprising. Does it mean that David was so poor that the only thing he could offer was his military skill as an able warrior? The rabbinic commentators find that the Philistine foreskins had a very limited value, being just about good enough to feed the dogs. Moreover, determined to get rid of David who had become a threatening political rival, Saul seems to have set up a trap for David, intending to have him killed.

5. *The Two Daughters of Hatshepsut Given to the Same Prince*

The history of ancient Egypt from the time of the eighteenth dynasty furnishes a further analogy to a man being offered two sisters as wives. King Thutmose II (1495–90) and Queen Hatshepsut (1486–68) had two daughters, Neferure, the elder, and Merytre-Hatshepsut, the younger. With a concubine named Isis, King Thutmose II also had a son named Thutmose-Menkheperre who, under the name of Thutmose III (1490–36), succeeded his father after a long period spent as coregent with his step-mother Hatshepsut.[71] His father Thutmose II had a short reign. He died, probably of an illness, leaving his son, the future Thutmose III, too young to reign alone. His step-mother Hatshepsut reigned in his stead. Officially, Thutmose III was just a coregent. He had two half sisters. The contemporaries of Thutmose I are categorical, Neferure was the elder daughter of Thutmose II and of Hatshepsut. A second younger princess, in all probability born from the same royal couple, shared the same preceptors as her elder sister.

Thutmose III was born of his father's union with a concubine, and this fact seems to have negatively affected his dynastic succession. He therefore married the royal princess who was the direct heiress of the royal family: his half-sister Neferure. From her birth, Neferure received the right to inscribe her name in a royal cartouche. Already as a child she bore the title *hemet*

70. S. Lafont, 'Le roi, le juge et l'étranger à Mari et dans la Bible', *RA* 92 (1998), pp. 161-81 (164).

71. Here I follow the historical reconstruction offered by C. Desroches-Noblecourt, *La reine mystérieuse Hatshepsout* (Paris: Pygmalion, 2002), pp. 58, 247, 250. In dating the reigns of these Pharaohs, see J.A. Wilson, *The Culture of Ancient Egypt* (Chicago: The University of Chicago Press, 1958), pp. 320, and 175-76 for the reigns of Hatshepsut and Thutmose III.

neter ('divine spouse'). The Egyptologist C. Desroches-Noblecourt suggests that the young King Thutmose III married his half-sister Neferure, who possessed all the royal titles that came to her with her birth. She became the 'Great Royal Spouse' only once Thutmose III came to the throne, after the departure of his step-mother, Queen Hatshepsut. Some of Neferure's new titles were, 'royal sister, royal daughter, divine spouse, dame of both lands'.[72] Some time later, however, the name of the spouse and half sister Neferure was replaced by the name of another wife, Satiāh. Apparently, Neferure fell into disgrace and lost her political influence. After the death of Queen Hatshepsut, Satiāh must have officially taken the place of Neferure when Thutmose III finally reigned alone. Having been first married to Thutmose III, she died young and the name of Neferure in the royal cartouche was chiseled out and inscribed with the name of the other spouse, Satiāh. The latter, however, was never called the 'Great Royal Spouse'. Apparently, Satiāh did not have the required royal ancestry for this supreme title.

Again this fact seems to have had some negative repercussion on Thutmose III who decided to take his first wife's (i.e. Neferure's) younger sister, as wife, Merytre-Hatshepsut, the younger daughter of Thutmose II and Hatshepsut. She is represented on a bas-relief found on one of the walls in the temple of the Thutmosids in Medinet Habu, where she is standing upright behind the image of her half-brother and husband Thutmose III. She gave birth to a son who became the Pharaoh Amenophis II. The tomb of Merytre-Hatshepsut, presently number 42 in the Valley of the Kings, was fitted out for her as indicated by the foundation deposits bearing her name. In his inscription, Senenmut, Hatshepsut's powerful vizier and major-domo of the royal family, says that he took care of her younger daughter Merytre as well as of the older one, Neferure. Another preceptor, Senmen, declares that he had been like a foster father for another 'Divine Spouse'.[73] Brought up together as royal children, the two daughters of Hatshesput, Merytre and Neferure, were probably the playmates of Thutmose III, before becoming his wives. The successive marriages of Thutmose III to his two half sisters were probably carried out in order to reinforce his own dynastic position as the legitimate heir and successor of his father, the Pharaoh Thutmose II. On the one hand, Thutmose III's claim to the throne was somewhat disputed, on account of the fact that he was a son of Thutmose II from the latter's union with a concubine. On the other hand, for a long period of time he had to live in the shadow of his powerful step-mother Hatshepsut, something which he apparently resented. Once he reached the throne as Pharaoh, Thutmose III strove to

72. Desroches-Noblecourt, *La reine mystérieuse Hatshepsout*, p. 243.

73. Desroches-Noblecourt, *La reine mystérieuse Hatshepsout*, p. 386. M. Gitton, *Les épouses divines de la 18e dynastie* (Paris: Les Belles Lettres, 1984), pp. 75-84, offers another point of view.

eradicate all memory of his step-mother with ardor and perseverance akin to revengeful rage.[74]

6. *Conclusions*

The comparative method allows us to draw several resemblances and differences between the daughters of Saul and Zimri-Lim.

The fact that Zimri-Lim was a nomadic Bedouin chieftain belonging to the northern Sim'alite tribes increases the pertinence of this comparison.[75] The very name Zimri-Lim means 'My Force is the Tribe'.[76] *Li'mum* (*līmum*), meaning 'tribe', is the same term meaning 'thousand' in Akkadian and 'people' in Hebrew (*le'ōm*). Saul belonged to the tribe of Benjamin, at the frontier between the southern tribe of Judah and the northern Israelite tribes. This is why the northern tribes seemed more attached to Saul than to David, who as a Judahite was a southerner. As pointed out by D.E. Fleming, 'The whole Israelite comparison is transformed when Zimri-Lim is understood to be a Sim'alite tribal king'.[77] Moreover, one should probably abandon the term 'monarchy' when discussing the times of Saul and David and speak rather of 'Israelite tribal chiefdom'.

Both Zimri-Lim's and Saul's tribal rule were affected by continuous political tensions and constant warring. Yaḫdun-Lim, one of Zimri-Lim's predecessors, was defeated by Šamši-Addu and was then assassinated. His tragic end was attributed to the storm-god Addu's outworking of justice because Yaḫdun-Lim committed a sin against the divinity.[78] The Israelite tribal king Saul is also accused of having been rejected by the tribal god YHWH for a sin he committed by disobeying the god's order (1 Sam. 15). Šamši-Addu placed Yasmaḫ-Addu at the head of Mari. The last tribal king of Mari, Zimri-Lim claimed to be a son of the previous king Yaḫdun-Lim, that is, the legitimate heir to the throne of Mari. Accompanied by an army of Bedouin warriors, disinherited sheikhs and some *condottieri* or mercenaries, he

74. N.-C. Grimal, *Histoire de l'Egypte ancienne* (Paris: Fayard, 1988), p. 270.

75. D. Charpin and J.-M. Durand, '"Fils de Sim'al": les origins tribales des rois de Mari', *RA* 80 (1986), pp. 141-83.

76. So J.-M. Durand, 'Assyriologie (les bétyles)', *Cours et travaux du Collège de France Annuaire* 103 (2002/2003), pp. 745-69 (748); *idem*, 'Peuplement et sociétés à l'époque Amorite: (I) Les clans bensim'alites', in C. Nicolle (ed.), *Amurru 3: Nomades et sédentaires dans le Proche-Orient ancient* (RAI, 46, Paris, 10-13 July, 2000; Paris: Editions Recherche sur les Civilisations, 2004), pp. 111-97; *idem*, 'Assyriology', *Annuaire du Collège de France* 101 (2000–2001), pp. 693-705 (694).

77. D.E. Fleming, 'Mari and the Possibilities of Biblical Memory', *RA* 92 (1998), pp. 41-78 (43).

78. J.-M. Durand, 'Le mythologème du combat entre le dieu de l'Orage et la Mer en Mésopotamie', *MARI* 7 (1993), pp. 43-61.

took power over Mari and proclaimed himself the new king of the Bedouin tribes. During his fifteen-year-long reign, Zimri-Lim had to fight numerous battles in order to ensure his rule over rebellious tribes. As he himself states in a letter to the ruler of Aleppo, 'Now, since the numerous days that I acceded to the throne, I have conducted battles and combats and have never brought a harvest to my land in peace'.[79] David too was accompanied by an army of mercenaries, disenfranchised land-owners and disgruntled soldiers. David's career follows a well-established pattern of the traditional power-struggle between petty tribal overlords in Syria and Canaan. This pattern spans the entire second millennium BCE, as attested by the careers of Zimri-Lim of Mari (eighteenth century BCE), Idrimi of Alalaḫ (fifteenth century BCE) and Saul and David (eleventh–tenth centuries BCE).

Zimri-Lim had ten daughters. The careers of two of them—Šimātum and Kirûm—are well known. Saul had daughters as well, Merab and Michal. Both men used their daughters as bargaining chips in their political schemes. The use of the comparative method has permitted us to point out resemblances and differences between the tragic destiny of Zimri-Lim's daughters Kirûm and Šimātum, and the comparable situation with Saul's daughters Michal and Merab.

For a father to offer two daughters to a single man seems to be prompted by his desire to exercise control over another man. This seems to be the case between Zimri-Lim and Ḫāya-Sūmû, Laban and Jacob, Saul and David.

The political factions and divisions that reigned in the town of Ilānṣurā, with the pro- and anti-Elamite parties, remind us of a similar situation that reigned at Saul's court with his own children Jonathan and Michal taking the side of David, the political rival of their father. Zimri-Lim's elder daughter Šimātum together with her husband Ḫāya-Sūmû led the pro-Elamite party, enemies of Zimri-Lim, while the younger Kirûm together with Yamṣûm, the chief of the Mari garrison in Ilānṣurā, sided with the anti-Elamite party in line with Zimri-Lim's political interests.

In 1988, D. Charpin pointed out the unusual aspect of Zimri-Lim's decision to marry his two daughters Šimātum and Kirûm to the same man:

> One still wonders why Zimri-Lim, who had already given Šimātum to Ḫāya-Sūmû for spouse, wished to give him, approximately two years later, another one of his daughters in marriage? At present we do not know of any parallel to this situation, where a 'vassal' king was the husband of two daughters of the same 'father'.[80]

79. M. Guichard, 'Les aspects religieux de la guerre à Mari', *RA* 93 (1999), pp. 27-48 (28): *i-na-an-na iš-tu u$_4$-mi ma-du-tim ša a-na* giš-gu-za-*ya e-ru-bu* giš-tukul *ù ta-ḫa-za-am e-ep-pé-eš ù ma-ti-ma e-bu-ra-am ša-al-ma-am ma-a-ti, ú-ul ú-še-ri-ib* (*ARMT*, 28, 16.27-30).

80. Charpin, *Archives épistolaires du Mari*, I/2, p. 44.

In my opinion, the fate of the two daughters of Saul, Merab and Michal, could offer a parallel to the situation at Mari. Moreover, the two daughters of Hatshepsut, Merytre and Neferure, who became the wives of Thutmose III, offer an additional example of a similar matrimonial transaction. Furthermore, the Mari analogy increases the historical probability that Saul really offered his two daughters to David. The Mari texts provide a historical precedent where the same man was offered two sisters, one after the other, as spouses. Saul, by marrying his daughter Michal to David, relied on her in gaining the upper hand over his dangerous political rival and hoped to get better control over his actions. In this manner his behavior is comparable to that of Zimri-Lim from Mari, who practiced a similar policy, marrying his numerous daughters to small kinglets of northern Syria. Zimri-Lim thus strove to extend his political ascendancy and control over these kingdoms through his daughters' marriages.

Though the successive marriages of his daughters to the same vassal, Zimri-Lim seems to have expected them to provide him with political information about their husband's alliances and probably to incite the latter to greater loyalty toward Zimri-Lim as his suzerain.

3

Michal in Rabbinic Literature*

1. *Introduction*

There are numerous pages in rabbinic literature dealing with the figure of Michal. Rabbinic commentators analyze Michal's relationship with David, with her second husband Palti as well as the question of her uncertain maternity. Their commentaries touch the emotional side of her relationship with these two men but also analyze with great rigor the legal basis of these two marriages. The rabbis have tried to determine whether it was legitimate for David to take his wife back once she had been married to Palti.

2 Samuel 6.23 states that Michal had no child up to her dying day. The rabbis differ on how this statement should be understood. For some rabbis, she gave birth to a child on the day she died, that is, she died in childbirth. Moreover, she is supposed to have given birth under the name of Eglah, which is taken to be another of Michal's names. For others, she had several children before her dispute with David on the occasion of his dance before the ark. After that incident she had no more children, as a punishment for her defiant attitude toward the king.

By contrast, the biblical texts are rather parsimonious with respect to Michal. This prompted rabbinic authors to fill in the blanks, producing a fair number of commentaries on Michal. Some midrashim describe her in greater detail. As far as looks go, Michal is counted among the four most beautiful women in the world. According to some midrashim, Michal was also an exceptionally pious woman who adopted the *miṣwâ* of wearing the phylacteries, a commandment incumbent on men only and implying study of the Torah.

* The present chapter makes extensive use of the CD-ROM text edition, *Judaic Classics* (Chicago: Davka Corporation, 1995). Citations marked with an asterisk indicate a quotation from or reference to this edition.

In general, the midrashim praise Michal's behavior when she helps David save his life, as in the story of his flight through the window in 1 Sam. 19.11-17, and condemn her when she reprimands him after his dance before the ark in 2 Samuel 6.

As we can expect, the rabbis do not have a single, unified opinion about Michal. The juxtaposition of different midrashim raises the following question: If Michal was such an exceptionally spiritual and pious woman, why was she so cruelly punished and kept from having a child?

2. *Emotional Aspects of Michal's Marriage with David*

According to one midrash, it appears that Michal's marriage with David was divinely predestined. One passage in an ancient midrashic commentary called *Leviticus Rabbah*, dating from the sixth century CE and produced in Palestine, says:

> Four people began their supplication by making a vow. Three of them made their request in an improper manner and the Holy One, blessed be He, answered them favorably, while one made the request in an improper manner and the Omnipresent answered him correspondingly. They are as follows: Eliezer, the servant of Abraham (Gen. 24.14), Saul (1 Sam. 17.25), Jephthah (Judg. 11.31), and Caleb (Jos. 15.16)… Saul made a request in an improper manner, as is proved by the text, 'The man who kills him [Goliath], the king will enrich with great riches, and will give him his daughter, and make his father's house free in Israel' (1 Sam. 17.25). Said the Holy One, blessed be He: 'If an Ammonite, or a bastard, or a slave had killed him, would you have given him your daughter?' But the Holy One, blessed be He, brought him David, and he gave his daughter Michal to him. (*Lev. R.* 37.4)[1]

According to this midrash, David obtained Michal after his victory over Goliath. It probably builds its argumentation on the ambiguity of the term *bštym*. A number of rabbinic commentators were intrigued by the fact that Saul first promised David his elder daughter Merab and then his younger one Michal. In 1 Sam. 18.17, Saul had initially offered to give him Merab for a wife: 'Here is my elder daughter Merab; I will give her to you for a wife'. In 1 Sam. 18.18, however, she was given to Adriel. The verse announcing that Saul wants to give him his younger daughter for a wife contains some ambiguity, 'Saul thought, "Let me give her to him, that she may be a snare for him, and that the hand of the Philistines may be against him". Therefore Saul said to David, "A second time" or "by the two [of them] (*bštym*)" you shall be my son-in-law' (1 Sam. 18.21). The term that is usually rendered with 'a second time' (RSV) is questionable. Rabbi Joseph Kara[2] understood the term

1. *Midrash Rabbah, Leviticus* (ed. H. Freedman and M. Simon; Eng. trans. J. Israelstam [chs. 1–19], J.J. Slotki [chs. 20–37]; London: The Soncino Press, 1961), p. 470.

2. Joseph Kara (b. c. 1060) was a Bible commentator who lived in northern France.

not as an ordinal 'by the second', but as a cardinal 'by the two', implying that at a certain time Saul had offered both his daughters to David for wives.[3]

Commenting on 1 Sam. 18.21, Rashi refers to the Aramaic translation of the *Targum Jonathan* and says, 'by one of the two' (*bḥd' mtryn*).[4] Another compilation of various midrashim called *Meṣudat David* adopts Rashi's explanation and adds, 'Either I will give you Merab against her will or Michal according to her own will'.[5] It seems that this comment has been culled from Abrabanel's explanation (see below).

Radaq explains this term in the following manner: 'Although I have spoken to you about my two daughters and that the marriage with the first one did not work out, you will have the second one and you will become my son-in-law today'.[6] Furthermore, Radaq detects David's distrust of Saul or a certain hesitancy to marry Michal:

> It appears that at first David was unwilling since Saul had to speak in secret with David's messengers so that they might influence David as it appears in (1 Sam. 18.22), 'And Saul commanded his servants, "Speak to David in private and say, 'Behold, the king has delight in you and all his servants love you; now then become the king's son-in-law'" '.

One midrash refers to the biblical episode described in 1 Sam. 19.11-17, where Michal, informed of her father's plan to kill David, helps her husband

3. Quoted in the modern Hebrew commentary by Yehuda Qil, *Shemuel 1–2* (Jerusalem: Mossad ha-Rav Kook, 1981), I, p. 193, commentary on 1 Sam. 18.21.

4. Rashi is an acronym for Rabbi Shelomo ben Yiṣḥaq (1040–1105), one of the greatest Jewish commentators in medieval France. He was born in Troyes in the region of Champagne and was a wine-grower by profession. After studying in Worms with Rhineland Jewish masters, he founded his own school. He produced a commentary on the entire Hebrew Bible and the Talmud and was also a rabbinic judge for the Jewish community and author of the *Responsa*, an anthology of answers to questions concerning the *Halakhah* or Jewish law. Here I quote Rashi according to the Rabbinic Bible—following *Miqra'ôt Gedolôt* (Jerusalem: Torah ha-Mefuarah, n.d. [Hebrew]) (with Targum Jonathan, Meṣudat David, Meṣudat Tsion, Radaq, Ralbag, and Midreshei-Hazal). Throughout this chapter these commentaries are quoted with reference to the biblical verses on which they offer an explanation.

5. *Meṣudat Ṣion* and *Meṣudat David* were produced by David Altschuler and his son Jehiel Hillel in the eighteenth century based on previous rabbinic commentaries. In 1780–82 the latter published in Leghorn his father's completed commentary on the Prophets and Hagiographa. The commentary consists of two parts, called respectively *Meṣudat Ṣion* ('Fortress of Zion') and *Meṣudat David* ('Fortress of David'). The former explains individual words. The latter elucidates the meaning of the text. This commentary is quoted from the Rabbinic Bible (*Miqra'ôt Gedolôt* [Hebrew]).

6. Radaq is an acronym for Rabbi David Qimḥi (1160–1235), another Jewish commentator in medieval France, born in Toulouse. He was also an outstanding grammarian. Throughout, Radaq's commentary is quoted from the Rabbinic Bible, *Miqra'ôt Gedolôt* (Hebrew).

to escape through the window. Moreover she devises a ruse with the teraphim in order to provide David with additional time to flee. A passage in *Midrash Tehillim*[7] (59.3) quotes a verse from the book of Proverbs, 'He who finds a wife finds a good thing (*ṭb*)' (Prov. 18.22), and comments in the following manner:

> Such was Michal, Saul's daughter who loved David her husband more than she loved her father, for she saved David from her father. When? When Saul sent men to watch David's house. Of this it is written 'To the Eternal God [who said]: Do not destroy David; Miktam; when Saul sent, and they watched the house to kill him' (Ps. 59.1).[8]

When lamenting over the death of his friend Jonathan, David might have been showing the limits of his love for Michal by saying, 'Your love to me was wonderful, greater than the love of women' (2 Sam. 1.26). According to one modern commentator, Y. Qil, although the form *nšym* ('women') appears in the plural, the reference is made here to Michal. It is only out of modesty that the plural had been used here.[9] By contrast, *Midrash Shemuel* 25.4 does not minimize this plural form and adds the names of two of David's wives who were the most important ones in his life: '"Greater than the love of women" or more precious than the love of women, Michal and Abigail: The love of Abigail in this world and the love of Michal in the world to come'.[10]

3. *Legal Aspects of David's Marriages with Saul's Daughters*

The validity of David's marriage with Michal seems to have troubled the Doctors of the Law from earliest times. In the Mishnah (*b. Sanh.* 2.2),[11]

7. *Midrash Tehillim* is a homiletical commentary on the Psalms. On the basis of internal evidence, a possible allusion to the Moslem caliphate (6.2, diaspora under Ishmael), a supposed reference to Apulia and Sicily (9.8), some scholars have concluded that *Midrash Tehillim* was compiled in Italy as late as the ninth century. The overwhelming body of material in *Midrash Tehillim*, however, goes back to the Talmudic period. This midrash was probably composed in Palestine. A number of its midrashim have been adopted in the thirteenth-century anthology called *Yalquṭ Shimoni*.

8. *The Midrash on Psalms* (Eng. trans. W.G. Braude; New Haven: Yale University Press, 1959), I, p. 511. In the RSV, the superscription of Ps. 59.1 reads differently: 'To the choirmaster; according to Do Not Destroy. A Miktam of David, when Saul sent men to watch his house in order to kill him.'

9. Qil, *Shemuel 1–2*, II, p. 320 n. 24.

10. *Midrash Shemuel* is dated to the eleventh century CE. It represents a compilation of ancient interpretations taken from the Mishnah, Tosefta and Midrash Halakhah, together with more recent midrashim on the books of Samuel. The compiler combines both exegesis and homiletical developments. See *Midrash Shemuel* (Lemberg: Solomon Buber, 1891 [Hebrew]). On the distinction between love in this world and in the one to come, see below.

11. *Mishnayôt mevu'arôt* (explained) by Pinhas Qahati, *Seder Neziqin* (Jerusalem: Hekal Shelomo, 5752 = 1991), *pereq sheni, mishnah bet*; J. Neusner, *The Mishnah: A New*

Rabbi Yehuda quotes 2 Sam. 12.8 where the prophet Nathan said to David, 'I gave you your master's house, and your master's wives', and comments by saying that only a king is allowed to marry the widows of another king.[12] The Gemarah (*b. Sanh.* 19b) provides a somewhat surprising commentary: 'They [the rabbis] said to Rabbi Yehuda, "He [David] married women of the house of the King [Saul] who were permissible to him, namely, Merab and Michal"'.[13]

The Mishnah says that no man is allowed to marry the widow of a king. By quoting 2 Sam. 12.8, Rabbi Yehuda attempts to limit this prohibition by saying that only a king is allowed to do so. The rabbis responded by saying that even if it was permitted to David to take Saul's widows he would not have married them since he married Merab and Michal. Indeed, the biblical text states that at first Saul offered David his elder daughter Merab: 'Then Saul said to David, 'Here is my elder daughter Merab; I will give her to you for a wife; only be valiant for me and fight YHWH's battles' (1 Sam. 18.17). On the one hand, David has proven that he was a valorous soldier as reflected in the couplet sung by the Israelite women, 'Saul has slain his thousands, and David his ten thousands' (1 Sam. 18.7). On the other hand, with the victory over Goliath, David had acquired the right to marry Merab, 'The man who kills him...the king will give him his daughter' (1 Sam. 17.25). Furthermore, the biblical text affirms that 'Saul gave him his daughter Michal for a wife' (1 Sam. 18.27). Therefore the rabbis consider that David had paid the price that Saul required for each one of his daughters and that his marriage with

Translation (New Haven: Yale University Press, 1988), p. 586: 'R. Judah says, "A king may marry the widow of a king". For so we find in the case of David, that he married the widow of Saul. For it is said etc. (2 Sam. 12.8).'

12. The Mishnah was not compiled prior to 70 CE, and the work on its compilation is associated with the name of Yehuda ha-Nasi (c. 138–217 CE).

13. *The Babylonian Talmud, Seder Nezikin, Sanhedrin* (Eng. trans. J. Shachter and H. Freedman; New York: Rebecca Bennet Publications, 1959), I, p. 100. The Talmud (the name deriving from the root *lmd* meaning 'to learn or study') is a monument of Jewish traditional learning. It was produced by one of the original Jewish sects called the Pharisees and reflects their views. The Talmud comprises the Mishnah (from the root *šnh*, 'to repeat, to learn'), a body of material that gives the opinions of the rabbis called the Tannaim (plural form of the Aramaic *tanna*, 'teacher, or one who repeats', that is, repetitor of the oral law) who lived and worked between 20 and 200 CE. The Mishnah only rarely indicates the Scriptural basis of rabbinic thinking. To the Mishnah was added the teaching of the Gemara, a work containing commentaries and discussions of the Mishnah by another group of rabbinic scholars called the Amoraim (plural form of the Aramaic *amora*, 'the one who interprets or explains'), who lived between 200 and 500 CE. The Jerusalem Talmud was compiled at around the beginning of the fifth century in Galilee, while the Babylonian Talmud was produced in rabbinic academies in the sixth century CE, in Babylonia.

both of them was legal. Moreover, the Babylonian Talmud (*b. Sanh.* 19b) considers Merab's marriage with Adriel to be illegal.[14]

The Scripture formulates an absolute prohibition of a man marrying two sisters at the same time as long as one of them is alive: 'And you shall not take a woman as a rival wife to her sister, uncovering her nakedness while her sister is yet alive' (Lev. 18.18). The Babylonian Talmud (*b. Sanh.* 19b) echoes the apparent contradiction between the law in Lev. 18.18 and David's marriage with Saul's two daughters:

> Rabbi Yose was asked by his disciples: How could David marry two sisters while they were both living? He answered: He married Michal after the death of Merab. Rabbi Joshua bar Korḥa said: His marriage with Merab was contracted in error [and hence was invalid], as it is said, 'Give me my wife Michal, whom I betrothed at the price of a hundred foreskins of the Philistines' (2 Sam. 3.14). How does this prove it? Rabbi Papa answered: Because he said, 'My wife Michal', but not 'my wife Merab'. Now, what was the error in his marriage [with Merab]? [It was this:] It is written, 'The man who kills him [Goliath], the king will enrich with great riches, and will give him his daughter' (1 Sam. 17.25). Now he [David] went and slew him, whereupon Saul said to him: I owe you a debt, and if one betroths a woman by a debt,[15] she is not betrothed.[16] Accordingly he gave her to Adriel, as it is written, 'But at the time when Merab, Saul's daughter, should have been given to David, she was given to Adriel the Meholathite for a wife' (1 Sam. 18.19). Then Saul said to David, 'If you should still wish me to give you Michal for a wife, go and bring me [another] hundred foreskins of the Philistines'. He went and brought them to him. Then he said: 'You have two claims on me, [the repayment of] a loan[17] and a *peruṭâ*'.[18] Now, Saul held that when a loan and a *peruṭâ* are offered [as *qiddushin*], he [the would-be husband] thinks mainly of the loan;[19] but in David's view, when there is a loan and a *peruṭâ*, the mind is set on the *peruṭâ*.[20] Or if you like, I will say, all agree that where a loan and a *peruṭâ* [are offered], the mind is set on the *peruṭâ*. Saul, however, thought that [the hundred foreskins] had no value, while David held that they had value at least as food for dogs and cats.[21]

14. See below for the discussion of the illegitimacy of the marriage between Michal and Palti (Sections 11-14).

15. By remitting the amount to her or, if she is a minor, to her father.

16. For, in returning a money loan, unlike a trust, the debtor is not obliged to return the actual coin lent, but its equivalent. Hence the woman actually receives nothing at the time of betrothal; cf. *b. Qid.* 6b, 47a.

17. The promise to enrich him stands as a loan.

18. A *peruṭâ* is a small coin representing the estimated value of the hundred foreskins. A *peruṭâ* is sufficient to serve as a token of betrothal (*qiddushin*).

19. And consequently, as stated above, she would not be betrothed.

20. Hence the betrothal is valid.

21. *The Babylonian Talmud, Seder Nezikin, Sanhedrin*, I, pp. 100-101.

This Talmudic text in *b. Sanh.* 19b together with Rashi's comments on the Talmud were repeated in the midrashic anthologies like *Yalquṭ Shimoni*,[22] establishing a tradition among the rabbis of accepting Michal's marriage with David as being legal from the point of view of traditional rabbinical law.

4. *Abrabanel's Interpretation*

There are a number of questions concerning Michal's marriage with David that deal neither with the affective aspects nor the juridical ones. The medieval commentator Isaac Abrabanel ties up all these questions in his discussion:

> Was it really the king's intention to offer his daughter in marriage to the one who would conquer Goliath and to give him riches? If that was the case why in spite of his promises did not Saul give his daughter to David after his victory over Goliath? Why did he send messengers to tell him: 'Behold, the king has delight in you, and all his servants love you; now then become the king's son-in-law' (1 Sam. 18.22)? And how could he ask him for an additional one hundred Philistine foreskins when Saul was already in his debt and was therefore bound to give him his daughter?[23]

Abrabanel attempts to provide an answer to these questions:

> Realizing that he could not strike David with his hand and his spear, Saul thought to kill him by giving him his daughter; not to honor him or to obtain his trust, but to deliver him into the hands of the Philistines without himself having [to raise] his hand against him. In my view, what people have said concerning his combat against Goliath the Philistine, that the king would enrich and would give his daughter to the man who would vanquish this Philistine, were not the real words of the king; maybe some people spoke by themselves, spreading a rumor with no foundation. Perhaps Saul uttered them in the manner of kings with emphasis and exaggeration. But when David presented himself to the king, Saul did not mention a word, neither before nor after the combat. Consequently, I say that Saul did not feel obliged to him with his words. Thus, he said: 'Here is my elder daughter Merab; I will give her to you for a wife;

22. *Yalquṭ Shimoni, Nebi'im u-ketubim* (Jerusalem: H. Vegeschel, n.d. [Hebrew]). This is the best known and the most detailed anthology of midrashim that covers the entire Hebrew Bible. The identity of the author, a certain Simon who exercised the activity of a preacher (*ha-darshan*) in thirteenth-century Frankfurt, is contested.

23. I. Abrabanel, *Nebi'im rishonim* (Jerusalem: Elisha, 1955 [Hebrew]), commentary on 1 Sam. 18 (third question). I. Abrabanel (1437–1508) was born in Lisbon, Portugal, in a family that originated in Seville, Spain. He was in the service of the State administration of the Spanish king, and was also a Bible commentator and a philosopher. Unable to make the king change his mind concerning his edict expelling the Jews from Spain in 1492, Abrabanel settled in Italy. His approach to commenting on biblical texts is not devoid of critical thinking. Throughout this chapter references to Abrabanel's commentary are made with respect to the biblical verses on which he comments.

only be valiant for me (*ḥyh-ly lbn-ḥyl*)…' (1 Sam. 18.17)[24] meaning the following: Because she is my daughter and moreover my elder daughter, Merab, I show you great favor by giving her to you as a wife. Therefore it is better for you to have the status of a son than of a son-in-law. You will be a brave son for me and whatever I ask from you it will be for the service of God, to fight the Lord's battles. And the Scripture tells us how bad his intention was, to deliver him into the Philistines' hands… When the moment came to give Merab, Saul's daughter, to David, which means the moment when he had to give her to David, she was given (*nittenāh*) to Adriel. It means that, by herself, without Saul's knowledge, she gave herself (*nittenāh*)[25] becoming engaged to Adriel of Meholah. Michal, her sister, fell in love with David. When Saul heard that Merab had become engaged to Adriel and that Michal loved David, the thing seemed clear. He said: 'I too have affection for him and will give him Michal, and if such is the will of God, let the hand of the Philistines be against him'. So Saul said to David: Do not be afflicted and do not worry on account of what Merab did, for 'by the second one you will become my son-in-law today' (1 Sam. 18.21). That is, by one of these two you will become my son-in-law, either I will give you Merab against her will or Michal with her consent… And the *pešaṭ* (literal meaning) of this text shows that having seen that his union with Merab would not take place, David refused any other union for he thought that Saul would behave as he did the first time. Consequently, Saul had to order his servants to speak to David in private, 'Behold, the king has delight in you, and all his servants love you; now then become the king's son-in-law' (1 Sam. 18.22); this was to convince him that Saul was not mocking him. David replied, 'Does it seem to you a slight thing to become the king's son-in-law?' (1 Sam. 18.23), meaning: How could I ever become the king's son-in-law, so heavy is the yoke and weighty the burden of the counter-gift that must be given for the daughter of the king, 'seeing that I am a poor man and of no repute' (1 Sam. 18.23). Saul ordered them to reply that it was not an obstacle since as a counter-gift he desired only one hundred Philistine foreskins. He said that he wanted to take revenge on his enemies. Deep inside he did not think this, desiring to make David fall into the hands of the Philistines.[26] In his great naivety, 'the thing was right in David's eyes' (1 Sam.

24. The Hebrew expression rendered by 'valiant' literally means 'brave son', which explains Abrabanel's commentary.

25. Abrabanel is skillfully exploiting the two possibilities of the Hebrew niphal, which can have both a passive and a reflexive sense. Cf. Gen. 12.3 where the niphal form *wnbrkw* is translated either by (all the families of the earth) 'will be blessed' or 'will bless themselves'.

26. Commenting on 1 Sam. 18.25, *Yalquṭ Me'am Lo'ez* adds: 'Saul made him believe that he only wanted to take revenge on his enemies and thus hid his sinister intentions. David would not fight for the honor of God as he did in fighting against Goliath, but for his own interest, deprived of divine help, he would be vanquished by the Philistines.' Originally written in Judeo-Spanish (Ladino), *Yalquṭ Me'am Lo'ez* is an anthology of midrashic commentaries compiled by Jacob Culi (1685–1735) and completed after his death; see J. Culi, *Yalquṭ Me'am Lo'ez, Shemuel 1–2* (Jerusalem: H. Vegeschel, n.d. [Hebrew]).

> 18.26), not so much for the love of Michal as for the honor of becoming the king's son-in-law.[27]

Rabbinic commentaries linger over the analysis of several details in David's initial relationship with Michal.

5. *David's Apparent Humility*

David responds to Saul's offer in terms that at first seem humble enough: 'Does it seem to you a slight thing to become the king's son-in-law, seeing that I am poor and of no repute?' (1 Sam. 18.23). Radaq comments on this verse in the following manner:

> 'I am a poor man and of no repute': According to the Targum Jonathan, 'a miserable and simple man (*gbr mskn whdywt*[28])';—'miserable' because I do not have the possibility of offering a convenient counter-gift for the daughter of a king. Therefore, Saul said to his servants, 'Thus shall you say to David, The king desires no counter-gift except a hundred foreskins of the Philistines' (1 Sam. 18.25).—'simple': it would be better for me not to take the daughter of the king.

David's humility could also be taken as an expression of vexation having been humiliated because Saul's initial offer to give him Merab was not honored. According to *Midrash Tehillim*, some rabbis understood David's reply in 1 Sam. 18.23, 'I am a poor man and despised', by juxtaposing it to a similar verse in the Psalms, 'I am small and despised' (*ṣ'yr 'nky wnbzh*, Ps. 119.141):

> 'I am young/small and despised; yet I have not forgotten Thy precepts' (Ps. 119.141). Did David mean that he was the youngest? Was not the youngest Jesse's eighth son, Elihu, for it is said, 'David the seventh, Elihu the eighth' (1 Chron. 2.15), proving that Elihu was younger than David? But David referred to himself as the youngest, saying, 'I am young/small and despised' because he meant: 'Saul despised me greatly'. For Scripture relates, 'But at the time when Merab, Saul's daughter, should have been given to David, she was given to Adriel the Meholathite for a wife' (1 Sam. 18.19), and also says, 'Saul had given Michal his daughter, David's wife, to Palti the son of Laish' (1 Sam. 25.44). Hence David said, 'I am young/small and despised'.[29]

Meṣudat Ṣion explains the term *wnqlh* in 1 Sam. 18.23 as the 'contrary of being honored' (*hw' hpk hmkwbd*). There exists a third opinion, however,

27. Abrabanel's commentary on 1 Sam. 18, with answers in pars. 17-23.

28. The Hebrew word *hdywt* comes from the Greek *idiōtēs* ('ignorant person'), from which the English word 'idiot' evolved. In Arabic *meskin* means 'poor' and 'miserable'.

29. *The Midrash on Psalms*, II, p. 287; *Midrash Tehillim* (Vilna: Solomon Buber, 1891 [Hebrew]).

among certain rabbis who consider David's words as having only the appearance of humility, hiding his social and political ambitions. Commenting on 1 Sam. 18.26, Malbim puts forward what he thinks might have been David's true motives:

> David is interested in acceding to kingship for if the 'thing appeared right in his eyes' (1 Sam. 18.26), it was not in respect to the act itself [bringing one hundred foreskins] which was not the feat of a warrior, but in view of the goal that he was going to attain, to become the king's son-in-law.[30]

6. *One Hundred Foreskins as a Counter-Gift*

Y. Qil comments on Saul's somber plans with regard to David as expressed in 1 Sam. 18.21—'Saul thought, "Let me give her to him, that she may be a snare for him, and that the hand of the Philistines may be against him"'—by pointing out that the Hebrew term *mōqēš* may mean 'a snare' but also 'a lure'.[31] Either way, the idea is the same, the marriage with Michal would be a means of making David stumble and fall into the hands of the Philistines. Just like Abrabanel, quoted above, Malbim too comments on 1 Sam. 18.20-30 by asking several questions:

> Why did Saul need this snare? Wasn't David conducting wars for him when he asked him to do so, and why would he perish now by trying to bring the foreskins? 'Now Saul thought to make David fall by the hand of the Philistines' (1 Sam. 18.25).[32] This means that as long as one fights and kills according to the rules of war, there would be no hatred against the leader of the armies. However, to fall on people resting, who think that they are safe and to cut off their foreskins like a thief, is not the feat of a warrior but an act of hatred and vengeance. It would provoke great hostility among the Philistines who would conspire for revenge.

Meṣudat David, comments on 1 Sam. 18.25 saying that this act of mutilation was an offense. Moreover, another verse (18.26) says that David brought the cut-off Philistine foreskins 'before the time [imparted by Saul] had expired', while the following verse mentions that he killed two hundred Philistines. According to Radaq, the transaction implies that David wanted to make it an official act by handing over the two hundred foreskins to Saul:

30. Malbim, *Oṣar ha-Perushim: Debar Shemuel 1–2* (Tel Aviv: Mefarshei ha-Tanakh, n.d. [Hebrew]). Malbim is an acronym for Meir Leib ben Yehiel Michael (1809–79). He was appointed the Great Rabbi of Romania in 1858, but being too uncompromising had to leave his post. He attached great importance to the literal meaning (*pešaṭ*) of the biblical text. Malbim's commentary is quoted here using the biblical verse to which it refers.

31. Qil, *Shemuel 1–2*, I, p. 193.

32. According to Abrabanel, since in this specific matter David was fighting in his own interest and not for God, maybe the latter would not provide him with divine support.

David did not bring them himself but had them brought to the king through the intermediary of Saul's emissaries or by his own men, as a counter-gift which a man about to become officially married hands over using somebody else.

Some rabbis think that the reason David killed two hundred Philistines (1 Sam. 18.27) when Saul only required one hundred foreskins (18.25), is due to an ancient custom imposed on future sons-in-law, that they should bring a greater present than that initially stipulated.[33]

7. *David and the Military Conflicts*

Commenting on 1 Sam. 18.28-30, Malbim thinks that cutting off the Philistine foreskins was not customary behavior in war:

> When Saul saw that his ruse had failed once again, he knew with certainty that God was with David and that Michal loved him (v. 20) and that it would strengthen him in his design to accede to kingship. Therefore Saul's fear and hostility increased, not only intermittently but continually (v. 29). 'Then the princes of the Philistines came out to battle' (v. 30). Saul thought that the Philistines would fight to the last man on account of the outrage they had been inflicted, which they actually did in order to take vengeance on David. But David did not shirk from his duty. He fought and 'had more success than all the servants of Saul' (v. 30). Although Saul sought to make him fall into the hands of the Philistines, it was quite the contrary for 'his name was highly esteemed' (v. 30).

Another midrash in *Yalquṭ Shimoni* comments differently on 1 Sam. 18.30,[34] presenting David not only as a dauntless warrior but also as a keen connoisseur of the religious regulations concerning the conduct of war:

> Rabbi Yodan bar Simon said: His name was highly esteemed in respect to the Torah. In what manner? When the Philistines heard that David was getting married they said: It is written in their Torah, 'When a man is newly married, he shall not go out with the army' (Deut. 24.5). It is therefore the right moment to attack him and to make him disappear from the face of the earth. But they did not know that David was wise and that he knew how to interpret the texts. [How?] In fact, what is [this verse] about? [It is about] voluntary or optional wars (*mlḥmt ršwt*)[35] in opposition to obligatory wars (*mlḥmt ḥwbh*)[36] in which

33. *Me'am Lo'ez* commenting on 1 Sam. 18.27 and quoting a commentary by Rabbi Abraham Anahi.

34. Repeating *Midrash Shemuel* 22.2*, and *b. Soṭ.* 44b.

35. 'Voluntary or optional wars' (*mlḥmt ršwt*) resemble offensive wars. See *Mishnah Soṭah* 8.7: 'Under what circumstances [do the foregoing rules apply? i.e., Deut. 24.5]. In the case of an optional (*rešût*) war. But in the case of a *miṣwâ* war (a war subject to religious requirement) everyone goes forth to battle—even the bridegroom from his chamber, and a bride from her marriage canopy. Said Rabbi Yehuda, Under what circumstances? In the case of a war subject to religious requirement (a *miṣwâ* war). But in the case of an

> everyone must take part, including the newly married bridegroom who is in his room, and the newly wed bride who is under the wedding canopy.

Being involved in a 'voluntary war' (*mlḥmt ršwt*),[37] although a newly married man, David was not under obligation to stay at home with his wife. He could fight against the Philistines and repel their attack. Moreover, David appears to be a shrewd strategist on another occasion. During the civil war between the House of Saul and the House of David, David makes a keen political move when he concludes an alliance with Abner, the leader of Ishbosheth's army, by requiring that Michal be returned to him. Here is what Malbim says about it:

> 'I will make a covenant with you; but one thing I require of you; that is, you shall not see my face, unless you first bring Michal, Saul's daughter, when you come to see my face' (2 Sam. 3.13). From start to finish, David considers how not to appear as a servant who rebelled against his master, destroying the House of his lord in order to take his place by force. [He wanted to appear] as someone who took over the kingdom in accordance with the Prophets and the Law, and with the approval of Israel and of the elders. He wanted Michal back because with her he would again become the son-in-law of the king he was

obligatory (*ḥwbh* [*ḥobâ*] war), everyone goes forth to battle—even a bridegroom from his chamber, and a bride from her marriage canopy' (Neusner, *The Mishnah*, p. 462). According to the Babylonian Talmud (*b. Soṭ.* 44b), optional wars are all the wars undertaken by the House of David with the goal of territorial expansion.

36. 'Obligatory wars' (*mlḥmt ršwt*) are wars dealing with the defense of the territory. *Midrash Shemuel* 22.2 refers both to 'obligatory wars' (*mlḥmt ršwt*) and to 'wars commanded [by the Torah]' (*mlḥmt mṣwt*) implying the conquest of Canaan and the war against Amaleq (cf. Deut. 25.19).

37. According to *b. Soṭ.* 44b, rabbis in the Talmud differ in the terminology they use in describing wars as a response to external aggressions: Rabbi Yehuda calls these defensive wars 'obligatory wars', while other rabbis call them 'voluntary wars'. They all agree, however, in saying that newly married men do not have to fight. On the question of war in rabbinic literature, see J. Genot-Bismuth, 'Pacifisme pharisien et sublimation de l'idée de guerre aux origines du rabbinisme', *ETR* 56 (1981), pp. 73-89 (80). Cf. *The Babylonian Talmud, Seder Nashim, Soṭah* (ed. I. Epstein; Eng. trans. A. Cohen; New York: Rebecca Bennet Publications, 1959), p. 224 (*b. Soṭ.* 44b): 'Rabbi Yoḥanan said: [A war] which is [designated] voluntary according to the rabbis is commanded [by the Torah] according to Rabbi Yehuda, and [a war] which is [designated] commanded according to the rabbis is obligatory according to Rabbi Yehuda. (They agree that a bridegroom must serve.) Rabba said: The wars waged by Joshua to conquer [Canaan] were obligatory in the opinion of all; the wars waged by the House of David for territorial expansion were voluntary in the opinion of all; where they differ is with regard to [wars] against heathens so that these should not march against them. One calls them "commanded" and the other "voluntary". The practical result is that one who is engaged in the performance of a commandment is exempt from the performance of another commandment (i.e. those engaged in a war commanded by the Torah are exempted from the performance of other commandments).'

> now opposing and thus would have a right to Saul's kingdom. He did not want it to appear that Abner was approaching him as if he were a leader who revolted against his king, but rather as someone who would bring him back his wife with the permission of his Lord, and that this should be done by the most important and the most honored man in the House of her father (i.e. Ishbosheth); this is what it means 'unless you first bring Michal'.

These different biblical texts together with rabbinic commentaries make David appear as a determined and ambitious individual who always keeps the accession to kingship in the forefront of his mind.

8. *Michal Saves David's Life*

Reading 1 Sam. 19.10d-18a together with the rabbinic commentaries allows us to get a clearer understanding of Michal's motivation in saving David's life. The love that she has for David seems to be her primary motive. As pointed out above, *Midrash Tehillim* 59.3 applies the verse in Prov. 18.22 to Michal. The rest of the midrash on 59.4,[38] however, shows how the rabbis are divided about Michal's valorous action because it implies the use of ruse and of the teraphim:

> 'When he fled from Saul' (Ps. 57.1). How did David escape? Rabbi Aibu and the Rabbis give different answers. Rabbi Aibu said: David had two gates in his house, one of which was locked; they watched for him at this gate, but he went out through the outer gate and so escaped. The Rabbis maintained: David had only one gate, and they stood by the gate and watched that he not escape. What did Michal do? With a rope she lowered David from a window and so he escaped.
>
> When the messengers of Saul came to the house, what did Michal do? She took the teraphim, and laid them on the bed, and put quilts of goats' hair (*kbyr*) at its head, as it is said 'and Michal took the teraphim, etc...' (1 Sam. 19.13). When they entered and asked for David, Michal said to them: 'He is ill and lying in bed'. They went back and told Saul. He said to them: 'Bring him hither in the bed'. They went and brought his bed to Saul, and Saul found the teraphim in the bed. Now he became angry at his daughter Michal, and said to her: 'Why hast thou deceived me and let mine enemy flee?' Michal answered: 'Thou didst wed me to thy brigand, and he stood over me with his sword as if to kill me, saying, "If thou dost not help me escape, I shall kill thee". Whereupon I was frightened, so fearful of him that I helped him escape'. As Scripture tells us, Michal said: 'He said unto me: Let me go, why should I kill thee?' (1 Sam. 19.17).

The Hebrew term *kbyr* is a *hapax legomenon* which is usually rendered as 'goatskin' or 'a pillow of goats' hair' (RSV). Radaq comments on 1 Sam. 19.13 saying, 'A pillow of goats' hair'. *Targum Jonathan* translates with

38. *The Midrash on Psalms*, I, pp. 510-11. Also quoted in *Yalquṭ Shimoni* 1 Sam. 18.

'goatskin'. One midrash (*Yalquṭ Shimoni* 19) says, 'She placed a goatskin in bed instead of David, that is a wine skin made out of goat's skin, the hair being outside. For that reason she put it in place of his head.' Commenting on 1 Sam. 19.10, Abrabanel says:

> Saul thought that David went home to sleep with his wife; he sent messengers to his house to watch him and kill him in the morning. Indeed, he did not order them to kill him at night in the house, because he feared that David, who was very cunning, might divert them from their purpose with his words; therefore he waited until daylight in order to kill him himself, with his own hands.

Commenting on 1 Sam. 19.11-12, Y. Qil proposes another explanation:

> Maybe Saul wanted to judge David in the morning and to condemn him as a rebel against the kingdom as suggested by a verse in Jer 21.12, 'Execute justice in the morning'. Saul could pretend that it was David who wanted to kill him. The best proof of that was that the latter had fled.[39] Furthermore, the fact that he had fled the royal palace without permission could have been considered as a sort of rebellion.[40]

It is only in v. 18 that we learn how David fled to Ramah in order to take refuge with Samuel. According to the comments in *Meṣudat David* on 1 Sam. 19.15:

> Saul thought that David was pretending to be sick in order not to show up. As it is said: 'Bring him up to me in the bed, that I may kill him' (v. 15). [He said this] in order to show that he was not sick, and to have an excuse to execute him in public, for he deserved death for having deceived Saul.

The Midrash on the book of Proverbs applies a verse in Prov. 31.23 to Michal—'Her husband is known in the gates'—and comments: 'It is Michal who saved David from death'.[41] Indeed, Michal's prompt action saves David's life, making it possible for him to attain kingship, to reign and receive honors. The rabbinic literature attributes positive value to Michal whenever she contributes to David's grandeur as a future statesman. In this episode David appears very human and in need of help. Michal is truly David's 'helpmate' (*'zr*). Her composure and sense of urgency has the immediate effect of saving David's life. But, as pointed out by Y. Qil, 'Michal has not only saved David, but the entire line of the House of David, including the Messiah'.[42]

39. An allusion to Gen. 39.15-18, where Joseph fled in order to escape from Potiphar's wife.

40. Qil, *Shemuel 1–2*, I, p. 198.

41. *Midrash Mishle* 31.22*.

42. Qil, *Shemuel 1–2*, Preface, n. 2.

9. *The Problem of the Teraphim*

Why were the teraphim in David's house? What do they represent and what was their use? These questions raise problems both for ancient rabbinic authors and for modern commentators. According to the then current meaning of the term, 'teraphim' stand for domestic gods and were therefore idols. Radaq comments in the following way on the nature of the teraphim mentioned in 1 Sam. 19.13:

> The [Aramaic] translation [offered by Targum Jonathan] is *ṣlmny'* 'images': they are made in the image of man. Therefore Michal placed them in the bed as if David were lying there... Some say that they served for idolatry like the teraphim that Rachel stole from Laban. Indeed, Laban practiced idolatry as it is said: 'Why did you steal my gods (Gen. 31.30: *'lhy*, "my gods")?' But far from me the idea that idolatry may have been practiced in David's house. Others say that it was a copper device conceived in order to read hours and in which the future could be seen through the stars. This is conceivable concerning Laban, but as far as Michal is concerned, it is difficult to explain the reasons why she would have placed them in place of David in the bed when this device has no human form. The wise Abraham ibn Ezra,[43] of blessed memory, wrote that the teraphim had a human form in order to receive the power of supernatural forces.

In commenting on 1 Sam. 19.13-16, Abrabanel combines all the different opinions of his predecessors in order to describe the teraphim:

> [They] were made out of copper, like a sundial, and one could use them to see certain things like the future [events]. I think that the teraphim had a general human form. Some were used in idolatry, others in order to attract the emanations from supernatural forces, and others still in order to know the hours of the day. Some were made in the image of famous men, and women had them made in the image of their husbands in order, out of love for them, to always have their traits at their side. Thus Michal's teraphim belonged to this latter category, for she loved David passionately. Consequently there was no guilt in this. Moreover, she could put them in place of David because they were made in his image.

Commenting on 1 Sam. 19.13, Y. Qil[44] says that the plural in teraphim does not stand for the multiplicity of objects; it indicates the respect with which the teraphim were treated and might reflect the multiplicity of forces that they represented. Apparently he proposes to treat the term teraphim as the term *'elohim*. Several biblical passages connect the teraphim with divination (Ezek. 21.21; Zech. 10.2).[45] In 1 Sam. 19.16 and in Gen. 31.34 their use

43. Commentary on Gen. 31.19.

44. Qil, *1–2 Shemuel*, I, p. 198.

45. Ezek. 21.21: '[The king of Babylon] consults the teraphim'; Zech. 10.2 'For the teraphim utter nonsense and the diviners see lies'.

is not forbidden. In 1 Sam. 15.23, the prophet Samuel sees them as exemplifying evil when he reprimands Saul, comparing his insubordination and stubbornness to the teraphim. The Mekhilta is explicit in counting the teraphim as belonging to idolatrous objects, 'Idolatry can also be called by default: an excluded thing (*ḥrm*), interdict, abomination, statuette, metal idol, gods, teraphim, idols (*'ṣbym*) and dung-gods (*glwlym*)'.[46] The teraphim belong to objects that rabbinic tradition considers reprehensible, and they are found in David's house (1 Sam. 19.11). Abrabanel comments on 1 Sam. 19.12, saying: 'It is very curious that an object serving as an idol, as a divinatory device and suggesting idolatry, should be found in David's house'.

10. *Michal's Marriage with Palti*

Saul took Michal away from David and gave her to another man, probably in order to signify the rupture of all family ties between his House and David. The rabbis did not fail to comment on this transaction. They refer to the Hebrew text and in particular to the conjunction of coordination *waw* with which the verse begins in 1 Sam. 25.44: 'And Saul gave Michal his daughter, David's wife, to Palti'. Some rabbis see in this the result of something that happened previously. This conjunction would therefore signify that Michal's marriage with Palti would have happened after that of David with Abigail and Ahinoam. Saul's action was a response to David's additional marriages. This is what Malbim suggests in commenting on this verse:

> Saul was angry against David because the latter married other women in addition to Michal without his permission. He considered it an insult to his daughter, a princess. Consequently he gave her to Palti, while David was fleeing to the desert of Paran to another destination in order to escape from Saul's wrath that again flared [against him]. Thus, the announcement of David's two new marriages to Abigail and Ahinoam is closely related to the fact that Saul gave his daughter Michal to Palti.

Neither the biblical text nor the midrashic commentaries say anything about Michal's feelings about this transaction. Did she agree to marry Palti under paternal constraint or was she willing? The only element that clarifies the affective side of the relationship between Palti and Michal is given by the biblical text describing the way Michal returns to David: 'But her husband went with her, weeping after her all the way to Bahurim' (2 Sam. 3.16). The verbal forms used in this verse, *wylk...hlwk wbkh*, denote a continuation and mean that Palti wept all the time as he accompanied her.

46. *Mekhilta Mishpatim*, tractate *Neziqin* 20*. For the analysis of this term, see D. Bodi, 'Les *gillûlîm* chez Ezéchiel et dans l'Ancien Testament et les différentes pratiques cultuelles associées à ce terme', *RB* 100 (1993), pp. 481-510.

With such a visible manifestation of Palti's feelings for Michal, it is striking, however, to note the impersonal form used in the Hebrew text when speaking of bringing Michal back 'from the husband'. 2 Samuel 3.15 should be rendered literally in the following manner: 'And Ishbosheth sent, and took her from the husband, from Paltiel the son of Laish'. *Targum Jonathan* makes the references explicit in Aramaic with a third feminine possessive suffix, 'from her husband'.

Rashi offers a curious explanation of Palti's tears. The latter is not crying because he is leaving Michal, but because he is losing an opportunity which was given him through this marriage to accomplish a *miṣwâ* that he was assigned, that is, to refrain from having sexual relations with her. Indeed, numerous rabbinic commentators agree in saying that the marriage between Michal and Palti was never consummated. Michal, being still married to David and being neither a widow nor a divorcee, could not legally become Palti's wife. One text in the Babylonian Talmud (*b. Sanh.* 19b-20a), wanting to preserve the legality of David's request to have his wife brought back to him, suggests that Palti married Michal, obeying an order that he received from Saul. Knowing, however, that she was legally still David's wife, he lived with her without ever touching her. In order to ensure that neither one of them should transgress this tacit agreement, he placed a sword in the bed between Michal and himself, saying that the one who crossed this limit would be killed by it:[47] 'What did he do [to be delivered from sin]? He planted a sword between her [Michal] and himself, and said, "Whoever [first] attempts this thing (i.e. the forbidden indulgence), shall be pierced with this sword".'[48]

In certain Talmudic texts, the role of the sword is to insure the respect of the law, the *Halakhah*; the one who transgresses it would be killed by the sword (*b. Šab.* 17a; *b. Yeb.* 77a).

The rabbis were more preoccupied with the legal aspects of David's request to have his wife back than with exploring the affective side of Michal's relationship with Palti.

11. *Was Michal's Marriage with Palti Legal?*

The Doctors of the Law found the legal issue of Michal's marriage with Palti particularly bothersome because it did not square with the practises of their own times. Being neither widowed nor divorced from David, she should not have been married to another man. Therefore, the rabbis used all their

47. This Talmudic anecdote is borrowed by *Yalquṭ Shimoni* in the commentary on 2 Sam. 25.

48. *The Babylonian Talmud, Seder Nezikin, Sanhedrin*, I, p. 103.

ingenuity in matters of traditional Jewish law in order to demonstrate that her marriage with Palti was illegitimate. In order to do so, they brought three elements into discussion: (1) the role of Doeg the Edomite, an avowed enemy of David; (2) a supposed letter of divorce (*gṭ*) given to Michal by David; and (3) the invalidity of Michal's marriage with Palti.

12. *Doeg the Edomite's Treachery*

Doeg the Edomite was Saul's friend. He died young, at the age of thirty-four according to the Babylonian Talmud (*b. Sanh.* 69b): 'And it is written, "Bloody and deceitful men shall not live half their days" (Ps. 55.24). And it has been taught: Doeg lived but thirty-four years, and Ahitophel thirty-three.'[49]

Doeg was considered by the rabbis as the most erudite scholar of his time, having served as president of the Sanhedrin. He was a master of legal questions. The rabbis attribute to Doeg the Edomite an influential role in the union between Michal and Palti. One midrash (*b. Zeb.* 54b) tells how Doeg's vanity was hurt after a public debate where David had the upper hand. Ever since that humiliating incident, Doeg spared no effort in order to take revenge on David. He incited Saul's jealousy against David, he pointed out David's Moabite origin in order to exclude him from the community of Israel,[50] and therewith succeeded in convincing Saul that David's marriage with Michal was invalid. Being no longer legally bound to David, Saul felt free to give her to another man.

According to a midrash in *Gen. R.* 32.1, by declaring David an outlaw, Doeg the Edomite facilitated the union between Michal and Palti. By stripping David of all legal rights as a member of the Israelite community, he annulled his marriage with Michal. On the basis of Doeg's skillful legal demonstration, Saul could give Michal, David's wife, to Palti ben Laish. David was legally considered dead, implying that it is permissible to kill him. Consequently his wife was free from the marriage bonds and therefore she would not be committing adultery when marrying someone else.

> It is written, 'Thou destroyest those who speak lies' (Ps. 5.7): this refers to Doeg and Ahitophel... The one [Ahitophel] permitted incest and bloodshed [when he counseled Absalom], 'Go in unto thy father's concubines' (2 Sam. 16.21). The other [Doeg] permitted incest: [Where do we find this]? Said Rabbi Naḥman bar Samuel bar Naḥman: He annulled his [David's] citizen rights and

49. *The Babylonian Talmud, Seder Nezikin, Sanhedrin*, II, p. 471.

50. See *b. Yeb.* 77a, which refers to the prohibition found in Deut. 23.3: 'No Ammonite or Moabite shall enter the assembly of the Lord; even to the tenth generation none belonging to them shall enter the assembly of the Lord for ever'.

> declared him an outlaw and as one dead, so that his blood was permitted and his wife was permitted.[51]

Numerous texts in the midrashim refer to the etymology of Doeg's name in order to prove the treacherousness of this man and his nefarious influence on Saul. The term 'Edomite' (*'dwmy*) in the name Doeg ha-Edomi (*d'g h'dmy*) is played off against the words 'red' (*'dwm*) and 'blood' (*dm*). In the Midrash on the book of Psalms (*Midrash Tehillim* 52.4), it is explained that he is called 'ha-Edomi' because he made David an outlaw, where the expression *htyr dmw* ('to outlaw [someone]') would be a word-play on his name. He also prompted Saul to say 'he [David] shall surely die' (1 Sam. 20.31). According to the Jerusalem Talmud (*y. Sanh.* 10), his name is *d'g h'dmy* because he spilled the blood (*dm*) of the priests of Nob by 'killing eighty five people who wore the linen ephod' (1 Sam. 22.18). According to the same passage, when in the presence of Doeg the Edomite, David answered some Israelites who came to ask him advice on a point of Jewish law, 'Doeg went to see Saul immediately, the king of Israel, advising him to kill the inhabitants of Nob, the priestly city. For it is said, "And the king said to the guard who stood about him, 'Turn and kill the priests of YHWH; because their hand also is with David, and they knew that he fled, and did not disclose it to me'"' (1 Sam. 22.17).

According to L. Ginzberg,[52]

> He [Doeg] was called Edomi, which means, not Edomite, but 'he who causes the blush of shame', because by his keen mind and his learning he put to shame all who entered into argument with him. But his scholarship lay only on his lips, his heart was not concerned in it, and his one aim was to elicit admiration. At the time of his death he had sunk so low that he forfeited all share in the life to come. Wounded vanity caused his hostility to David, who had gotten the better of him in a learned discussion.

All these various commentaries agree in showing Doeg's treachery in invalidating the marriage between Michal and David. Indirectly they also imply the validity of this union.

13. *David's Supposed Letter of Divorce* (gṭ)

The Babylonian Talmud (*b. Šab.* 56a) describes a practise of Israelite warriors giving a divorce letter (*gṭ*) to their wives before going to war. The rabbis assumed that this practice was already in effect in David's time. It was

51. *Midrash Rabbah, Genesis* (ed. H. Freedman and M. Simon; Eng. trans. H. Freedman; London: The Soncino Press, 1961), I, p. 249 (*Gen. R.* 32.1).

52. L. Ginzberg, *The Legends of the Jews* (Philadelphia: The Jewish Publication Society of America, 1954), IV, p. 75.

customary in rabbinic times that when a man went to war or undertook a long voyage, he would give his wife a letter of divorce. If he disappeared and no formal proof of his death could be adduced, the wife would be considered a divorcee and was allowed to remarry:

> Rabbi Samuel bar Naḥmani said in Rabbi Jonathan's name: Every one who went out in the wars of the house of David wrote a bill of divorcement for his wife, for it is said, 'Also take these ten cheeses to the commander of their thousand. See how your brothers fare, and bring some token (*'rbtm*) from them/or take their pledge' (1 Sam. 17.18). What is meant by *'rbtm*? Rabbi Joseph learned: The things which pledge man and woman [to one another].[53]

Commenting on 2 Samuel 12 (*remez* = 'allusion', no. 148) *Yalquṭ Shimoni* asks: 'What does *'rbtm* mean? Rab Joseph taught: these are things that concern only him and her', that is, the letter of divorce which defined their present marital situation. Malbim comments on 2 Sam. 11.3 and explains:

> It is probable that the wives of those who were slain in war remained *('gnwt)*, 'abandoned and bound [to their husbands]'.[54] In fact, the bodies [of the slain] were buried in haste without anyone recognizing with certainty the slain one in order to testify and to report to his wife [about his death], the more so when the enemy was victorious and buried the corpses. This is why David's court decreed that the soldiers had to give their wives a letter of divorce, a definitive one or a conditional one.

There were two different letters of divorce: (1) the definitive one that took effect immediately the day it was written, and (2) a conditional one in which the husband stipulated that if he did not return from war or a perilous voyage in an agreed amount of time, the divorce became retroactively effective from the day the letter of divorce was issued. Rashi suggests that David had recourse to such a retroactive letter of divorce when he attempted to cover his adulterous relationship with Bathsheba. He comments on David's order to have Uriah killed in battle, 'so that he will be smitten and die' (2 Sam. 11.15), and says: 'In order that he should be retroactively divorced and, consequently, he [David] would not have had relations with a married woman; for anyone who departs for war writes his wife a divorce letter on the condition that he die in battle'.

Another tractate of the Babylonian Talmud (*b. Ket.* 9a-b) quotes the verse in 1 Sam. 17.18—'See how your brothers fare, and bring some token (*'rbtm*) from them'—and says that 'whoever went to war from the House of David wrote a letter of divorce to his wife'. Rashi explains that the letter of divorce had a retroactive effect only if the husband died in war. The letter allowed

53. *The Babylonian Talmud, Seder Mo'ed, Shabbath* (ed. I. Epstein; Eng. trans. H. Freedman; London: The Soncino Press, 1938), p. 260

54. That is, 'restrained' or not permitted to marry another man; cf. *b. Git.* 26b.

the woman to have the status of a divorcee instead of a widow and to avoid having to undergo the levirate if her husband died without descendants. The *Tosafot*[55]and Rambam, however, explain that Rashi's comments should not be taken literally, for, if he were right, the letter of divorce would have been written only by men who had no descendants. They argue that Rashi admitted that every soldier had to write a letter of divorce for his wife, even if she was not concerned with having to undergo the levirate, allowing her to remarry if her husband disappeared.

When commenting on 1 Sam. 25.44, Radaq repeats several previous explanations[56] and mentions the argument concerning the existence of a supposed letter of divorce that David issued to Michal before fleeing away from her on the night when Saul's men were waiting in ambush:

> ...All these words are far from the literal sense (*pešaṭ*).What appears to me the most correct interpretation is that David gave Michal a letter of divorce. We have seen that Saul began to hate David so much when he became his son-in-law that David had to flee. Saul saw that David had fled. Since [David] would return to him from time to time, he forced him to give a letter of divorce to his daughter so that she might not become an abandoned woman. David complied and Saul gave her to Palti ben Laish. And if you say that it was forbidden to David to take her back, since it is forbidden for a man to take the wife he divorced after she has been married or betrothed to another man, it is also said that he did not give her a letter of divorce willingly. And if you ask who forced him to do so? Didn't he flee from Saul? Although he fled, however, we have seen that he returned to Saul since it is written, 'If your father misses me...' (1 Sam. 20.6). The entire episode proves that even after he fled [from Saul] he would occasionally return [to the court]; while he was with him, Saul forced him to give his letter of divorce. But in Israel, a letter of divorce given under constraint is not valid. And if you ask: Did not Saul's court know that such a letter is not valid? It is possible that the court had to follow the king's will; moreover, it is said that before giving his letter of divorce, David said in front of two witnesses who were dear to him, 'See, I am forced to give this letter of divorce'; but the witnesses concealed this fact and David gave the letter. The letter of divorce was therefore not a [valid] letter of divorce, but neither Palti ben Laish nor Michal knew it; they thought that the letter of

55. *Tosafot* means 'additions'. These are additional comments on different tractates and are arranged according to the basic divisions of the Talmud. The point of departure for these comments is not the Talmud itself, however, but rather the comments of previous rabbis, mainly Rashi. The origin of the *Tosafot* is attributed to Rashi's sons and disciples and should be distinguished from *Tosefta* which is of much earlier origin.

56. Radaq mentions the discussion in *b. Sanh.* 19 concaerning the repayment of a debt that cannot seal a marriage while a *peruṭâ* can do so (see above, Section 3); he refers to the Talmudic anecdote about the sword placed in the bed between Michal and Palti (see above, Section 10), and mentions Rashi's explanation of Palti's tears (see above, Section 10) as an expression of his regret for losing an opportunity to accomplish a *miṣwâ* of self-restraint.

> divorce was a [valid] one. It is also possible that the letter of divorce was valid from the start and that David wanted to send it to Michal through a messenger, but that he annulled it before it reached her, without her [them] knowing it. Thus Michal could have been married by error, and therefore she would not have been forbidden to David. It was as if she had been married by force, for she thought that the letter of divorce was valid. In fact it does not matter whether it was a constraint or an error,[57] as far as the wife of a man is concerned, for it is said, 'if a man lies with her carnally and she is undetected' (Num. 5.13) with the exception of the constraint, 'and acts unfaithfully against him' (Num. 5.12) with the exception of the error, she is permitted [to be taken back by] her husband.

In this manner, Radaq attempts to show that the separation between Michal and David was invalid and therefore she was not free to marry another man.

14. *The Invalidity of Michal and Merab's Marriages with Palti and Adriel*

Instead of trying to prove the invalidity of Michal's marriage with Palti and to show the invalidity of her separation from David, rabbis in the Talmud prefer to show the intrinsic impossibility of her marriage with Palti. Even if the divorce from David had been valid, her union with Palti would have been illegal:

> How does Rabbi Yose[58] interpret the verse, 'Give me my wife Michal?' He explains it by another view of his. For it has been taught: Rabbi Yose used to interpret the following confused passage thus: It is written, 'The king took the two sons of Rizpah the daughter of Ariah, whom she bore to Saul, Armoni and Mephibosheth, and the five sons of Michal the daughter of Saul, whom she bore to Adriel the son of Barzillai the Meholathite' (2 Sam. 21.8). But was Michal really given to Adriel; was she not given to Palti the son of Laish, as it is written, 'Saul had given Michal his daughter, David's wife, to Palti the son of Laish, who was of Gallim' (1 Sam. 25.44). But Scripture compares the marriage of Merab to Adriel to that of Michal to Palti: To teach that just as the marriage of Michal to Palti was unlawful, so was that of Merab to Adriel.[59]

In this passage, Rabbi Yose refers to the verse in 2 Sam. 21.8, 'and the five sons of Michal the daughter of Saul, whom she bore to Adriel the son of Barzillai the Meholathite', saying that by this elliptical formulation, the biblical text places the marriages of Michal with Palti and of Merab with Adriel on the same level. The didactic goal of this juxtaposition would have been to intimate that the marriage of Michal to Palti was invalid because she was already married to David and that, for the same reasons, the marriage of

57. The result would be the same and divorce would not be valid.
58. Who holds that before his marriage to Michal, David was legally married to Merab.
59. *The Babylonian Talmud, Seder Nezikin, Sanhedrin*, I, p. 101 (*b. Sanh.* 19b).

Merab to Adriel was equally invalid. Rabbi Yose interprets the words 'Michal my wife' not as excluding Merab as wife, but rather as showing that just as Michal was legally his wife, so was Merab. Therefore the marriages of Michal and Merab with Palti ben Laish and Adriel respectively were transgressions. According to Rabbi Yose, David had married Michal after the death of Merab. For other rabbinic authors, the marriage between David and Merab was invalid because Merab became betrothed to David as a reimbursement of a debt incurred by her father Saul. Such a transaction being illegal, David was allowed to marry her sister Michal.

15. *David Demands the Return of his Wife Michal*

When David fled from Saul, he left his wife Michal behind. During his years away from home, David acquired other wives, including Abigail, Ahinoam (1 Sam. 25.39-43), Maacah, Haggith, Abital, and Eglah whom he married in Hebron (2 Sam. 3.2-5). During the civil war that broke out after the death of Saul, in order to sign a truce with the adverse camp, David requires that Michal be brought back to him. Commenting on the words of David in 2 Sam. 3.14, 'David sent messengers to Ishbosheth, Saul's son, saying: "Give me my wife Michal, whom I betrothed at the price of a hundred foreskins of the Philistines"', *Yalquṭ Me'am Lo'ez* is one of the rare midrashim to suggest that David might have had a particular emotional attachment for Michal: 'With these very words David gave reasons why he desired to see Michal again. The first one is that she was his first wife and that a man draws true satisfaction only from his first wife.' The commentary immediately adduces a second reason which overshadows the first one. David risked his life when at Saul's request he had to kill one hundred Philistines in order to bring the required number of foreskins. This second reason is borrowed by the *Meṣudat David* commenting on 2 Sam. 3.14:

> David emphasizes and repeats: '...my wife Michal, whom I betrothed at the price of a hundred foreskins of the Philistines', which I obtained in order to seal my betrothal. Or maybe he wanted to say: Didn't I then place my life in jeopardy for her? And one could say that even now my hand continues to fight for her. I have indeed brought two hundred foreskins although the agreement stipulated only one hundred.

Apart from the single remark quoted above in *Yalquṭ Me'am Lo'ez*, concerning David's possible emotional attachment to Michal, the midrashim in general tend to treat Michal as a thing acquired for a high price. Another commentary pursues this 'reification' of Michal:

> David did not approach Michal after she returned from Palti. He behaved with her as he behaved with his ten concubines: 'David came to his house at Jerusalem; and the king took the ten concubines whom he had left to care for the

> house, and put them in a house under guard, and provided for them, but did not go in to them. So they were shut up until the day of their death, living as if in widowhood' (2 Sam. 20.3). Consequently she [Michal] had no child [to the day of her death] (2 Sam. 6.23).[60]

This rabbinic interpretation might be of some significance since it would seem to corroborate the interpretation suggested in the first chapter of the present study—namely, that Michal never bore a child to David.

There is a frequently repeated feature in rabbinic literature that identifies the name of Eglah with Michal. The name 'Eglah' is found twice in biblical literature: in the listing of wives whom David acquired in Hebron, 'Eglah, David's wife' (2 Sam. 3.5) and 'his [David's] wife Eglah' (1 Chron. 3.3). The name *'glh* means 'heifer' or 'young cow'. This meaning was exploited by various rabbinic commentators using the common technique of making a commentary on a passage starting with the particular meaning of a name. The Babylonian Talmud (*b. Sanh.* 21a) refers to this specific meaning of Eglah when it mentions the teaching of Rab who intimates the possibility of a particularly tender relationship between David and Michal: 'Rab said: Eglah is Michal. And why was she called Eglah? Because she was beloved by him, as an Eglah [calf] by its mother.'[61]

Abrabanel's comment on 2 Sam. 3.5 presupposes the same relationship: 'Consequently she was called "David's wife" because she was his first wife'. Rashi builds on this identification of Eglah with Michal when he says that because Michal was very dear to David, she was called 'his wife' in 1 Chron. 3.3. In order to corroborate the idea of an affectionate relationship between David and Michal, in commenting on 2 Sam. 3.5, Rashi points out another biblical verse where the name Eglah is used as a term of endearment applying to a wife: 'If you had not plowed with my heifer (*'glh*), you would not have found out my riddle' (Judg. 14.18). Here Samson refers to his newly wed bride as a 'heifer' (*'glh*).

16. *Was it Legitimate for David to take Michal Back?*

This question was widely debated in rabbinic literature. The midrash referred abundantly to the counter-gift of one hundred foreskins that David had brought to Saul for Michal's hand, implying that Michal was legally David's and not Palti's wife. Moreover, as already mentioned above, Radaq brought a supposed 'letter of divorce' into the discussion, and introduced the idea of Michal being forced to marry Palti. That too invalidates Palti's role as

60. Y. Qil commenting on 2 Sam. 6.23 and quoting the opinion of Rabbi Amos Haram ha-Hir (*Shemuel 1–2*, II, p. 374).

61. *The Babylonian Talmud, Seder Nezikin, Sanhedrin*, I, p. 113. This midrash is also mentioned in *Yalquṭ Shimoni* on 2 Sam. 3.5.

Michal's husband. She remains David's wife legally in spite of her episode with Palti. Heeding the law enunciated in Deut. 24.4 forbidding a divorced woman to go back to her first husband, the midrashim argue that Palti never knew Michal in the biblical sense of the term.

Commenting on 2 Sam. 3.14, Radaq refers to a passage in the Babylonian Talmud (*b. Sanh.* 19b), already discussed above, and says the following concerning the legality of David taking Michal back as his wife:

> '...She is my wife and I acquired her as a spouse at the price of one hundred Philistine foreskins'; this means that my mind was preoccupied with the foreskins and not with the riches that Saul wanted to give to me, which for him was just a debt to be reimbursed; therefore she is really my wife. And following the literal sense (*pešaṭ*), he said: 'whom I betrothed as a wife'[62] meaning for whom I jeopardized my life; therefore you have to bring her back to me. And he mentions 'one hundred foreskins', although he brought two hundred foreskins, for the number of one hundred was what they had agreed upon.[63]

Having demonstrated the invalidity of Michal's marriage with Palti, the authors of the midrash must now legitimate David's claims on her and show that Michal's relationship with Palti was entirely chaste.

The Babylonian Talmud (*b. Sanh.* 19b) accomplishes this feat in the following manner:

> [The second husband of David's undivorced wife] is variously called Palti (1 Sam. 25.44) and Paltiel (2 Sam. 3.15)!—Rabbi Yoḥanan said: His name was really Palti, but why was he called Paltiel? Because God saved him from transgression.[64] ...But is it not stated: 'And her husband [Palti] went with her' (2 Sam. 3.16)?—This means that he was like a husband to her.[65] But is it not written, 'He went weeping?'—This was for losing the good deed [of self-restraint]. Hence '[he followed her] to Baḥurim', implying that they had both remained like unmarried youths and not tasted the pleasures of marital relations.[66]

Here the Talmud makes a word-play by taking a geographical name as if it were a common term *bḥwrym*, plural of *bḥwr* ('a youth'). *Targum Jonathan* renders this term with *'lmt* which in Aramaic means 'youths'. *Leviticus Rabbah* 23.10 continues in the same vein:

62. According to *Meṣudat David* on 2 Sam. 3.14, *'šty* with reference to Deut. 20.7, 'a man that has betrothed a wife'.

63. Radaq's commentary on 2 Sam. 3.14 is also found in Malbim and in *Meṣudat David* commenting on the same verse.

64. Paltiel is a compound theophorous name composed of *plṭ* ('to escape') and *'l* ('God'). The reason for the addition of *'l* to 'Palti' is taken to express, as it were, the name of God to which he dedicated himself and who preserved him from transgressing the law by sleeping with a woman already married to another man.

65. Maintaining and loving her, but no more.

66. *The Babylonian Talmud, Seder Nezikin, Sanhedrin*, I, p. 103.

> There were three who fled from transgression and with whom the Holy One, blessed be He, united His name. They are: Joseph, Jael, and Palti. How do we know it of Joseph? Because it says, 'He made it a decree in Jehoseph [*yhwsp*]' (Ps. 81.5).[67] What is the implication of the expression *yhwsp*? God [*yh*, two letters of the divine tetragram], testifies in regard to him that he did not touch Potiphar's wife (Gen. 39.12). Whence of Jael? From the fact that it says, 'Jael came out to meet Sisera, and said to him: Turn aside, my lord, turn aside to me; have no fear. So he turned aside to her into her tent, and she covered him with a *śemikâ* [*śmykh*]' (Judg. 4.18). Our Rabbis here [Palestine] say it means with a *sudra*,[68] while our Rabbis there [Babylon] say it means with a cloak. Resh Laqish remarked: We have searched the whole of the Scripture and have not found any article the name of which is *śmykh*.[69] What then is *śmykh*? It denotes: *šemî kō* [*šmy kh*] (My name is there); My name (i.e. God's name) testifies in regard to her that this wicked fellow [Sisera] had no contact with her.[70] Whence for Palti? One verse says, 'Saul had given Michal his daughter, David's wife, to Palti [*plṭy*] the son of Laish' (1 Sam. 25.44), and another verse says, 'Paltiel' [*plṭy'l*] (2 Sam. 3.15). Who took away the name Palti and who gave him the name Paltiel? The fact is that the additional (*'el*) [God] indicates: I [says God] testify, in regard to him that he had no contact with David's wife.[71]

Commenting on 2 Sam. 3.15, one midrash in *Me'am Lo'ez* elaborates on the name Palti son of Laish and says, 'She was taken from Paltiel because God (*'l*) had cast forth (*plṭ*) his fault away from him. And Ben Laish, because he overcame his instincts like a lion (*lyš*).' There are numerous midrashic texts that borrow the same idea of a Platonic relationship between Michal and Palti. One midrash found in *Qoh. R.* 7.39, which contains a particularly negative appreciation of women in general and of Michal in particular, adduces a biblical verse found in Qoh. 7.26: 'And I found more bitter than death the woman whose heart is snares and nets, and whose hands are fetters; he who pleases God escapes her, but the sinner is taken by her'. For this somewhat misogynous commentator, Palti son of Laish is one of the men who deserves that the words 'who pleases God escapes her' be applied to him. The other meritorious men cited by the midrash are Joseph who escaped the advances of Potiphar's wife, and Phinehas who killed the Midianite (Num. 25.7). The 'sinners' are Potiphar who had married a bad woman, Zimri who was seduced by the Midianite woman (Num. 25.14) and Amnon who, obsessed with Tamar's beauty, committed the crime of raping her (2 Sam. 13.14).

67. In this verse, the name Joseph habitually spelled *ywsp*, is written with an additional *h*—thus *yhwsp*.

68. A kind of scarf wound about the head and neck.

69. In modern Hebrew *śmykh* means a blanket. The RSV translates the term in Judg. 4.18 with 'rug', while *HALOT*, III, p. 1337, translates it 'cover, covering'.

70. This is possible owing to the fact that prior to the work of the Masoretes (seventh to ninth centuries CE), the Hebrew text did not contain a diacritical mark to differentiate between *sin* (*ś*) and *shin* (*š*).

71. *Midrash Rabbah, Leviticus*, p. 300.

Realizing that his marriage with Michal was illegal, Palti refused to have any sexual relationship with her (*b. Sanh.* 19b). From this it becomes evident for the rabbis that 'the woman whose heart is snares and nets, and whose hands are fetters' refers to Michal. By exercising self-control and refusing to be affected by Michal's wiles, Palti enters the rabbinic tradition as the epitome of the pious and righteous man who successfully resisted what the midrash describes as 'the woman who lays snares and ambushes, on land and sea'.

Furthermore, praising the moral victories gained by some men mentioned in the Hebrew Bible who resisted the charms of feminine seductiveness, one Talmudic text (*b. Sanh.* 19b-20a) attributes virtues to Joseph, Boaz and Palti, which the biblical texts attribute to women!

> Rabbi Yoḥanan said: What is meant by the verse, 'Many daughters have done excellently, but you surpass them all?' (Prov. 31.29)—'Many daughters', refers to Joseph and Boaz; and 'you surpass them all', to Palti son of Laish.
>
> Rabbi Samuel bar Naḥmani said in Rabbi Jonathan's name: What is meant by the verse, 'Charm is deceitful and beauty vain, but a woman that fears the Lord is to be praised?' (Prov. 31.30)—'Charm is deceitful', refers to [the trials of] Joseph; 'and beauty is vain', to Boaz (Ruth 3.44); while 'and a woman that fears the Lord is to be praised', to the case of Palti son of Laish.[72]

For the rabbinic tradition, Palti ben Laish is the real hero. During the many years of his cohabitation with Michal, night after night he resisted the temptation of sexual indulgence with her. David's wife was wrongly given to him but he gave her back to David without ever having touched her. Commenting on 1 Samuel 24, Ralbag[73] affirms that the whole of Israel knew that Palti and Michal did not live together as husband and wife; consequently, David could take her back with no objection. All the rabbis, however, do not agree with this interpretation. Abrabanel,[74] for example, refutes a number of interpretations enumerated above and adduces his own point of view on the basis of a close reading of the biblical text:

> All these commentaries are worthless, for the biblical text does not say that David gave Michal a letter of divorce, that Saul forced Michal to this marriage, that he knew that David fled, that David made a declaration [in front of witnesses] or had sent messengers; and everything that Radaq says does not appear in the [biblical] text…

72. *The Babylonian Talmud, Seder Nezikin, Sanhedrin*, I, p. 105.

73. Ralbag is an acronym for Rabbi Levi ben Gershom (1288–1344), born at Bagnols-sur-Cèze (Gard, France). He was a mathematician, philosopher and biblical commentator. His comments are quoted from the Rabbinic Bible, *Miqra'ôt Gedolôt*.

74. Abrabanel's commentary on 1 Sam. 24, in response to his fourth question: 'How was it possible for David to take Michal back from Palti…?' (*Nebi'im Rishonim*, pars. 32 and 44).

And yet Michal did not have a child by David. It would have been better, however, that she had not been remembered and that her name had not been mentioned after she married Palti ben Laish. David did not lack women that he should undergo such an outrage. We cannot say with Ralbag that David rested on what was known, that Palti did not marry her [carnally], for that was not known. Who could have proven it when she lived as his wife and slept in his bed? Moreover, according to the Torah, since she had been married to another man, she was forbidden for her first husband, even if she had not belonged to her second husband. And in order to avoid all these imbroglios, I would not say anything that would make one think that Saul gave his daughter to Palti ben Laish [when she was still David's wife]. Saul feared God, the Lord of heavens; how could he commit such a great crime? The truth is that when Saul saw that David had taken other women, Abigail and Ahinoam, he feared that Michal, his daughter, would have [sexual] relations with another [man] for she was still a young woman; or he feared that she would not remain worthy of her father's honor, for, seeing her husband David driven away, she could have thought that he would never come back. Saul took some women in order to take care of her, or so that she might not be excessively sad, or maybe even run away in order to look for David, or even insist on an explanation from her father. For all those reasons Saul gave his daughter to Palti ben Laish so that he might take care of her and keep her like a man would raise his daughter. It appears that Palti was an older man, already married and having sons. Saul placed his daughter in his house so that she might be protected, honor required that he should not marry her. For that reason she took with her the sons of her sister Merab whom she gave to Adriel, in order to bring them up and thus to drive away the grief of her heart and the sorrow of an abandoned woman, as it appears at the end of the book (2 Sam. 21.8). They were with her and for that reason they were called 'her sons'. Therefore nowhere is it said 'Saul gave Michal to Palti ben Laish *for a wife*' because he did not give her for a wife but to protect her. For that reason, it is only said. '(He) had given Michal his daughter' (1 Sam. 25.44). Moreover the fact that it is said, 'Saul had given Michal his daughter, David's wife…' proves that; being still David's wife, she could not have married somebody else. She had been given to Palti ben Laish and was entrusted into his custody. He spoke comforting words to her heart so that she might not be excessively sad on account of her husband who went away and took other wives. For that reason this verse comes immediately after the one relating how David took Abigail and Ahinoam for wives. This also allowed David to come back to her. He asked Abner to bring her back to him for, as an abandoned woman, she was in Palti's house with the aim of being diverted from her despair and Saul prevented her [as well] from joining David. Of course, it is said that 'her husband went with her, weeping' (2 Sam. 3.16). Palti is called 'her man' (*'yšh*) but only because she lived with him. Indeed, he was not called 'her husband' (*b'lh*), for she was not married to him. This is the way the prophet spoke when he said, 'You will call me my Man, and no longer will you call me my Ba'al' (Hos. 2.18).[75] The term *'yš* ('man') refers to

75. Cf. Andersen and Freedman, *Hosea*, p. 216: 'You will call me Ishi [My man, viz. husband] and you will never again call me Baali [My master/owner/lord/Baal]'.

> a protector and lord, while the word *b'l* ('husband') indicates ownership or the duties of the husband. Did not I also see in (*b. Yoma* 84, 1st mishnah) concerning the high priest on Yom Kippur *'yšy khn gdwl* ('my man, the high priest'), in order to underline his status and directing role? It is in this sense that Palti is called 'his man'. Extending the meaning of the term 'his man', the rabbis said that Palti had married her. This is unacceptable, however, and in truth it could only be what I said. Palti, as it is written, loved Michal who dwelt with him, with an extreme love like the love of a father for his daughter. This is why he followed her weeping. Hence it turns out that Michal was neither promised to Palti nor did she marry him; she did not belong to him and therefore David could go back to her. And with this the fourth question has been answered.

Commenting on 2 Sam. 11.26, Malbim uses the same distinction between 'man' (*'yš*) and 'husband' (*b'l*), in order to show that Bathsheba had no more sexual relations with her 'man', being divorced from him the moment he went to war, and hence that she was sexually available to David:

> In the text it is implied that she was divorced from Uriah since it is said: 'When the wife (*'št*) of Uriah heard that Uriah her man (*'yšh*) was dead, she made lamentation for her husband (*b'lh*)'. There is a difference between the word 'man' (*'yš*), and the word 'husband' ('owner') (*b'l*). 'Man' (*'yš*) implies the love that exists between a man and a woman, while 'husband' (*b'l*) expresses only the sexual relations they had or domination. When a woman speaks, she uses the expression, 'my man' and not 'my husband'; thus it is said: 'You will call me my Man, and no longer will you call me my Ba'al/husband' (Hos. 2.18). The rumor spread that her man had died, for that is what the people thought, but in fact she lamented over her husband and not over her man for she was already divorced.

Although varying in their approach, all these commentaries tend to argue that the marriage between Michal and Palti was not consummated. Michal's and David's honor are safe and David can claim his wife back the same way he would have claimed something that belonged to him and that had been in somebody else's custody. Since the legality of his union with Michal has been accepted by the rabbis, the validity of their marriage has been preserved in spite of Michal's episode with Palti.

17. *David's Dance before the Ark and the Dispute with Michal*

The arrival of the ark in David's private capital (2 Sam. 6) followed by Nathan's promise of dynastic continuity in 2 Sam. 7 consecrates David as the new ruler of the different Israelite tribes. In 2 Sam. 6.16 he is called 'King David'. As long as Michal played a supporting role in David's career, the midrashim depict her in a positive light. But as soon as she opposes David's dealings, she becomes a vile woman. The following comment from *Num. R.* 4.20 recapitulates a number of preceding midrashim:[76]

> 'And David danced before the Lord with all his might; and David was girded with a linen ephod' (2 Sam. 6.14). Come and observe how much David humbled himself in honor of the Holy One, blessed be He! David should have simply walked before the ark like a king, robed in his royal apparel. But no! He attired himself in fairest garb in honor of the ark, and played/or danced (*śḥq*) before it, saying whatever could appropriately be said; as it says: 'David wore a linen ephod' (1 Chron. 15.27c) and 'David danced (*mkrkr*) before the Lord with all his might (*bkl 'z*)' (2 Sam. 6.14a). What is the meaning of *bkl 'z*? ('With all his might'). What is *mkrkr*? He struck his hands against each other, clapping them and saying *kiri ram* ('Hail, all High!'). Israel cheered loudly and sounded their horns (*špr*) and trumpets and all manner of musical instruments; as it says, 'And all the house of Israel brought up the ark of the Lord with shouting, and with the sound of the horn' (2 Sam. 6.15; 1 Chron. 15.28). When they arrived at Jerusalem all the women looked at David from the roofs and windows and watched him dance and play and he did not mind. Hence it is written: 'As the ark of the Lord came into the city of David, Michal the daughter of Saul looked out of the window' (2 Sam. 6.16). This only proves that his wife looked out at him, but how do you know that all the women of Jerusalem did so too? Because she, in fact, says to him, 'How the king of Israel honored himself today, uncovering himself today before the eyes of his servants' maids' (2 Sam. 6.20). 'She saw King David leaping (*mpzz*) and dancing (*mkrkr*)' (2 Sam. 6.16). When she saw him behaving like a commoner she lost all respect for him. What is the meaning of 'leaping and dancing (*mpzz wmkrkr*)': what exactly was he doing? He was dressed, say our rabbis, in glistening, gold-embroidered garments shining like fine gold, and he struck his hands against each other, clapping them. As he danced, crying *kiri ram* ('Hail, all High!') he made a tinkling sound (*mpzz*). What is *mpzz*? The refined gold (*paz*) which he wore made a jingling noise (*mepazzez*). It might be supposed that David did no more than this. But no! He turned the front of his foot and danced.[77] For so it is written elsewhere: 'She saw the king David dancing (*mrqd*) and playing/or making merry (*mśḥq*)' (1 Chron. 15.29). 'All the women looked at him from the roofs and windows, and he did not mind'. Whence do we infer that David turned the front of his foot and danced? From the following: For you find that when they brought the ark into the city of David they put it in the place which David had prepared for it, and offered burnt-offerings before it, he and Israel, for it is written: 'And they brought the ark of the Lord, and set it in its place... and David offered burnt-offerings...' (2 Sam. 6.17), and elsewhere it is written: 'And they offered burnt-offerings and peace-offerings before God' (1 Chron. 16.1). And after he had made an end of offering he blessed all the people for having honored the ark, and so great was his joy in the ark that he gave them all presents, including the

76. See the Jerusalem Talmud, *y. Suk.* 24.1; *y. Sanh* 12.1; *Midrash Shemuel* 25.6; *Yalquṭ Shimoni* 2 Sam. 3 and 6.

77. According to Radaq, he danced on tiptoe revealing his naked toes.

> women; as it says: 'And when David had finished offering the burnt-offerings and the peace-offerings, he blessed the people in the name of the Lord of hosts, and distributed among all the people, the whole multitude of Israel, both men and women, to each a cake of bread, a portion of meat (*'špr*), and a cake of raisins (*'šyšh*)' (2 Sam. 6.18-19).—What is *'špr*? One-sixth of a bullock.[78] *'šyšh*? One-sixth of an ephah.[79] Some say that *'šyšh* means a cask of wine, quoting, 'And love flasks of wine (*'ašiše*)' (Hos. 3.1).[80]

There are several features in this midrash that are of interest. First, the enigmatic term *mkrkr* is interpreted as *kiri ram*, meaning 'Lord (most) High', where *kiri* stands for Greek *Kyrios* ('Lord'), a term which the LXX uses in order to translate the tetragram of the divine name YHWH. Greek was not spoken in Jerusalem at the time of David and the rabbis are making an obvious anachronism here. Nevertheless, this detail is important as it shows the bilingualism of the rabbis and of the Jewish community. The Hellenization of the Jews living in the Mediterranean basin had begun by the end of the fourth century BCE. The LXX was the first translation of the Hebrew Bible into Greek made for the Jews of Alexandria in the middle of the third century BCE, who apparently no longer spoke Hebrew. The rabbis of the Talmud were multilingual (reading and speaking Hebrew, Aramaic and Greek). Moreover Mishnaic Hebrew adopted numerous Greek terms. Secondly, the midrash sheds light on another enigmatic term *mpzz*. The rabbis play with the root *pzz* and combine several meanings: *pzz* I, a denominative from *pz* in hophal, means 'to be overlaid with fine gold; to be refined', and *pz*, a noun designating 'refined, pure gold'.[81] From this meaning they infer that *mpzz* may also mean 'to jingle or tinkle', and that *pzz* II means 'to act with precipitation', referring to David's dance in 2 Sam. 6.16.[82]

18. *The Conflict*

David's dancing and cavorting before the ark and the assembled crowd displeased Michal. Commenting on 2 Sam. 6.16, Y. Qil points out the use of the term *wtbz* (from the root *bzh*, 'to despise'), and says: 'The form is in the future with a *waw* consecutive, giving it a past meaning. From this form we may deduce that Michal, being very proud, despised him in her heart but did

78. A piece of meat of that size. Accordingly, *'špr* is read as an abbreviation for *'eḥad mišišah be-par.*

79. Reading this too as an abbreviation for *'eḥad mišišah be-ephah.*

80. *Midrash Rabbah, Numbers* (ed. H. Freedman and M. Simon; Eng. trans. J.J. Slotki; London: The Soncino Press, 1961), I, pp. 133-34.

81. *HALOT*, III, p. 921b; Caquot, Sznycer and Herdner, *Textes ougaritiques*, p. 130 n. r: 'pure gold, refined gold'; Prov. 8.19 parallel with *ḥrwṣ*.

82. BDB, p. 808. *HALOT*, III, p. 921b; Syriac *paz* ('to dance') and *pazzizā* ('agile'), Arabic *fazza* ('to be startled [gazelle]').

not reveal it to anybody. She waited for an opportunity to speak to him personally.'[83]

The midrash in *Num. R.* 4.20 amply elaborates on the reasons for the dispute between Michal and David:

> And after all Israel had taken leave of him he turned in to greet his household and to gladden them (*wlśmḥh*) with some of his own delight in the ark. Michal came out and showed her contempt for him for having degraded himself in honor of the ark before the women. Hence it is written: 'And David returned to bless his household. But Michal the daughter of Saul came out to meet David…' (2 Sam. 6.20). She did not let him come into the house, but went out into the street, and overwhelmed him with reproaches and said: 'How the king of Israel honored himself today, uncovering himself today before the eyes of his servants' maids' (*ibid.*). From here you learn that he turned the front of his foot and danced, since she tells him, 'who uncovered himself today'. She began to quarrel with him and sought to destroy his countenance (lit. 'to eat his face');[84] she said 'Have I seen your glory? O, how the king of Israel honored himself today!' Now you have made it known that you are indeed a king! "Who uncovered himself today"; O, she taunted, that it had at least been in private! But no; "Before the eyes of his servants' maids!"' It was the women of Israel whom she called 'handmaids'. 'As one of the vulgar fellows shamelessly uncovers himself'. Rabbi Aba bar Kahana said: A [professional] dancer (*'ḥd hrqym*) is the lowest of the low, for there is none more neglectful of religious duties than he is, and like him David danced before the ark. She said to him: 'This day the nobility of my father's house is made clear. Come and see what a difference there is between you and my father's house! All the members of Saul's household were modest and saintly'. It was said of the members of Saul's household that in all their life no one had ever seen the naked heel or toe of any of them… And thus Michal spoke to him saying, 'The members of my father's house were so chaste, and you stand and uncover yourself like any low fellow'. When she finished speaking, he said to her: 'Did I forsooth play before a mortal king? Did I not in fact play before the supreme King of Kings, "who chose me over against your father and his house" (2 Sam. 6.21)? If your father had been more righteous than I, would God have chosen me and disqualified your father's house?' Hence it is written: 'And David said to Michal: It was before the Lord…' (*ibid.*). He said to her: 'Your father was king over Israel only, I am ruler over Israel and Judah'. Hence it is written, 'Over the people of the Lord' (*ibid.*), indicating the tribe of Judah; 'over Israel' indicating the rest of the tribes. Another explanation: He told her: 'The members of your father's household sought only their own glory, and did not trouble themselves about the glory of heaven; I do not so, but, not troubling about my own glory, seek rather the glory of heaven'. Hence it is written: 'I will make myself yet more contemptible than this' (2 Sam. 6.22). Nor must you imagine that I was lowly in other people's eyes but not despised in mine

83. Qil, *Shemuel 1–2*, II, p. 362.

84. The expression is idiomatic and means 'to put to shame', or 'to make one lose one's face'.

> own; it is stated, 'I will be abased in my eyes; but by the maids of whom you have spoken, by them I shall be held in honor' (*ibid.*). He said to her: 'Those daughters of Israel whom you call handmaids (*'mhwt*) are not handmaids but mothers (*'ymhwt*);[85] would I had a share with them in the world to come!' [...] Because Michal had spoken thus she was punished, as you see from what follows in the Scripture: 'And Michal the daughter of Saul had no child to the day of her death' (2 Sam. 6.23).[86]

Michal was punished by virtue of the retribution principle called *mydh kngd mydh* ('measure for measure'). She outraged the women of Jerusalem by treating them as servant maids and not as mothers. Therefore her punishment is related to her fault. By despising women who were mothers, she was herself deprived of motherhood.

Neither Michal's childlessness nor her dispute with David are mentioned in Chronicles. The details of their conflict are expunged and the affair is summarized in a single verse: '...Michal the daughter of Saul looked out of the window, and saw King David dancing and playing/making merry; and she despised him in her heart' (1 Chron. 15.29). In commenting on this verse, Rashi explains that the Chronicles were written in honor of David's reign and the blame addressed to him by Michal was omitted because 'It is an offense for David that a woman should talk to him in such a manner'.

All the rabbis, however, are not prepared to exonerate David's behavior in the affair of his dance before the ark. Two expressions have attracted their attention: on the one hand, the expression *mpzz wmkrkr* ('leaping and dancing'), and, on the other, the term *nglh*, in the expression *khglwt nglwt* ('like the uncovering of himself').

According to the commentary on 2 Sam. 6.16 found in the *Meṣudat David*, the term *mpzz* refers to David's dance with a steady rhythm and implies excessive haste. The commentary adduces a reference to a story in the Babylonian Talmud (*b. Šab.* 88a) where the term *mpzz* implies such excessive haste. A Sadducee addressed Rabba[87] reproaching him and other Israelites for acting with haste and lacking adequate reflection. In the expression *n'śh wnšm'* ('we shall act and listen'), the Israelites are hastily committing themselves 'to doing' instead of 'listening', thus accepting something without even knowing whether they are capable of accomplishing what they have been asked to do.

In Radaq's opinion, *mpzz* is a synonym of *mkrkr*. Since they seem to be redundant, each term may serve to underline a different aspect of David's

85. This rabbinic interpretation implies a wordplay between 'maids' (*'mhwt*) and 'mothers' (*'ymhwt*).

86. *Midrash Rabbah, Numbers*, I, pp. 135-36.

87. Rabba bar Naḥmani, quoted as Rabba in the Talmud, was a Babylonian amora of the third generation (270–331 CE), leader of the academy of Pumbedita.

dance; if, however, they both mean the same thing, then by mentioning both, they underline how frenetic David's dance was. He also quotes *Targum Jonathan* who renders the expression with 'dancing and glorifying'. Moreover, he notes that in Chronicles the expression is rendered with 'dancing and playing/making merry' (1 Chron. 15.29). Concerning the second expression, *khglwt nglwt*, Radaq notes that these two terms represent a *mākôr* form of Hebrew infinitive of the niphal conjugation, the first without the preformative *nun* and the latter with it. This succession of infinitives points out David's excessive exuberance and his over-abundant manifestation of joy.

The Babylonian Talmud speaks of David's guilt by referring to a verse in the Psalms attributed to him: 'Rabba expounded: Why was David punished? Because he called the words of the Torah "songs", as it is said, "Thy statutes have been my songs in the house of pilgrimage" (Ps. 119.54)'.[88]

19. *The Ark at Obed-Edom's House*

After an initial effort to bring the ark to Jerusalem, and prompted by the death of a man that occurred at the moment of its transportation, David decided to make a halt and leave it at Obed-Edom's house. According to 2 Sam. 6.9-10, David became afraid and did not dare to bring it to his place. In doing so, David implicitly admitted his guilt. He preferred to leave the ark with Obed-Edom, and to wait for the divine wrath to be appeased. In 1 Chron. 15.18, Obed-Edom is listed among the Levites and the gate-keepers. Three months later, however, 'YHWH has blessed the household of Obed-Edom and all that belongs to him, because of the ark of God. So David went and brought up the ark of God from the house of Obed-Edom to the city of David with rejoicing' (2 Sam. 6.12). The midrash elaborates on the form that this divine blessing had on Obed-Edom's household. Both the Talmud and the midrashim agree that the ark brought exceptional fecundity to all the female folk in Obed-Edom's household. In three months, says the Babylonian Talmud, his house was filled with sixty-two sons. According to the rabbis, it is because Obed-Edom attended to the ark by sweeping its dust that his daughters-in-law gave birth to six children in a row:

> Rabbi Eliezer the son of Rabbi Yose the Galilean began to speak in praise of hospitality, expounding the verse, 'And the Lord blessed Obed-Edom and all his house....because of the ark of God' (2 Sam. 6.12). Have we not here an argument *a fortiori*? If such was the reward for attending to the ark which did not eat or drink, but before which he merely swept and laid the dust, how much more will it be for one who entertains a scholar in his house and gives

88. *The Babylonian Talmud, Seder Nashim, Soṭah*, p. 174 n. 5. 'When he [David] fled from his enemies, he entertained himself by treating Scriptural passages as songs. He thus made a profane use of them' (*b. Soṭ.* 35a-35b).

> him to eat and drink and allows him the use of his possessions! What was the blessing with which God blessed him [Obed-Edom]?—Rabbi Judah bar Zebida says: This refers to Hamoth [Obed-Edom's wife] and her eight daughters-in-law who each bore six children at a birth, as it says, 'Peullethai the eighth [son], for God blessed him' (1 Chron. 26.5) and it is written, 'All these were of the sons of Obed-Edom, with their sons and brethren, able men qualified for service, sixty-two of Obed-Edom' (1 Chron. 26.8).[89]

The total of sixty-two is made up of the eight sons mentioned, six more to his wife at one birth, and six to each of his eight daughters-in-law (8+6+48=62). Moreover, one midrash of the haggadic type found in *Num. R.* 4.20 relates what amounts to a fairy tale, and brings an additional precision concerning the miraculous births that affected Obed-Edom's daughters-in-law:[90]

> It was said of Obed-Edom: He had eight sons and he also had eight daughters-in-law each of whom gave birth to two children in one month. How was this? She would pass seven days of menstrual uncleanness (Lev. 12.2) and seven of cleanness (Lev. 15.28), and then give birth. Then another seven of uncleanness and seven of cleanness, and again give birth; that was sixteen [births] a month.[91] This continued for three months, making a total of forty-eight.[92]

Wanting to show that it is not the ark that kills or provides blessing, another midrash in *Num. R.* 4.20 offers the following explanation:

> Our rabbis said: There were two things which are really holy and great but which men wrongly considered to be dangerous, and in order that a stigma should not be attached to them a striking instance of their praiseworthiness and blessedness has been recorded. These are the things: The incense and the ark. 'The incense': That men might not say the incense was dangerous, having been the cause of the death of Nadab and Abihu (Lev. 10.1), and the cause through which the congregation of Korah was burned (Num. 16.35), as well as the medium through which Uzziah was stricken with leprosy (2 Chron. 26.19), the Holy One, blessed be He, recorded the great distinction of the incense in that it was the instrument whereby Israel was delivered; as it says: 'So Aaron took it as Moses said, and ran into the midst of the assembly; and behold, the plague had already begun among the people; and he put on the incense, and made an atonement for the people' (Num. 17.12 [Eng. 16.47]). 'The ark': That men might not say the ark was dangerous, since it was this that had smitten the Philistines (1 Sam. 5.1), it was this that had slain the men of Beth-Shemesh (1 Sam. 6.19), and this also it was that had slain Uzzah, He recorded its

89. *The Babylonian Talmud, Seder Nashim, Berakoth* (ed. I. Epstein; Eng. trans. M. Simon; New York: Rebecca Bennet Publications, 1959), p. 402 (*b. Ber.* 63b-64a).

90. This midrash is also cited in *Cant. R.* 2.18.

91. The total progeny granted to Obed-Edom by his eight daughters-in-law.

92. The period during which the ark remained in Obed-Edom's house; see *Midrash Rabbah, Numbers*, I, p. 131.

> blessedness; 'And the ark of the Lord remained in the house of Obed-Edom the Gittite three months; and the Lord blessed Obed-Edom and all his household' (2 Sam. 6.11). All this is to teach you that it is not the incense nor the ark that kills, but that it is the sins that kill.[93]

In light of the above, Obed-Edom's household was blessed with exceptional fertility on account of his piety and the hospitality extended to the ark. By contrast, the arrival of the ark in the City of David was the occasion that provoked Michal's sterility. But was this sterility a punishment for her fault or is it the expression of the divine disapproval of some of David's acts? The absence of a son from Michal the daughter of Saul deprives him of an ideal heir who would have united the two royal houses and legitimized his own claim to the throne. David's heir, Solomon, was son of Bathsheba, Uriah's wife, whom David had to kill in order to hide his adulterous relationship with one of his officers' wives. Moreover, in spite of his legendary wisdom, Solomon failed as the political and spiritual leader of his people:

> For when Solomon was old his wives turned away his heart after other gods; and his heart was not wholly true to YHWH his God, as was the heart of David his father. For Solomon went after Ashtoreth the goddess of the Sidonians, and after Milcom the abomination of the Ammonites. So Solomon did what was evil in the sight of YHWH, and did not wholly follow YHWH, as David his father had done. (1 Kgs 11.4-6)

What fault of David's deprived him of an ideal heir? The biblical text incriminates David directly through the blame that Michal addresses to him after his dance before the ark.

20. *David's Fault*

It appears that in his dance, David was influenced by the ancient Near Eastern customs of his times and adopted some cultic and religious practices of his neighbors. This might have provoked Michal's reaction of disapproval. The rabbis attempted to clarify the reasons for Michal's contempt of David's behavior during the dance. Commenting on 2 Sam. 6.16, Radaq says: 'When she saw him through the window, she despised him in her heart, for she thought that his honor as a king was at stake and that his vulgar behavior, even if it was before the ark of the Lord, could only be detrimental to him'.

Commenting the same verse, Abrabanel continues in the same vein: '[Michal] thought that this action was an offense to the laws of kingship and that it was vulgar behavior'. In respect to 2 Sam. 6.12 and 15, Abrabanel notes that David behaves in a way different from the people around him:

93. *Midrash Rabbah, Numbers*, I, p. 130.

> It is said that David danced and gesticulated with all his might before God. While during the first transfer [of the ark] he was part of the group of people who rejoiced, this time, however, he acts differently and adopts an attitude different from the rest of the people; it is said of him that he dances and gesticulates; he is wearing an ephod, a vestment particular to the high priest which he did not wear during the first transfer of the ark.

Another midrash from *Me'am Lo'ez*, commenting on 2 Sam. 6.5, calls attention to David's uncommon behavior which suggests a sort of ecstatic dance:

> Some comment saying that at the beginning David did not dance in the manner that was customary in the kingdom. During the first transfer [of the ark] there was a group of musicians who played according to the rules (1 Chron. 13.8).[94] This time, however, David is no longer taking any notice of others; he is leaping and gesticulating with all his might. Moreover, he is not dressed in full regalia but in a tunic more appropriate to priests.

Commenting on 2 Sam. 6.19, Y. Qil points out the mention of women as being part of the festivities and rejoicing: '"[David] distributed among the people, the whole multitude of Israel, both men and women". From the fact that they are mentioned, one may deduce that the participation of women was not commonplace. Michal, watching from the window, is convinced that participation in this kind of rejoicing was dishonorable'.[95]

Commenting on 2 Sam. 6.20, Abrabanel[96] explains the reasons for Michal's disapproval:

> When [David] returned in order to bless his wife, his sons and the people from his household, since he was back from a journey, Michal sought a quarrel with him, speaking to him with mockery: 'How the king of Israel honored himself today' (2 Sam. 6.20). She wanted to tell him that it was not to his honor to have uncovered himself in such a manner before his servant's maids by dancing and leaping as he did; for she thought that it was a way for him to be jesting and dallying with them.

David does not refute Michal's assertion, admitting implicitly that he behaved in the manner she described. The rest of Abrabanel's commentary on 2 Sam. 6.20-22 points out that David's objection deals with the reasons of his unusual behavior:

> David answered that the deeds deserve to be praised or blamed only in view of their aim; even if he had danced before a man and in his honor that would have been a noble act from him on account of his [David's] superior social

94. 1 Chron. 13.8 reads: 'And David and all Israel were making merry/playing before God with all their might, with song and lyres and harps and tambourines and cymbals and trumpets'.

95. Qil, *1–2 Shemuel*, II, p. 373.

96. Abrabanel commenting on 2 Sam. 6.20-22 (sixth comment).

> rank. Therefore, dancing before God is not a disgrace for the worth of kings is null and in his case there are no kings but only servants. He tried to explain to her that his dance was not a bodily expression but a spiritual joy in relationship to God. Then he gave her a second argument: The one who receives great favors from God is blessed; it is therefore preferable that he should serve God well, as it is written: 'who chose me above your father, and above all his house' (v. 21). And in order to conclude his argument, he said: 'I will make myself yet more contemptible than this, and I will be abased in my eyes' (v. 22a), meaning the following: On account of divine greatness and the favors that [God] showed me, it is better that I should remain simple and more humble, for honors and display of social rank are neither suitable with people who are inferior to you nor with God; 'but by the maids of whom you have spoken, by them I shall be held in honor' (v. 22b) meant that it was better to derive some glory from them than from God. It is equally possible to comment: before God and in order to serve him, I will humble myself, by glorifying myself with the maids.

In spite of giving a spiritual meaning to David's dance, Abrabanel admits that his behavior with the maids in front of Michal might have been indelicate. Indeed, if one analyzes the Hebrew verbs employed in order to describe David's behavior which provoked Michal's indignation, one is confirmed in the suspicion that his conduct was unseemly and reproachable. In Chronicles, the verb *śḥq* is used in the verse reporting the incident: 'Michal the daughter of Saul looked out of the window and saw King David dancing (*mrqd*) and playing (*mśḥq*); and she despised him in her heart' (1 Chron. 15.29). The verb *śḥq* is questionable and translators vary considerably in its rendering: RSV and NEB read 'dancing and making merry'; NEB has 'leaping and capering' in 2 Sam. 6.16; TOB renders with '*sautait et dansait*'.

The same verb also appears written with a *ṣade* instead of a *śamek*, as found in Gen. 26.8: 'Abimelech king of the Philistines looked out of a window and saw Isaac fondling (*mṣḥq*) Rebekah his wife'. Here Rashi explains that Abimelech saw Isaac 'use his bed' with his wife, that is, he saw him engage in marital relations (*mṣḥq*), another term or a polite way to designate intimate relations.[97] The verb also appears in the Exodus account of the dance before the golden calf: 'and the people sat down to eat and drink, and rose up to play (*lṣḥq*)' (Exod. 32.6). Commenting on this verse, Rashi says:

> 'To play' (*lṣḥq*)—in this word there is a connotation of sexual immorality *glwy 'rywt* ('to uncover nakedness') as it is said *lṣḥq by* ('in order to mock, i.e., to fondle me') (Potiphar's wife falsely accusing Joseph in Gen. 39.17); and [there is the idea] of bloodshed, as it is said, 'let the young men arise and fence (*wyśḥqw*) before us' (describing a combat with swords in 2 Sam. 2.14). Here too, 'Hur was slain' [from *Midrash Tanḥuma* 20].

97. Cf. *Gen. R.* 64.5.

The Aramaic versions are not very helpful. In the Pentateuch, *Targum Onqelos* translates the term with Aramaic *ḥyk* meaning 'to laugh', while *Targum Jonathan* renders the references in Samuel and Chronicles with the Aramaic verb *šbḥ* ('to praise').

Y. Qil comments on 2 Sam. 6.20-22 and points out a series of Hebrew terms which are highly significant in describing David's behavior and Michal's blame.[98] The expression 'his servants' maids' (*'mhwt 'bdyw*) used by Michal is contemptuous. The verb 'to uncover oneself', expressed by a double infinitive (*khglwt nglwt*, v. 20), reinforces and underlines the idea of David's nudity in the course of his dance. In order to translate this double infinitive, *Targum Jonathan* uses *dḥlyṣ*, the Aramaic equivalent of Hebrew *ḥlṣ*, describing the action of taking off shoes or clothes.

The rabbis are known for their divergent opinions. One midrash found in *Num. R.* 4.20 attempts to exonerate David by connecting Psalm 131 with David's dance:

> No man in Israel abased himself for the sake of the commandments more than David, as you may infer from the text in which he said to God: 'O Lord, my heart is not lifted up' (Ps. 131.1a) meaning, when Samuel anointed me as king; 'my eyes are not raised too high' (v. 1b), when I slew Goliath; 'I did not walk (*hlkty*) [after] great things' (v. 1c), when I was restored to my kingdom; 'or to what is too marvelous to me' (v. 1d), when I brought up the ark. 'Like a weaned child with its mother; like a weaned child (is) my soul in me' (v. 2); as the baby is not ashamed to remain uncovered before its mother, so did I dispose my soul before Thee, not having been ashamed to abase myself in Thy presence in order to honor Thee. 'Like a weaned child (is) my soul in me': As the baby that has just come out of its mother's womb and is not too proud to suck at his mother's breasts, so is my soul within me, for I am not ashamed to learn the Torah even from the least in Israel. Rabbi Ada son of Rabbi Hanina expounded: The Holy One, blessed be He, said to him: 'Thou madest thyself like a babe. By thy life! As the babe is without iniquity so art thou without iniquity'; as it says: 'The Lord has also put away your sin; you shall not die' (2 Sam. 12.13). From this you learn that it is not right for a man to act proudly in the presence of the Omnipresent, but he should abase himself if that is in His honor.[99]

21. *David's Guilt according to the Talmudic Literature*

In the books of Samuel an incident occurs between David and Shimei ben Gera, a member of Saul's clan, which may indicate that David's bloodguilt in respect to Saul's descendants was common knowledge in those days:

98. Qil, *1–2 Shemuel*, II, p. 373.
99. *Midrash Rabbah, Numbers*, I, p. 137.

> When King David came to Bahurim (*bḥrym*),[100] there came out a man of the family of the House of Saul, whose name was Shimei, the son of Gera; and as he came he cursed continually. And he threw stones at David... And Shimei said as he cursed, 'Begone, begone you man of blood, you worthless fellow (*ṣ' ṣ' 'yš hdmym w'yš hbly'l*)'. YHWH has avenged upon you all the blood of the House of Saul, in whose place you have reigned; and YHWH has given the kingdom into the hand of your son Absalom. See, your ruin is on you; for you are a man of blood. (2 Sam. 16.5-8)

On his deathbed David instructs his son Solomon to avenge him on account of this incident, saying, 'you will bring his gray head down with blood to Sheol' (1 Kgs 2.9). In referring to Shimei, David says, 'who cursed me with a grievous curse (*qllny qllh nmrṣt*)' (v. 8). A rabbinic interpretation in the Babylonian Talmud (*b. Šab.* 105a), takes *nmrṣt* as an acronym revealing David's crimes: 'Rab Aḥa bar Jacob quoted: "He cursed me with a curse (*nmrṣt*)". This is an abbreviation (i.e. an acronym): he is an adulterer (*nw'p*), a Moabite (*mw'by*), a murderer (*rwṣḥ*), an adversary (*ṣwrr*), an abomination (*tw'bh*).'[101] This rabbinic interpretative technique is called *noṭariqon*, a method of exegesis whereby each letter of a word is taken as the initial letter and abbreviation of another word.

Commenting on 2 Sam. 16.7, Ralbag says: 'It is possible that he (David) was called "a man of blood" because he shed a lot of blood, and that he was called a base fellow (*'yš hbly'l*), on account of Bathsheba, the wife of Uriah the Hittite'.[102]

There is a second instance in the books of Samuel where David is called 'son of Belial'. In 1 Sam. 25.17, one of Abigail's servants returns and reports imminent danger, announcing that David, accompanied by some four hundred warriors, is marching against them: 'Now therefore know this and consider what you should do; for evil is determined against our master and against all his house, for he is such a son of Belial (*bn bly'l*), that one cannot speak to him'.[103]

100. Bahurim is the place to which Palti ben Laish accompanied Michal when David requested to have her back.

101. *The Babylonian Talmud, Seder Mo'ed, Shabbath*, III, p. 506. Cf. also *Yalquṭ Shimoni*, par. 170, and *Midrash Tehillim* 3.3: 'How is *nmrṣt* to be understood? As an acrostic (lit. *Noṭariqon*): the letter N stands for *no'ef*, "adulterer"; the letter M, for "Moabite"; the letter R, for *roṣeaḥ*, "murderer"; the letter Ṣ for *ṣorer*, "persecutor"; and the letter T, for *to'ebah*, "abomination"'; see *The Midrash on Psalms*, I, p. 53.

102. In the *Testament of the Twelve Patriarchs*, Beliar masters the one whose mind is lustful: 'If lust does not subdue your thoughts, neither will Beliar be able to subdue you'; see *T. Reub.* 4.11.

103. The RSV reads: 'ill-natured fellow'; NJPS: 'nasty fellow'; NEB: 'a good-for-nothing'; NIV: 'a wicked man'.

Commenting on this verse, Radaq notes the ambiguity it contains and says that 'David could well be that son of Belial by making this kind of request from Nabal' (i.e. to provide food and drink for David's 600 mercenaries).

The Babylonian Talmud (*b. Šab.* 55b) speaks of David's guilt in a section dealing with the sins of the fathers:

> Rab Yehuda says in Rab's name: When David said to Mephibosheth (Jonathan's son): 'You and Ziba will divide the land' (2 Sam. 19.30), a *bat qol* (Heavenly Echo) came forth and declared to him, Rehoboam and Jeroboam will divide the kingdom. Rab Yehuda said in Rab's name: Had not David paid heed to slander, the kingdom of the House of David would not have been divided, Israel had not engaged in idolatry, and we would not have been exiled from our country.[104]

A series of errors which have brought about the exile are credited to David's initial misdeed in respect to Saul's inheritance. In the injustice which David inflicted on Mephibosheth, Jonathan's son and last descendant of the House of Saul, by despoiling him of half of his inheritance, the rabbis perceive the triggering of the retribution principle *middâ keneged middâ*. What he did to the descendants of Saul was bound to happen to his own descendants. Rab Yehuda and Rab see in David's act the reason for his kingdom's division after Solomon's death.[105] Moreover, after the schism under Rehoboam and Jeroboam, idolatry spread in Judah as well as in Northern Israel which, according to the prophets, was one of the main reasons for the exile.

This has been pointed out by J. Bernard:

> The sin committed against Uriah is the sin of David which is most vehemently condemned in the Bible itself... At the time of the Mishnah, this sin of David together with all others had to be concealed. The fact that Rab Yehuda and Rab still know it and mention it in a chapter in the Talmud which is entirely consecrated to exculpating David shows that in the times of these two rabbis the most complete traditions concerning David's sins were still alive in common memory.[106]

Sifra, a halakhic midrash on the book of Leviticus dating from the second half of the third century CE which insists on the scriptural character of the laws contained in the Mishnah, imputes the practice of idolatry to David by the very fact that he had lived among the Philistines:

104. *The Babylonian Talmud, Seder Mo'ed Shabbath*, p. 268. The first step to idolatry was Jeroboam's setting up of the golden calves in order to maintain the independence of his kingdom (1 Kgs 12.26-30). Exile is seen as a punishment for idolatry.

105. Rab or Rav (Abba ben Aivu), was a first generation Babylonian amora (220–250 CE) and head of the academy of Sura. Rab Yehuda ben Ezekiel was a second generation Babylonian amora (250–290 CE).

106. J. Bernard, 'David et le péché originel chez les Tannaïm', in Desrousseaux and Vermeylen (eds.), *Figures de David à travers la Bible*, pp. 277-314 (307).

> 'In order to give you the land of Canaan, and to be your God' (Lev. 25.38). From there we infer: Every son of Israel who dwells in the land of Israel takes on himself the yoke of the Kingdom of Heaven. And whoever leaves the land, it is as if he practiced idolatry. Thus David said: '...But if it is men, may they be cursed before the Lord, for they have driven me out this day that I should have no share in the heritage of the Lord, saying, 'Go, serve other gods' (1 Sam. 26.19). Do we suppose that David practiced idolatry? Thus he explained saying: Whoever dwells in the land of Israel takes part in the Kingdom of Heaven. But whoever goes out from it, it is as if he practiced idolatry.[107]

In *Sifre Devarim* 51[108] we read:

> If you say: Why did David go to conquer Aram Naharaim and Arab Zobah when the *miṣwôt* were not issued? One would say that David acted in opposition to the Torah. For the Torah says: After they have conquered the land of Israel they would be allowed to conquer other lands. But he did not act in such a manner. Instead, he reverted to the conquest of Aram Naharaim and Aram Zobah, and the Jebusite who was near Jerusalem, he did not dispossess. The place (i.e. God) told him: The Jebusite who is next to the throne, you did not dispossess. Why did you revert to the conquest of Aram Naharaim and Aram Zobah?

The same midrash, *Sifre Devarim* 43, reiterates the rabbinic tradition which imputes the practice of idolatry to David:

> Another interpretation: '...and you shall eat and be full. Take heed...' (Deut. 11.15b-16a). He told them: Beware lest the *yeṣer hara'* (the 'evil inclination') beguiles you and you become separated from the Torah. For when a man [Adam] separates himself from the Torah, he clings to idolatry. As it is said: 'They have turned aside quickly out of the way which I commanded them; they have made for themselves a molten calf' (Exod. 32.8). And the Scripture says, 'If it is the Lord who has stirred you up against me, may he accept an offering; but if it is men, may they be cursed before the Lord, for they have driven me out this day that I should have no share in the heritage of the Lord, saying, "Go, serve other gods"' (1 Sam. 26.19). Do you suppose that King David practiced idolatry? When he separated himself from the Torah, he clung to idolatry.[109]

A similar interpretation found in *Tosefta Abodah Zarah* 4.5 concerns David practicing idolatry while he dwelt in the land of the Philistines.

The writings known to have come from the school of Aqiba (45 to 135 CE) do not hesitate to talk of David's culpability. On several occasions it is said

107. Quoted in Bernard, 'David et le péché original chez les Tannaïm', p. 288 (*Sifra*, par. 5, 109c).

108. Quoted in Bernard, 'David et le péché original chez les Tannaïm', p. 295. *Sifre Devarim* is a midrash adapted by Rabbi Aqiba from the older tradition transmitted by Rabbi Eliezer and completed by his school of disciples before the end of the third century CE. One finds in it a discussion on David's wars and military conquests which the midrash considers as wars of aggression and not in keeping with the divine plan.

109. Quoted in Bernard, 'David et le péché original chez les Tannaïm', p. 294.

that David practiced idolatry and that in doing so he obeyed his evil inclination (*yeṣer hara'*) which led him away from obedience to the teaching of the Torah. The fact that David's culpability is mentioned several times in rabbinic literature indicates that it was a well-attested tradition known by the rabbis, even if the Mishnah does not mention it. The rabbis are divided between those who attempt to exculpate David and those who have too great a respect for the biblical text to accept the arguments by which some of their colleagues tried to salvage David's reputation. The rabbis defending David do not hesitate to censure certain biblical texts and to forbid the reading of 2 Samuel 11 describing David's adulterous relationship with Bathsheba and the murder of her husband Uriah. Thus *Tosefta Megillah* 3.38 enjoins: 'The affair of David with Bathsheba is neither to be read nor translated [into Aramaic] and the scribe should teach as usual'. Here the *Tosefta* formulates the principle adopted in the Mishnah of passing over in silence certain of David's sins. The Mishnah is the first exhaustive compilation of Jewish oral law (*torah še-be'al pe*, lit. 'instruction by the mouth'). It reflects several centuries of rabbinic legislative tradition and forms the basis of the Talmud. According to the latter, the Mishnah was finalized by Rabbi Meir. Divided into six orders (*seder*), it was compiled in the third century CE by Rabbi Yehuda ha-Nasi (also called simply Rabbi).

This famous doctor of the law had a personal interest in exonerating David for he claimed to be his descendant. Thus, according to the Babylonian Talmud (*b. Šab.* 55b-56a), he placed his exegetical expertise at the service of his bias making a major case out of an infinitive verbal form 'to do' (*l'śwt*):

> ...How do I interpret, 'Why have you despised the word of the Lord, to do (*l'śwt*) what is evil in his sight?' [in order to kill Uriah] (2 Sam. 12.9). He wished to do [evil], but he did not. Rab observed: Rabbi [Yehuda ha-Nasi] who is descended from David, seeks to defend him, and expounds [the verse] in David's favor. [Thus:] The 'evil' [mentioned] here is unlike every other 'evil' [mentioned] elsewhere in the Torah. For every other evil [mentioned] in the Torah it is written, 'and he did', whereas here it is written, 'to do': [this means] that he desired to do, but did not.[110]

22. *Did Michal Have Children?*

Michal, married to David and then to Palti, was taken back by David in order to reinforce his claim to kingship. Did David and Michal have children? No biblical text mentions this possibility. Moreover, 2 Sam. 6.23 affirms the contrary, 'And Michal the daughter of Saul had no child to the day of her death (*'dywm mwth*)'. This verse closes the account of David's dance before the ark. Michal reproached David for his behavior which she found to be

110. *The Babylonian Talmud, Seder Mo'ed, Shabbath*, pp. 259-60.

either indecent or indelicate. Indeed, this verse is often taken to express the punishment that befell Michal on account of the criticism she addressed to King David. Among rabbinic commentators, however, this verse is somewhat controversial. For some of them, Michal had children before the episode of the ark. For others she gave birth to a child on the day she died. According to the Gemara (*b. Sanh.* 21a), 'And Rab Judah, or according to others, Rabbi Joseph said: Michal received her due punishment (*myṭrps'*)—But we might argue thus: prior to that incident she did have [children], but after it she did not'.[111]

Commenting on 2 Sam. 6.23, Rashi says that 'she had no more children from that day on'. Radaq interprets this verse in its literal sense (*pešaṭ*), saying that she had no children from that day on as a punishment for what she said to David, but that she had had children before. Continuing his comments, he offers a homiletical reflection or *deraš*, starting from an explanation of the Hebrew preposition *'ad*:

> *'ad* with a meaning identical to that found in Gen. 28.15, 'for I will not leave you until (*'ad*) I have done that of which I have spoken to you', which means until a certain time limit beyond which things come about. Thus, according to *deraš*, on the day of her death she had [a child].

23. *The Equation of Eglah with Michal*

The rabbis in the Babylonian Talmud (*b. Sanh.* 21a[112]) address the same issue when they comment on the injunction in the Mishnah (*Sanh.* 2.4), which forbids the king from having more than eighteen wives, 'Neither shall he multiply wives to himself (Deut. 17.17)—only eighteen':

> Whence do we deduce the number eighteen? From the verse, 'And sons were born to David at Hebron: his first born was Amnon, of Ahinoam of Jezreel; and his second, Chileab, of Abigail the widow of Nabal of Carmel; and the third, Absalom the son of Maacah the daughter of Talmai king of Geshur; and the fourth, Adonijah the son of Haggith; and the fifth, Shephatiah the son of

111. This opinion was reiterated in *Yalquṭ Shimoni* on 2 Sam. 3. The term for childlessness (*myṭrps'*) means 'debt matured for collection by seizure' according to Jastrow.

112. '[Now as to the number eighteen] Is it not stated, "And David took more concubines and wives from Jerusalem?" (2 Sam. 5.13)—To make up the eighteen. What are "wives", and what are "concubines?"—Rab Judah said in Rab's name: Wives have "*kethubah*" and "*qiddušin*" [legal and legitimate marriage]; concubines have neither. Rab Judah also said in Rab's name: David had four hundred children, and all born of *yepôt to'ar* [lit. "beautiful figures" of captive women taken as concubines by the king because of their beauty]; they had beautiful curly hair and all drove in golden carriages. They used to march at the head of the troops and were men of power in David's household.' Found also in *Yalquṭ Shimoni* 2 Sam. 3.

> Abital; and the sixth, Ithream of Eglah, David's wife. These were born to David in Hebron' (2 Sam. 3.2-5). And of them the prophet [Nathan] said: 'And if these were too few, I would add to you as many more (lit. the like of these and the like of these [*khnh wkhnh*])' (2 Sam. 12.8b), each (*khnh*) implying six, which with the original six, makes eighteen in all.[113]

The Gemara continues and adds that Michal too was David's wife, which implies that David had seven wives. Here Rab intervenes and equates Eglah with Michal. He justifies her being called Eglah because she was as dear to him as a heifer or a calf to its mother. This interpretation was borrowed by Rashi in his commentary on 2 Sam. 3.5. When commenting on 2 Sam. 3.5, Radaq mentions an opinion according to which Eglah was one of Saul's wives whom David took over after the death of the former, as it is said in 2 Sam. 12.8: 'And I gave you your master's wives into your bosom'. Rab Ḥisda comments on 2 Sam. 6.23, by saying that 'She had no child until the day of her death, but on the day of her death she did'. In other words, Michal died in childbirth. The Gemara itself, however, notes the incongruity of this interpretation and continues, 'These children are mentioned as having been born in Hebron while the incident with Michal happened in Jerusalem' (*b. Sanh.* 21a).

Indeed, Ithream son of Eglah was born in Hebron, an event which preceded the dispute between Michal and David in 2 Samuel 6. Therefore, Michal could not have died while giving birth to Ithream in Jerusalem. The rabbis, however, defy the chronology of biblical narrative and continue identifying Eglah with Michal.

Reading the list of David's six sons born in Hebron in 2 Sam. 3.5, Abrabanel points out that the expression 'wife of David' is found uniquely with the name of Eglah (2 Sam. 3.5; 1 Chron. 3.3). He infers that this could only be Michal because she was his first wife, the one who was most devoted to him (she loved him) and who was moreover a kingly daughter:

> The Scripture could not accept the statement that 'Michal the daughter of Saul had no child to the day of her death', therefore it seemed preferable to say that she was another woman [i.e. Eglah]; since she was named Eglah, the text had to add to her name [the expression] 'David's wife' in order to say that his wife was not just any heifer of the herd.

The Rabbis were eager to reconcile 2 Sam. 3.5 with 2 Sam. 6.23. The idea that Michal died in childbirth is used in numerous rabbinic commentaries with some minor variations:

113. *The Babylonian Talmud, Seder Nezikin, Sanhedrin*, I, p. 112 (*b. Sanh.* 21a). Some rabbis take into account the conjunction (*w*) between the two *khnh* and offer an additional interpretation (24 and 48 wives).

> As regards [Michal], she was punished: 'Michal the daughter of Saul had no child to the day of her death' (2 Sam. 6.23). But is it not said 'And the sixth, Ithream of Eglah, David's wife' (2 Sam. 3.5)? She therefore had a son. Because she lowed (*g'h*) like a heifer (*'glh*) and died as she gave birth to a child, she received the name of Eglah.[114]

Rashi's comments on 2 Sam. 3.5 admit the anteriority of this verse in respect to 2 Sam. 6.23: 'And the sixth, Ithream of Eglah, David's wife' in 2 Sam. 3.5, if the identification between Eglah and Michal is accepted, does not necessarily contradict the statement in 2 Sam. 6.23, 'Michal the daughter of Saul had no child to the day of her death'. According to Rashi, 'she did not have children after that incident when she showed contempt for David. Prior to that incident, however, she did have a child.'

Abrabanel adduces an additional reason why Michal had no child to the day of her death:

> Here is another reason why David did not want that the descendants of the House of Saul should multiply and that they should be of the same blood as that of the House of David; David's descendants were blessed by God; God knew that the episode with the Gibeonites who massacred the [rest of the] descendants of Saul was going to take place (2 Sam. 21.1-10). What would David have done then with the sons he would have had with Michal? He would have either given them to be executed or he would have spared them and one would have spoken of partiality; either way the episode would have been tragic. God did so that Michal should not conceive by David, so that the descendants of Saul should not mix with those of David, in order to become one flesh.[115]

24. *The Five Sons of Michal or of Merab?*

The Masoretic text in 2 Sam. 21.8 mentions 'the five sons of Michal the daughter of Saul, whom she bore to Adriel the son of Barzillai the Meholathite'. Because of incongruity in respect to the name of the husband, the name of Michal is often emended to Merab, as in the RSV. The Babylonian Talmud (*b. Yeb.* 79a) mentions, however, 'the five sons of Michal...' The rabbis who generally follow the reading of the Masoretic text are unanimous in their explanation of this incongruity.[116] They adopt a view found many

114. *Talmud Yerušalmi* (Jerusalem: Shiloh, 5729 = 1968 [Hebrew]), p. 55 (*y. Suk.* 5.4). See *y. Sanh.* 2.4 (p. 20); *Midrash Shemuel* 11.3* (dealing with 1 Chron. 3.3).

115. Abrabanel's explanation was borrowed by Malbim in his commentary on 2 Sam. 6.23.

116. *Tosefta b. Soṭ.* 11.8; *b. Sanh.* 19b; *y. Sanh.* 29b; *y. Qid.* 42b; *Yalquṭ Shimoni* on 1 Sam. 18.27 and Abrabanel on 2 Sam. 21.8; *Num. R.* 8.4: 'You must suppose that they were the sons of Merab, and that because Michal reared them they were called by her name'.

times in the Talmud according to which, when a person is fully invested in the execution of a task, the result of his or her action bears his or her name, even if that person was not the original instigator or creator of the project. This interpretation is already found in *Targum Jonathan* on 2 Sam. 21.8, which rendered the verse in the following manner: ‘The five sons of Merab whom Michal the daughter of Saul had brought up’.

The Babylonian Talmud (*b. Sanh.* 19b) points out the merits of adoptive parents:[117]

> Now as to Rabbi Joshua bar Korḥa, surely it is written, ‘And the five sons of Michal the daughter of Saul whom she bore to Adriel’ (2 Sam. 21.8)?—Rabbi Joshua [bar Korḥa] answers thee: Was it then Michal who bore them? Surely it was rather Merab who bore them? But Merab bore and Michal brought them up; therefore they were called by her name. This teaches thee that whoever brings up an orphan in his home, Scripture ascribes it to him as though he had begotten him.
>
> Rabbi Ḥanina says this is derived from the following: ‘And the women her neighbors, gave it a name, saying, There is a son born to Naomi’ (Ruth 4.17). Was it then Naomi who bore him? Surely it was Ruth who bore him! But Ruth bore and Naomi brought him up; hence he was called after her [Naomi’s] name.[118]

The same Talmudic tractate continues with other biblical examples where similar cases are found: Moses is called son of Bithia, Pharaoh’s daughter, yet he was Jochebed’s son (1 Chron. 4.18)—his real mother, having to hide her identity, could not publicly be identified as such; the sons of Jacob and Joseph (Ps. 77.16) where Jacob begat and Joseph acquired his father’s title by supporting Jacob’s sons.

The *Tosefta* (*Soṭ.* 11.8) speaks in the same vein:

> A verse says, ‘The five sons of Michal the daughter of Saul, whom she bore to Adriel the son of Barzillai the Meholathite’ (2 Sam. 21.8), and another verse says, ‘Michal the daughter of Saul had no child to the day of her death’ (2 Sam. 6.23). How can these two verses coexist? In this manner: The five sons were those of Merab but Michal brought them up; they were consequently called by her name. In the same manner it is said, ‘A son has been born to Naomi’ (Ruth 4.17); and also, ‘These are the generations of Aaron and Moses’ (Num. 3.1).

The Babylonian Talmud (*b. Sanh.* 19b) explains the last reference by showing that teaching the Torah to a disciple is another manner of giving life to him:

117. *The Babylonian Talmud, Seder Nezikin, Sanhedrin*, I, pp. 101-102.

118. The true mother was Ruth who bore a son from Boaz. Naomi, Ruth’s former mother-in-law, was simply nursing the child.

> Rabbi Samuel bar Naḥmani said in Rabbi Jonathan's name: He who teaches the son of his neighbor the Torah, Scripture ascribes it to him as if he had begotten him, as it says, 'These are the generations of Aaron and Moses' (Num. 3.1), whilst further on it is written, 'These are the names of the sons of Aaron' (v. 2), thus teaching that Aaron begot and Moses taught them; hence they are called by his name.[119]

This principle formulated in the following way, 'Every work to which a man devotes himself is called by his name' (*kl dbr š'dm nwtn npšw 'lyw nqr' lšmw*), is borrowed by the Mekhilta[120] and placed in conjunction with Ps. 30.1: 'Mizmor, a song at the dedication of the Temple of David' (*mzmwr šyr-ṣnkt hbyt ldwd*). The Mekhilta asks: 'Was it really David who built the Temple? Was it not Solomon as it is written: "Solomon...began to build the Temple of the Lord" (1 Kgs 6.1)?' The Talmud explains: It said 'Song at the dedication of the Temple of David' because he devoted himself completely to this task. Even if he did not accomplish it, it was nevertheless imputed to him. The Mekhilta continues the discussion and adduces three things as belonging to Moses while they are manifestly God's: 'The Torah of Moses', 'your people' and 'your judgment'.

25. *The Michal–Rachel Analogy*

Some rabbis establish a parallel between Michal, David's wife, Rachel, Jacob's wife, and the wife of Phinehas, the priest Eli's daughter-in-law.[121] Biblical texts affirm explicitly that the latter two died in childbirth:

> There are three [women] for whom childbearing was so difficult that they died: Rachel, the wife of Phinehas, and Michal, the daughter of Saul. Rachel: 'Rachel travailed, and she had hard labor...and as her soul was departing, for she was dying' (Gen. 35.16,18); the wife of Phinehas: 'His daughter-in-law, the wife of Phinehas, was with child, about to give birth...and about the time of her death' (1 Sam. 4.19,20); Michal as it is written, 'Michal the daughter of Saul had no child to the day of her death' (2 Sam. 6.23). But she had a child the day she died; is it not written, 'And the sixth, Ithream of Eglah, David's wife' (2 Sam. 3.5)? But why was she called Eglah? Rabbi Yehuda [said]: Because she lowed like a heifer and expired.[122]

The rabbis have here placed together biblical texts that present similarities in order to interpret them by applying the same hermeneutical principle. This formal rule of rabbinic exegesis is called *Gezerah šawah* (lit. 'equal cut') or

119. *The Babylonian Talmud, Seder Nezikin, Sanhedrin*, I, p. 102.

120. *Mekhilta of Rabbi Ishmael*, tractate *Bishlah* ch. 1 of *Shirat-ha-Yam* (Exod. 14)*. The Mekhilta is a Tannaitic midrash on Exodus. Mekhilta means 'measure', or 'method'.

121. *Midrash Bereshit* 82.7 and *Midrash Shemuel* 11.3.

122. *Midrash Rabbah, Genesis*, II, p. 757.

the principle of analogy. In legal matters, it stands for the application to one subject of a rule already known to apply to another, on the strength of a common expression used in connection with both in the Scripture. This method is also applied to Bible exposition. Thus it became common to correlate Rachel and Michal, Jacob and David, and Laban and Saul.

The names of both women stem from the world of fauna; while Eglah stands for a 'heifer, young cow, calf', Rachel means a 'lamb'. Commenting on 2 Sam. 3.5, Y. Qil points out some verbal similarities concerning these two women: 'Saul had given Michal his daughter, David's wife' (1 Sam. 25.44) and 'the sons of Rachel, Jacob's wife' (Gen. 46.19).[123] Referring to this last verse, Rashi says that when the biblical text enumerates other sons of Jacob it does not specify that their mother was the 'wife of'. This is so because Rachel is the foundation of the house. Rashi elaborates further on Rachel in his comments on Gen. 31.4:

> Rachel was the foundation (*'qr*) on which his household rested, for it is on account of her that Jacob entered into Laban's family. Moreover, even Leah's sons concede this. Thus Boaz and his tribunal [i.e. the elders at the gate], descendants of the tribe of Judah say, 'May the Lord make the woman, who is coming into your house, like Rachel and Leah, who together built up the house of Israel' (Ruth 4.11). They give the priority to Rachel over Leah.

Rashi is exploiting the different meanings of the word *'qr*. As an adjective it means 'barren, sterile', while as a noun it means 'basis, foundation'. Apparently he has taken this term from Ps. 113.9, 'He gives the barren woman (*'qrt*) a home, making her the joyous mother of children'. Applied to Michal, this analogy would make her a foundation of David's household too.

Other verses could be adduced in order to bolster the analogy between Michal and Rachel—'she [Michal] had no child' (2 Sam. 6.23) and 'Rachel was barren (*'qrh*)' (Gen. 29.31)—and according to the rabbis they both died in childbirth. They both had an elder sister who was married or promised in marriage to their future husbands, Jacob and David respectively. The analogy serves to establish a contrast as well. While the biblical text says that Michal loved David (*wt'hb mykl bt š'wl 't-dwd*, 1 Sam. 18.20), and that Jacob loved Rachel (*wy'hb y'qb 't-rḥl*, Gen. 29.18), the juxtaposition of these two statements brings into sharp focus David's apparent absence of love for Michal.

Both Rachel and Michal experience the situation of being pursued by their respective fathers (Laban in Gen. 29.25, and Saul in 1 Sam. 19.17) and they both use the teraphim in order to betray and lie to their fathers (1 Sam. 19.13-16 and Gen. 31.34).

123. Qil, *1–2 Shemuel*, II, p. 334.

26. *Michal as an Exceptionally Beautiful Woman*

The biblical texts often speak of a woman's beauty (e.g. Abigail in 1 Sam. 25.3 and Bathsheba in 2 Sam. 11.2). The mention of feminine beauty can be taken as a code indicating that the female in question is worthy of royal status, which she eventually obtains. Paradoxically, concerning Queen Michal's outward appearance, the Bible says nothing. This might be an intentional hint concerning the tragic outcome of Michal's life-story as the unloved and rejected queen. The midrash, however, attempts to fill these gaps by depicting her as an outwardly beautiful woman who has attained an equal level of inner spiritual perfection.

When the rabbis spoke of the most beautiful women in the world they counted Michal among them. 'The rabbis have taught: There were four exceptionally beautiful women in the world: Rahab, Jael, Michal and Abigail. Rahab [was beautiful] by her name, Jael by her voice, Michal by her looks, and Abigail by the remembrance she left.'[124]

According to other texts these four women inspired violent desire in men on account of their exceptional beauty. Thus the Babylonian Talmud (*b. Meg.* 15a) says,

> Our Rabbis taught: Rahab inspired lust (*zinnetâ*)[125] by her name, Jael by her voice, Abigail by her memory, Michal daughter of Saul by her appearance.

The fact that Michal is called 'daughter of Saul' is not without significance in respect of her beauty. The midrash considered Saul as being among the most beautiful men mentioned in the Bible.[126] In certain texts Michal is described as 'daughter of Cush', where the latter is taken as being another name of Saul.[127] He was called 'Cush', that is, 'Ethiopian' (Ps. 7.1)[128] for he was as

124. *Oṣar ha-Midrashim*, Hupat Eliahu ch. 5*.

125. *The Babylonian Talmud, Seder Mo'ed, Megillah* (ed. I. Epstein; Eng. trans. M. Simon; New York: Rebecca Bennet Publications, 1959), p. 87. Also in *Oṣar ha-Midrashim*, Rabbenu ha-Qadosh 3*. The verb *zinnetâ*, from the root *znh*, is a piel perfect 3rd feminine singular meaning 'to excite the senses, to suggest impure thoughts, to invite faithlessness'. See M. Jastrow, *A Dictionary of the Targumim, Talmud Babli and Yerushalmi, and Midrashic Literature* (New York: Judaica Press, 1975), p. 406c. A. Steinsaltz translates this Aramaic verb into modern Hebrew with *lht'wwt* ('to provoke desire'). See A. Steinsaltz, *Talmud Babli: Meseket Megillah* (Jerusalem: Institute for Talmudic Publications, 1989 [Hebrew]), p. 62 (*b. Meg.* 15a).

126. See *Sifrei Behalotkha* 41*, and *Midrash Tehillim* Ps. 7.14.

127. See *b. 'Erub.* 96a; *Tosafot 'Erub* 96a; *y. Ber.* 14b and *y. 'Erub.* 59a.

128. Ps. 7.1 'A Shiggaion of David, which he sang to YHWH concerning Cush a Benjaminite'. Cf. *The Midrash on Psalms*, I, pp. 112-13: 'Another comment on "concerning the matter of Cush". Cush refers to the congregation of Israel. For when the children of Israel differ with the Holy One, blessed be He, by sinning, He calls them Cushites, as when he said: "Are ye not as the children of the Cushites unto Me, O children of Israel?"

outstanding by his good looks as the Ethiopians are distinguished by the color of their skin.

Taking his clue from this rabbinic tradition about Michal, Y. Qil suggests a new interpretation of the name Eglah in 2 Sam. 3.5 as a reference to her beauty.[129] She was 'a very beautiful heifer', as it is written, 'A beautiful heifer is Egypt…' (Jer. 46.20a), and 'Ephraim was a trained heifer that loved to thresh' (Hos. 10.11).

27. *Michal as a Strong-Willed Woman*

The midrashim depict Michal as a beautiful woman who inspires burning desire. Moreover, she is also ascribed exceptional strength of character. Contrary to the custom of the times, she chooses her husband herself and apparently makes it known to her father; she defies her father when the latter, in his hatred for David, wants to kill him. Moreover, she is not afraid to show her contempt toward King David when she deems that his public behavior is inappropriate. *Midrash Tehillim* 59.4 offers an explanation of Michal's name, Eglah, as an expression of her strong will and defiant character:

> Because of this incident the name Eglah was given to Michal, for in the verse 'Unto David were born sons…the sixth, Ithream of Eglah, David's wife' (2 Sam. 3.2a, 5), Eglah refers to Michal. And why was her name Eglah, 'heifer', given to Michal? Because like the heifer that will not take the yoke upon her neck, so Michal did not take the yoke from her father, but bucked against it.[130]

Other texts see in the episode of David's flight from his house an additional explanation of the name Eglah. *Midrash Shemuel* 22.4* suggests that this nickname arose after she replied to her father who reproached her for her complicity in David's getaway: 'Because she lowed, saying: Father, couldn't you marry me to someone else than to this brigand? He unsheathed his sword against me, saying, "If you do not help me to escape, you will die".'

28. *Michal, a Pious Woman Wearing Phylacteries and Studying the Torah*

Numerous midrashim insist on Michal's outstanding religious qualities. Her piety is almost unanimously acknowledged by the rabbis. A great number of

(Amos 9.7)… Likewise, Saul was different from other men both because of his deeds and because of his beauty, for Scripture says [quoting 1 Sam. 19.2]. If you want to know how great Saul's beauty was, then read closely the passage where it is spoken of Saul and his servant (1 Sam. 9.11-13).'

129. Qil, *1–2 Shemuel*, II, p. 334.

130. *The Midrash on Psalms*, I, p. 511.

rabbinic texts[131] suggest that she was wearing the *tephillin* or phylacteries as pious Jewish men do during daily morning worship.[132] Being a woman she was not obliged to do so. The requirement of wearing the *tephillin* (plural from *tefillah*, 'prayer') is incumbent on those who study the Torah, that is, the men. In this way the rabbis credit Michal with the study of the Torah. They refer to Michal's example in their discussion on whether females should be allowed to study the Scripture and tradition; Michal creates a precedent Reformed Judaism refers to in its claim for equal rights for women in matters of worship.

Thus the Babylonian Talmud (*b. 'Erub.* 96a)[133] quotes the example of Michal who assumes the *miṣwâ* of wearing the *tephillin*:

> For it was taught: Michal daughter of the Kushite[134] wore *tefillin* and the Sages did not attempt to prevent her, and the wife of Jonah[135] attended (lit 'was going up to') the festival pilgrimage and the Sages did not prevent her. Now since the Sages did not prevent her it is clearly evident that they held the view that it (wearing the *tefillin*) is a positive precept the performance of which is not limited to a particular time.[136]

This means that phylacteries could be worn at any time of the day, including at night, on Sabbaths and on feast days. If this *miṣwâ* had been limited to specific moments, women would have been exempted from it. Moreover, Michal being guilty of adding to the commandments would have been reprimanded by religious authorities.[137]

The rabbis discuss Michal's example and try to determine whether the *miṣwâ* of wearing the *tephillin* is a positive commandment not limited to a

131. See *b. 'Erub* 96a; *y. Ber.* 12b; *y. Erub.* 59a; *Mekhilta* Parachat Bo 17.21; *Tosafot Rosh ha-Shanah* 331; *Tosafot 'Erub.* 96a; *Pesikta Rabbati* 22.7; *Oṣar ha-Midrashim*, Hupat Eliahu ch. 5*.

132. The commandment to wear the *tephillin* is inspired by four passages in the Bible (Exod. 13.1-10, 11-16; Deut. 6.4-9, 13-21).

133. *The Babylonian Talmud, Seder Mo'ed, 'Erubin* (ed. I. Epstein; Eng. trans. I.W. Slotki; 3 vols.; New York: Rebecca Bennet Publications, 1959), III, pp. 665-66.

134. A reference to Saul.

135. Jonah the son of Amittai, the prophet.

136. *The Babylonian Talmud, Seder Mo'ed, 'Erubin*, III, p. 665.

137. This text refers to the principle of *mṣwt 'śh šhzmn grm'*, literally 'a positive commandment that time conveys' or commandments limited in time which can be carried out during a certain moment of the day, or only during the day with the exclusion of the night, or uniquely during specific days of the year. In traditional Judaism, women are exempt from commandments of this type, except for specific occasions such as the sanctifying of the Sabbath, the eating of unleavened bread for Pessaḥ, praying, and so on. Women are bound, however, to all commandments that are not limited in time, such as giving to charity, fixing a mezuzah, with the exclusion of the study of the Torah and some additional rare *mṣwt*.

specific time? If that were not the case, was Michal justified in submitting herself to a new commandment? Some rabbis with a more restrictive vision concerning the role of women in Jewish cultic life transform this pious action of Michal's into a violation of the law. The Jerusalem Talmud (*y. Ber.* 14b), rejects the idea of Michal's supposed piety:

> It is taught elsewhere: women and slaves are exempted from reading of the *Šema'*-prayer and from the commandment of wearing phylacteries. Women are exempted because it is written, 'You shall teach them to your sons (*bnykm*)' (Deut. 11.19) and not to your daughters. Since men received a special command to study religious precepts, they are also subjected to the obligation of wearing phylacteries, which is not the case in respect to women. To this rule the example of Michal, the daughter of Cush or Saul, was opposed, who wore phylacteries, and the wife of Jonah who went to Jerusalem for festivals. The rabbis, however, did not object to these two [women]. This is true, said Rabbi Hiskia bar-Abahu, therefore Michal, daughter of Saul, was given rabbinic advice to abstain [from her practice] from then on, and the wife of Jonah was brought back [home].[138]

The idea of Michal wearing phylacteries seems to have been inspired by a *Haggada*[139] saying that the last chapter in the book of Proverbs refers to twenty-two pious women in the Bible; the last twenty-two verses in Prov. 31.10-31 praise the merits of each of these valorous women. The *Haggadah* found a reference to Michal in Prov. 31.25, 'Strength (*'wz*) and dignity are her clothing (*lbwšh*), and she laughs at the time to come (*lywm 'ḥrwn*)', lit. 'on the last day'. In the elaboration of his interpretation, the author of the *Haggadah* pays particular attention to the Hebrew terms in this verse. According to the Jerusalem Talmud (*y. Ber.* 6a), the Hebrew term for 'strength' (*'wz*) is an equivalent for phylacteries. This leads to the idea that the woman praised in this verse whose 'clothing is strength' refers to Michal wearing the phylacteries. Moreover, this association of ideas is favored by the fact that the Jerusalem Talmud (*y. Ber.* 13.2) uses the expression *lbwš tpylyn* ('to be clothed with phylacteries') in order to say 'wearing phylacteries'. The last part of the verse, saying that 'she laughs on the last day', is also applicable to Michal. As seen previously, several rabbinic authors argued that Michal knew the joys of motherhood on the last day of her life as she died in childbirth.[140]

138. This explanation is repeated almost verbatim in *y. 'Erub.* 59a and in *Pesikta Rabbati* 22.7*.

139. Found in S.Z. Schechter (ed.), *Midrash ha-Gadol: Genesis* (Cambridge: Cambridge University Press, 1902), I, col. 344 (Hebrew).

140. See *b. Sanh.* 21a: 'Rabbi Ḥisda said: She had no child until the day of her death, but on the day of her death she did'; *Yalquṭ Shimoni* on 2 Sam. 3; *Midrash Bereshit* 82.13; *Midrash Shemuel* 11.3.

The connection of Michal to phylacteries makes her a woman dedicated to prayer and knowledgeable about biblical precepts. In other words, for the rabbinic tradition Michal is a representative of true Yahwism—a conclusion which is congruent with the conclusion reached in the first chapter of the present study.

29. *Michal as David's Wife in the World to Come*

Midrash Shemuel 25.4 contrasts Michal's and Abigail's love for David with David's love for Jonathan, '"Your love to me was wonderful, greater than the love of women (*nšym*)" (2 Sam. 1.26), that is, more precious than the love of two women, Michal and Abigail; the love of Abigail in this world, and the love of Michal in the world to come'.[141]

First, the midrash explains the use of the plural *nšym* in David's funeral song over Jonathan as a reference to Michal and Abigail, and second, it circumscribes the domains to which these two loves refer: Abigail's love to this world and Michal's love to the world to come. Abigail seems to be the adequate woman for David in this world; their relationship was socially acceptable. They had overcome a radical disagreement and avoided unnecessary bloodshed. According to the biblical narrative, David's relationship with Michal turned sour and was bedeviled by forced and prolonged separations and an unsuccessful reunion. Perhaps as compensation she becomes David's soul mate in the world to come. The midrash is elliptical in its expression and one can only guess the reasons for this juxtaposition. Why is Michal's love relegated to the world to come? On account of her unrequited love? Or maybe because it is said that Michal was the first to have love for David (1 Sam. 18.20), while in the narrative on David and Abigail there is no mention of love? Moreover, Abigail seems to be preoccupied with David's survival in this world when she says, 'If men rise up to pursue you and to seek your life, the life of my lord shall be bound up in the bundle of the living...the lives of your enemies he [God] shall sling out as from the hollow of a sling' (1 Sam. 25.39). At least this is the way Radaq understood this verse when he said, 'May your pursuers be unable to put you to death and may you keep your name alive, meaning that you may continue your daily walk, and may God, blessed be He, drive your pursuers to death'.

The rabbis themselves had difficulties in understanding David's statement in 2 Sam. 1.26, and one midrash[142] reverses the domains ascribed to each woman: 'More precious than the love of two women. Who are these women? Michal in this world and Abigail in the world to come'.

141. *Midrash Shemuel* 25.4*.

142. *Yalquṭ Shimoni* on 2 Sam. 1.26.

It is said 'Michal in this world', because she saved David's life from the hands of Saul, and Abigail because she prevented David from killing Nabal, a crime that could have had consequences in the world to come. Thus two interpretations of the same verse are possible.

30. *Michal a 'Helpmate Opposing' David*

Considering Michal's love for David which the Scripture underlines, one could infer that, of all David's women, she truly accomplished the role of a wife, an ideal companion in the sense of 'a helpmate opposing him' (*'zr kngdw*, Gen. 2.18). One midrash found in *Gen. R.* 17.3,[143] and repeated by Rashi when commenting on this verse, explains the expression in the following way: 'If he [the man] is worthy, she will be a helpmate (*'zr*). If he is not worthy, she will be against him (*kngdw*), to fight him.'

Another text further explains this midrashic interpretation: 'She is a helpmate in order to make him stand [upright] and a helpmate in order to open his eyes'.[144] In other words, the wife would be 'a helpmate opposing him' in order to make her man stand upright before God. The ideal companion, as conceived by the divine creator, would be a wise woman, capable of discernment, helping her husband when the latter acts according to the Law and opposing him when he is straying away from it. In the light of this understanding of the ideal helpmate, Michal was 'a helpmate for him' when in a critical situation she informed David of her father's murderous intentions and helped him to save his life. She was equally 'a helpmate against him' when David strayed away from a faithful walk before God. Among his numerous wives, Michal was the only one who dared oppose David when he danced before the ark (2 Sam. 6.16). It was David's inappropriate behavior that provoked her reaction. In so doing she assumed the role of a perfect companion as the one who is 'a helpmate opposing him'.

143. The translation found in *Midrash Rabbah, Genesis*, p. 133, is not the best: 'I will make him a help (*'zr*) against him (*kngdw*); if he is fortunate, she is a help; if not, she is against him'. Cf. also *Pirkei de Rabbi Eliezer* ch. 12; *b. Yeb.* 63a*.

144. *Tanna Devi Eliahu Rabbah* 10.6*.

CONCLUSIONS

A historical-critical analysis of David's career concludes with a particularly negative assessment of David's character. In J. Vermeylen's words, 'David was, in all likelihood, a man without scruples, who adopted as his mission the conquest of power over Israel and who did not shrink either from war or from assassination in order to achieve this goal'.[1]

The seventeenth-century French Protestant theologian Pierre Bayle, in an article on 'King David' in one of the first historical-critical dictionaries of the Bible, pointed out the danger of writing a pious apology for David's misdeeds:

> The profound respect that we have for this great king and great prophet should not prevent us from disapproving the blemishes that are found in his life; otherwise we would give an occasion to secular people to object that an action is just because it is committed by men we venerate. There would be nothing more detrimental for Christian morality. It is important for true religion, that the life of the orthodox be judged by ideas of rectitude and order (remark D)... We would do a great wrong to eternal laws, and consequently to true religion, if we would give an occasion to secular people to object that, as long as a man is inspired by God, we view his conduct as a rule of morals (remark I)... It is not permitted in a dictionary to imitate the panegyrists who describe only positive traits: one has to write as an historian by stating good and evil, and that is what Scripture does (remark L).[2]

In the biblical narrative, Michal is a marginal figure from two points of view. First, her story is preserved only in fragments and was embedded within the larger narrative concerning the political struggle between the House of Saul and that of David. Secondly, as a female in an ancient Near Eastern patriarchal society she had an inevitably secondary role. It is therefore highly significant that the biblical redactors decided to preserve her memory.

1. Vermeylen, 'La Maison de Saül et la Maison de David', p. 70; *idem*, *La loi du plus fort*.

2. P. Bayle, 'David', *Dictionnaire historique et critique* (1696), p. 909 (repr. Hildesheim: G. Olms, 1982), p. 335. Ph. de Robert, 'Le roi David vu par Pierre Bayle', in *Pierre Bayle, citoyen du monde: de l'enfant du Carla à l'auteur du Dictionnaire* (ed. H. Bost and Ph. de Robert; Paris: H. Champion, 1999), pp. 187-98.

It appears that the Michal tradition represents an inner-biblical attempt to deconstruct[3] royal ideology in ancient Israel. From the point of view of the redactor of the Deuteronomistic historiography, the Israelite monarchy was a tragic enterprise, doomed from its beginning. The redactor uses the story of the tragic fate of a royal princess in order to denounce the abuses that the monarchic institution introduced into Israelite society. It is a unique feature in ancient Near Eastern literature that the story of a woman should serve to criticize patriarchal society and its institutions. From a literary point of view, it has been noted how female figures that appear in the David narrative often play a significant role as catalysts of change.[4]

The most thorough work of deconstruction of the David story so far has been carried out by B. Halpern. The fourth chapter of his *magnum opus*[5] presents David as a 'serial killer'. Because David appears as the principal beneficiary of the death of a series of people, Halpern suggests that David might have commissioned the murders of the following people: Nabal, Saul, Ishbaal, Abner, Saul's seven other descendants, Amnon, Absalom, Amasa, Uriah. While in some cases, Halpern is undoubtedly right, at times, however, his analysis makes one wonder about the usefulness of his basic interpretative grid. Is it useful to read the Abigail–Nabal–David triangular relationship in 1 Samuel 25 as an episode akin to an Agatha Christie crime novel?[6] Halpern himself admits, however, that in this chapter he proposes something that amounts more to imaginative interpretation than to genuine historical

3. H.J. Silverman, *Derrida and Deconstruction* (Continental Philosophy, 2; New York: Routledge, 1989), p. 4. The critical reading called 'deconstruction' can be defined as a philosophical practise in relation to dominant historical figures and texts in the Western tradition. It proposes to interpret texts in terms of their margins, traces, limits, or frameworks; it accounts for how a text's explicit formulations undermine its implicit or non-explicit aspects. It brings out what the text excludes by showing what it includes. It points out the elements of marginality, supplementarity, and indecidability as they operate in the reading of texts. Moreover, it contains an element of political subversiveness.

4. Cf. D.M. Gunn, 'Traditional Composition in the "Succession Narrative"', *VT* 26 (1976), pp. 214-29 (222): 'It is remarkable how in the major episodes of the story of King David...a woman is so often an important catalyst in the plot (Rizpah, Saul's concubine; Bathsheba; Tamar; Abishag, David's concubine)'. In his historical novel *Les Chouans*, describing the clash between the traditional laws of monarchial government and society and the revolutionary and democratic ideas introduced by the French Revolution provoking historical upheavals in Brittany, Balzac uses female figures as a metaphor for historical change. In Balzac's perspective, on account of women's ambiguous social position, they seem to reveal in a clearer manner the political and social conflicts of these troubled times; cf. G. Vannier, 'Balzac', in D. Couty, J.-P. de Beaumarchais and A. Ray (eds.), *Dictionnaire des littératures de langue française* (Paris: Bordas, 1984), I, pp. 120-43 (138).

5. Halpern, *David's Secret Demons*, Chapter 4, 'King David, Serial Killer'.

6. Halpern, *David's Secret Demons*, p. 77: 'Did Abigail murder her husband to defect to David?... This is the basis of the plot of Agatha Christie's novels.'

reconstruction. The rest of his book represents a meticulous historical, epigraphical, archaeological and comparative study of David's career, a landmark in this genre that will remain a model to emulate. Halpern's perspicacious study brings us to the question of epistemology and to the issue of 'truth and method' in historical studies. In this connection it might be useful to be reminded of some guidelines for historical investigation proposed by Hans-Georg Gadamer. The central question of a truly historical hermeneutic and the fundamental issue of epistemology—namely, how can we know the truth about something—is 'where is the ground for the legitimacy of prejudices?' Prejudices also include presuppositions and different interpretative grids with which one approaches historical material. Gadamer asks: 'What distinguishes legitimate prejudices from all the countless ones which it is the undeniable task of critical reason to overcome?'[7]

Gadamer distinguishes between 'legitimate' and 'illegitimate'[8] questions in the course of historical investigation. He rehabilitates the history of interpretative tradition and attributes considerable value to the *Wirkungsgeschichte* (i.e. the way a text has been received in the course of its transmission). The latter provides us with an interpretative horizon and guides us in asking the right questions. It might help us to discover in much that is subjective what is substantial.[9]

In order to avoid the pitfalls and excesses of a prejudiced interpretation, in the foregoing pages I have submitted the various fragments of the Michal tradition to a host of different interpretative methods—rhetorical-critical, historical and comparative analyses—which furnished a major historical analogy to the marriage transaction between Saul and David involving Merab and Michal. My conclusions were checked against the two-thousand-year-long rabbinic interpretations which provided one major aspect of the *Wirkungsgeschichte* or history of the interpretation of the Michal story. Both modern interpretative methods as well as traditional rabbinic readings point to David's guilt from the beginning of his dynasty and rehabilitate Michal's role.

The Michal tradition facilitates the elaboration of a biblical theology which is fully conscious of the patriarchal stamp of scriptural texts and so denounces their politico-religious legitimization.[10]

7. H.-G. Gadamer, *Truth and Method* (New York: Crossroad, 1982), p. 246.

8. Rashi's interpretation of Palti's crying as his regret for losing an occasion to exercise self-control over his passions might be an example of *eisegesis* or 'reading into a text'. Moreover, the following might be an example of an 'illegitimate question' when in respect to David and Bathsheba, G.A. Yee asks, 'Did they have "a great time in bed"?'; see G.A. Yee, '"Fraught with Background": Literary Ambiguity in II Samuel 11', *Int* 42 (1988), pp. 240-53 (243).

9. Gadamer, *Truth and Method*, pp. 268-69.

10. E. Schüssler Fiorenza, *In Memory of Her: A Feminist Theological Reconstruction of Christian Origins* (New York: Crossroad, 1987).

BIBLIOGRAPHY

Abrabanel, I., *Nebi'im rishonim* (Jerusalem: Elisha, 1955 [Hebrew]).

Ackroyd, P.R., *The First Book of Samuel* (Cambridge Bible Commentary; Cambridge: Cambridge University Press, 1971).

—'The Succession Narrative (So-Called)', *Int* 35 (1981), pp. 383-96.

—'The Verb Love—*'AHEB* in the David–Jonathan Narrative—A Footnote', *VT* 25 (1975), pp. 213-14.

Ahlström, G.W., '*Krkr* and *tpd*', *VT* 28 (1978), pp. 100-101.

Alster, B., 'Marriage and Love in the Sumerian Love Songs with Some Notes on the Manchester Tammuz', in M.E. Cohen, D.C. Snell and D.B. Weisberg (eds.), *The Tablet and the Scroll: Near Eastern Studies in Honor of W.W. Hallo* (Bethesda, MD: CDL Press, 1993), pp. 15-27.

Alter, R., *The Art of Biblical Narrative* (New York: Basic Books, 1981).

—'A Literary Approach to the Bible', *Commentary* 60 (1975), pp. 70-78.

Anbar, M. 'Aspect moral dans un discours « prophétique » de Mari', *UF* 7 (1975), pp. 517-18.

—'La "reprise" ', *VT* 38 (1988), pp. 385-98.

Andersen, F.I., and D.N. Freedman, *Hosea* (AB, 24; Garden City, NY: Doubelday, 1983).

Arnaud, D., *Recherches au pays d'Aštata. Emar VI: Textes sumériens et accadiens* (4 vols; Paris: Editions Recherche sur les Civilisations, 1985–86).

Astour, M.C., 'The Amarna Age Forerunners of Biblical Antiroyalism', in *Studies in Jewish Languages, Literature, and Society: For Max Weinreich on his Seventieth Birthday* (The Hague: Mouton, 1964), pp. 6-17.

—'The North Mesopotamian Kingdom of Ilānṣurā', in G.D. Young (ed.), *Mari in Retrospect* (Winona Lake, IN: Eisenbrauns, 1992), pp. 1-35.

Auld, A.G., and C.Y.S. Ho, 'The Making of David and Goliath', *JSOT* 56 (1992), pp. 19-39.

Auzou, G., *La danse devant l'arche: Etude du livre de Samuel* (Paris: Editions de l'Orante, 1968).

Avishur, Y., '*Krkr* in Biblical Hebrew and in Ugaritic', *VT* 26 (1976), pp. 257-61.

The Babylonian Talmud, Seder Nashim, Berakoth (ed. I. Epstein; Eng. trans. M. Simon; New York: Rebecca Bennet Publications, 1959).

The Babylonian Talmud, Seder Mo'ed, 'Erubin (ed. I. Epstein; Eng. trans. I.W. Slotki; 3 vols.; New York: Rebecca Bennet Publications, 1959).

The Babylonian Talmud, Seder Mo'ed, Megillah (ed. I. Epstein; Eng. trans. M. Simon; New York: Rebecca Bennet Publications, 1959).

The Babylonian Talmud, Seder Nezikin, Sanhedrin (Eng. trans. J. Shachter and H. Freedman; New York: Rebecca Bennet Publications, 1959).

The Babylonian Talmud, Seder Mo'ed, Shabbath (ed. I. Epstein; Eng. trans. H. Freedman; London: The Soncino Press, 1938).

The Babylonian Talmud, Seder Nashim, Soṭah (ed. I. Epstein; Eng. trans. A. Cohen; 2 vols.; New York: Rebecca Bennet Publications, 1959).

Badalì, E., M.G. Biga, O. Carena, G. di Bernardo, S. di Rienzo, M. Liverani and P. Vitali, 'Studies on the Annals of Aššurnasirpal II. I. Morphological Analysis', *Vicino Oriente* 5 (1982), pp. 13-73.

Badinter, E., *XY: De l'identité masculine* (Paris: O. Jacob, 1992).

Bailey, R.C., *David in Love and War: The Pursuit of Power in 2 Samuel 10–12* (JSOTSup, 75; Sheffield: JSOT Press, 1990).

Barnett, D., 'The Nimrud Ivories and the Art of the Phoenicians', *Iraq* 2 (1935), pp. 179-210.

Barthélemy, D., 'La qualité du Texte Massorétique de Samuel', in E. Tov (ed.), *The Hebrew and Greek Texts of Samuel* (Proceedings IOSCS, Vienna, 22 August 1980 (Jerusalem: Academon, 1980), pp. 1-44.

Barthélemy, D., D.W. Gooding, J. Lust and E. Tov (eds.), *The Story of David and Goliath: Textual and Literary Criticism* (OBO, 73; Freiburg: Universitätsverlag, 1986).

Barton, G., 'A Liturgy for the Celebration of the Spring Festival at Jerusalem in the Age of Abraham and Melchizedek', *JBL* 53 (1934), pp. 61-78.

Barton, J., 'Dating the "Succession Narrative"', in J. Day (ed.), *In Search of Pre-Exilic Israel* (JSOTSup, 406; London: T. & T. Clark International, 2004), pp. 95-106.

Batto, B.F., 'Land Tenure and Women at Mari', *JESHO* 23 (1980), pp. 209-39.

Bayle, P., 'David', in *Dictionnaire historique et critique* (1696), p. 909 (repr. Hildesheim: G. Olms, 1982), p. 335.

Ben-Barak, Z., 'The Legal Background to the Restoration of Michal to David', in Clines and Eskenazi (eds.), *Telling Queen Michal's Story*, pp. 74-90.

Berlin, A., 'Characterization in Biblical Narrative: David's Wives', *JSOT* 23 (1982), pp. 69-85.

Bernard, J., 'David et le péché originel chez les Tannaïm', in Desrousseaux and Vermeylen (eds.), *Figures de David à travers la Bible*, pp. 277-314.

Bleeker, C.J., 'The Position of the Queen in Ancient Egypt', in International Congress for the History of Religions, *The Sacral Kingship*, pp. 261-68.

Bodi, D., *The Book of Ezekiel and the Poem of Erra* (OBO, 101; Freiburg: Universitätsverlag, 1991).

—'Les *gillûlîm* chez Ezéchiel et dans l'Ancien Testament et les différentes pratiques cultuelles associées à ce terme', *RB* 100 (1993), pp. 481-510.

—'La tragédie de Mikal en tant que critique de la monarchie israélite et préfiguration de sa fin', *Foi et Vie* 96 (1996), pp. 65-105.

—*Petite grammaire de l'akkadien à l'usage des débutants* (Paris: Geuthner, 2001).

Boecker, H.J., *Die Beurteilung der Anfänge des Königtums in den deuteronomistischen Abschnitten des 1. Samuelbuches: Ein Beitrag zum Problem des 'Deuteronomistischen Geschichtswerks'* (WMANT, 31; Neukirchen–Vluyn: Neukirchener Verlag, 1969).

Bottéro, J., 'La femme dans la Mésopotamie ancienne', in P. Grimmal (ed.), *Histoire mondiale de la femme* (Paris: Nouvelle Librairie de France, 1965), pp. 158-223.

Breasted, J.H., *Ancient Records of Egypt.* III. *The Nineteenth Dynasty* (Chicago: University of Chicago Press, 1906).

Brenner, A., *The Israelite Woman: Social Role and Literary Type in Biblical Narrative* (The Biblical Seminar, 1; Sheffield: JSOT Press, 1985).

Briand, J., 'Les figures de David en 1 S 16,1–2 S 5,3. Rapports entre littérature et histoire', in Desrousseaux and Vermeylen (eds.), *Figures de David à travers la Bible*, pp. 9-34.
Brueggemann, W., '2 Samuel 21–24: An Appendix of Deconstruction', *CBQ* 50 (1988), pp. 382-97.
Brunner, H., 'Gerechtigkeit als Fundament des Thrones', *VT* 8 (1958), pp. 426-28.
Buccellati, G., 'La "carriera" di David a quella di Idrimi re di Alalac', *Bibbia e Oriente* 4 (1962), pp. 95-99.
Buren, E.D. van, 'The Guardian of the Gate in the Akkadian Period', *Or* 16 NS (1947), pp. 312-32.
Çambel, H., with a contribution from W. Röllig and J.D. Hawkins, *Corpus of Hieroglyphic Luwian Inscriptions*. II. *Karatepe-Aslantaş* (UISK, 8.2; Berlin: W. de Gruyter, 1999).
Caquot, A., 'Les danses sacrées en Israël et à l'entour', in J. Cazeneuve *et al.* (eds.), *Les danses sacrées (Anthologie)* (Sources orientales, 6; Paris: Seuil, 1963), pp. 121-43.
Caquot, A., M. Sznycer and A. Herdner, *Textes ougaritiques*, I (LAPO, 7; Paris: Cerf, 1978).
Caquot, A., and Ph. de Robert, *Les Livres de Samuel* (Geneva: Labor & Fides, 1994).
Carlson, R.A., 'David and the Ark in 2 Samuel 6', in Lemaire and Otzen (eds.), *History and Traditions of Early Israel*, pp. 17-23.
—*David the Chosen King: A Traditio-Historical Approach to the Second Book of Samuel* (Stockholm: Almqvist & Wicksell, 1964).
Caspari, W., *Die Samuelbücher* (KAT, 7; Leipzig: Deichert, 1926).
Cazelles, H., 'David's Monarchy and the Gibeonite Claim (II Sam. xxi, 1-14)', *PEQ* 87 (1955), pp. 165-75.
—'De l'idéologie royale', *JANES* 5 (1973), pp. 59-73.
Chalier, C., *Les matriarches: Sarah, Rébecca, Rachel et Léa* (Paris: Seuil, 1985).
Charpin, D., 'Review of Malamat, *Mari and the Bible*', *RA* 93 (1999), pp. 91-93.
Charpin, D., and J.-M. Durand, '"Fils de Sim'al": les origins tribales des rois de Mari', *RA* 80 (1986), pp. 141-83.
—'La prise du pouvoir par Zimri-Lim', *MARI* 4 (1985), pp. 293-343.
Charpin, D., D.O. Edzard and M. Stol, *Mesopotamien: Die altbabylonische Zeit* (OBO, 160; Freiburg: Freiburg Academic Press, 2004).
Charpin, D., F. Joannès, S. Lackenbacher and B. Lafont (eds.), *Archives épistolaires de Mari I/2, ARM XXVI* (Paris: Editions Recherche sur les Civilisations, 1988).
Charpin, D., and N. Ziegler, *Mari et le Proche-Orient à l'époque amorrite: essai d'histoire politique* (Paris: Société pour l'étude du Proche-Orient ancien, 2002).
Clines, D.J.A., 'Story and Poem: The Old Testament as Literature and as Scripture', *Int* 34 (1980), pp. 115-27.
—'X, X ben Y, ben Y: Personal Names in Hebrew Narrative Style', *VT* 22 (1972), pp. 266-87.
Clines, D.J.A., and T.C. Eskenazi (eds.), *Telling Queen Michal's Story: An Experiment in Comparative Interpretation* (JSOTSup, 119; Sheffield: JSOT Press, 1991).
Conrad, J., 'Zum geschichtlichen Hintergrund der Darstellung von Davids Aufstieg', *ThLZ* 97 (1972), cols. 321-32.
Contenau, G., *Manuel d'archéologie orientale depuis les origines jusqu'à l'époque d'Alexandre* (4 vols.; Paris: A. Picard, 1927–47).

Crowfoot, J.W., and Grace M. Crowfoot, *Early Ivories from Samaria* (London: Palestine Exploration Fund, 1938).
Crüsemann, F., *Die Widerstand gegen das Königtum* (Neukirchen–Vluyn: Neukirchener Verlag, 1978).
—'Zwei alttestamentliche Witze', *ZAW* 92 (1980), pp. 215-17.
Cryer, F.H., 'David's Rise to Power and the Death of Abner: An Analysis of 1 Samuel xxvi 14-16 and its Redaction-Critical Implications', *VT* 35 (1985), pp. 385-94.
Culi, J., *Yalquṭ Me'am Lo'ez, Shemuel 1–2* (Jerusalem: H. Vegeschel, n.d. [Hebrew]).
Dahood, M., *Psalms* (3 vols.; Garden City, NY: Doubleday, 1970).
Dalglish, E.R., 'Palti', in *IDB*, III, p. 647.
Decamp de Mertzenfeld, C., *Inventaire commenté des ivoires phéniciens et apparentés découverts dans le Proche-Orient* (Paris: Boccard, 1954).
Delekat, L., 'Tendenz und Theologie der David-Salomo-Erzählung', in F. Maass (ed.), *Das ferne und nahe Wort* (Festschrift L. Rost; BZAW, 105; Berlin: Alfred Töpelmann, 1967), pp. 26-37.
Derrida, J., *De la grammatologie* (Paris: Les Editions de Minuit, 1967).
—*Of Grammatology* (trans. G.C. Spivak; Baltimore: The Johns Hopkins University Press, 1975).
—*Positions* (trans. A. Bass; Chicago: University of Chicago Press, 1982).
Desnoyers, L., *Histoire du peuple hébreu: des Juges à la captivité* (3 vols.; Paris: A. Picard, 1930).
Desroches-Noblecourt, C., *La reine mystérieuse Hatshepsout* (Paris: Pygmalion, 2002).
Desrousseaux, L., and J. Vermeylen (eds.), *Figures de David à travers la Bible* (LD, 177; Paris: Cerf, 1999).
Dieterlé, C., and M.V. Monsarrat, 'Famine, guerre et peste en 2 Samuel 21–24', in T. Römer (ed.), *Lectio difficilior probabilior? L'exégèse comme expérience de décloisonnement. Mélanges offerts à Françoise Smyth-Florentin* (Dielheimer Blätter zum AT, 12; Heidelberg: Diebner, 1991), pp. 207-20.
Dietrich, M., 'Die Einsetzungsritual der *Entu* von Emar (Emar VI/3, 369)', *UF* 21 (1989), pp. 47-100.
Dietrich, W., '*dāwīd, dôd* und *bytdwd*', *ThLZ* 53 (1997), cols. 17-32.
Dietrich, W. (ed.), *David und Saul im Widerstreit: Diachronie und Synchronie im Wettstreit, Beiträge zur Auslegung des ersten Samuelbuches* (OBO, 206; Freiburg: Academic Press, 2004).
Donner, H., and W. Röllig, *Kanaanäische und aramäische Inschriften* (3 vols.; Wiesbaden: Otto Harrassowitz, 1973–79).
Dossin, G., 'Amurru, dieu cananéen', in M.A. Beek *et al.* (eds.), *Symbolae biblicae et Mesopotamicae F.M.T. de Liagre Böhl dedicatae* (Leiden: E.J. Brill, 1973), pp. 95-98.
Dossin, G., and A. Finet, *Correspondance féminine* (ARM, 10: Paris: Geuthner, 1978).
Draffkorn Kilmer, A., 'How was Queen Ereshkigal Tricked? A New Interpretation of the Descent of Ishtar', *UF* 3 (1971), pp. 299-309.
—'Symbolic Gestures in Akkadian Contracts from Alalakh and Ugarit', *JAOS* 94 (1974), pp. 177-83.
Driver, G.R., and J.C. Miles, *The Babylonian Laws* (2 vols.; Oxford: Clarendon Press, 1952–55).
—'Review of J.W. Crowfoot and G.M. Crowfoot, *Early Ivories from Samaria*, 1938', *Syria* 20 (1939), pp. 379-80.
Dunand, M., *Fouilles de Byblos* (2 vols.; Paris: Geuthner, 1937).

Dunand, F., 'Note sur les origines de l'apocalyptique judaïque à la lumière des "Prophétie akkadiennes"', in F. Raphaël (ed.), *L'Apocalyptique* (Etudes d'Histoire des Religions, 3; Paris: Geuthner, 1977), pp. 77-87.
Durand, J.-M., 'Assyriologie (les bétyles)', *Cours et travaux du Collège de France Annuaire* 103 (2002–2003), pp. 745-69.
—'Assyriology', *Annuaire du Collège de France* 101 (2000–2001), pp. 693-705.
—'Les dames du palais de Mari à l'époque du royaume de Haute Mésopotamie', *MARI* 4 (1985), pp. 385-436.
—*Documents épistolaires du palais de Mari*, I (LAPO, 16, Paris: Cerf, 1997).
—*Documents épistolaires du palais de Mari*, III (LAPO, 18, Paris: Cerf, 2000).
—'Le mythologème du combat entre le dieu de l'Orage et la Mer en Mésopotamie', *MARI* 7 (1993), pp. 43-61.
—'Peuplement et sociétés à l'époque amorite (I) Les clans bensim'alites', in C. Nicolle (ed.), *Amurru 3: Nomades et sédentaires dans le Proche-Orient ancient* (RAI, 46, Paris, 10-13 July, 2000; Paris: Editions Recherche sur les Civilisations, 2004), pp. 111-97.
—'Trois études sur Mari', *MARI* 3 (1984), pp. 127-80.
Durand, J.-M. (ed.), *La femme dans le Proche-Orient antique* (RAI, 33, Paris, 7–10 July 1986; Paris: Editions Recherche sur les Civilisations, 1987).
Durand, J.-M., and J. Margueron, 'La question du Harem Royal dans le palais de Mari', *Journal des savants* (1980), pp. 253-80.
Edelman, D.V., *King Saul in the Historiography of Judah* (JSOTSup, 121; Sheffield: JSOT Press, 1991).
Ehrlich, E.L., *A Concise History of Israel* (New York: Harper & Row, 1962).
Eisenberg, J., and A. Abecassis, *Et Dieu créa Eve* (Paris: A. Michel, 1979).
Erman, A., and H. Grapow, *Wörterbuch der aegyptischen Sprache* (7 vols.; Leipzig: J.C. Hinrichs, 1931).
Exum, J.C., 'Michal at the Window, Michal in the Movies', in *eadem*, *Plotted, Shot, and Painted: Cultural Representations of Biblical Women* (JSOTSup, 215; Sheffield: Sheffield Academic Press, 1996), pp. 54-78.
—'Michal: The Whole Story', in *eadem*, *Fragmented Women, Feminist (Sub)versions of Biblical Narratives* (JSOTSup, 163; Sheffield: JSOT Press, 1993), pp. 42-60.
—*Tragedy and Biblical Narrative: Arrows of the Almighty* (Cambridge: Cambridge University Press, 1992).
Farber-Flügge, G., *Der Mythos 'Inanna und Enki' unter besonderer Berücksichtigung der Liste der m e* (Studia Pohl, 10; Rome: Pontifical Biblical Institute, 1973).
Fauth, W., *Aphrodite Parakyptusa: Untersuchungen zum Erscheinungsbild der vorderasiatischen Dea Prospiciens* (Akademie der Wissenschaften und der Literatur, Abhandlungen der geistes- und sozialwissenschaftlichen Klasse, 6; Wiesbaden: K. Steiner, 1967).
Fensham, F.C., 'The Treaty between Israel and the Gibeonites', in E.F. Campbell and D.N. Freedman (eds.), *The Biblical Archaeologist Reader* (Garden City, NY: Doubleday, 1970), III, pp. 121-26.
Fergusson, M.A., *Images of Women in Literature* (Boston: Houghton Mifflin, 1973).
Fields, W.W., 'The Motif "Night as Danger" Associated with Three Biblical Destruction Narratives', in M. Fishbane and E. Tov (eds.), *Sha'arei Talmon: Studies in the Bible, Qumran, and the Ancient Near East Presented to Shemaryahu Talmon* (Winona Lake, IN: Eisenbrauns, 1992), pp. 17-32.

Finet, A., *Le Code de Hammurapi* (Paris: Cerf, 1973).

—'Hammu-rapi et l'épouse vertueuse', in M.A. Beek *et al.* (eds.), *Symbolae biblicae et Mesopotamicae F.M.T. de Liagre Böhl dedicatae* (Leiden: E.J. Brill, 1973), pp. 137-43.

—'Iawi-Ilâ, roi de Talḫayûm', *Syria* 41 (1964), pp. 117-42.

Finkelstein, J.J., 'The Edikt of Ammiṣaduqa: A New Text', *RA* 63 (1969), pp. 45-64.

—'Some New *Misharum* Material and its Implications', in Güterbock and Jacobsen (eds.), *Studies in Honor of Benno Landsberger*, pp. 233-46.

Fishbane, M., 'The Treaty Background of Amos 1:11 and Related Matters', *JBL* 89 (1970), pp. 313-18.

Fitzmyer, J., 'The Aramaic Inscriptions of Sefire I and II', *JAOS* 81 (1961), pp. 178-222.

—*The Aramaic Inscriptions of Sefire* (BibOr, 19; Rome: Pontifical Biblical Institute, 1967).

Flanagan, J.A., 'Court History or Succession Narrative? A Study of 2 Samuel 9–20 and 1 Kings 1–2', *JBL* 91 (1972), pp. 172-81.

—'Succession and Genealogy in the Davidic Dynasty', in H.B. Huffmon, F.A. Spina and A.R.W. Green (eds.), *The Quest for the Kingdom of God: Studies in Honor of George E. Mendenhall* (Winona Lake, IN: Eisenbrauns, 1983), pp. 35-55.

Fleming, D.E., *The Institution of Baal's High Priestess at Emar: A Window on Ancient Syrian Religion* (HSS, 42; Atlanta: Scholars Press, 1992).

—'Mari and the Possibilities of Biblical Memory', *RA* 92 (1998), pp. 41-78.

Fokkelman, J.P., *Narrative Art and Poetry in the Books of Samuel: A Full Interpretation Based on Stylistic and Structural Analyses*. II. *The Crossing Fates* (SSN, 23; Assen: Van Gorcum, 1986).

—*Narrative Art and Poetry in the Books of Samuel: A Full Interpretation Based on Stylistic and Structural Analyses*. I. *King David (II Sam. 9–20 & I Kings 1–2)* (SSN, 20; Assen: Van Gorcum, 1981).

—*Narrative Art and Poetry in the Books of Samuel: A Full Interpretation Based on Stylistic and Structural Analyses*. III. *Throne and City* (SSN, 27; Assen: Van Gorcum, 1990).

Frankfort, H., *Kingship and the Gods* (repr., Chicago: The University of Chicago Press, 1978 [1948]).

Frye, N., *The Great Code: The Bible and Literature* (New York: Harcourt Brace Jovanovich, 1981).

Gadamer, H.-G., *Truth and Method* (New York: Crossroad, 1982).

Gadd, C.J., *Ideas of Divine Rule in the Ancient East* (Oxford: Oxford University Press, 1948).

Gardiner, A., *Egypt of the Pharaohs* (Oxford: Oxford University Press, 1961).

Garvie, A.F., *Aeschylus' Supplices: Play and Trilogy* (London: Cambridge University Press, 1969).

Gaster, T.H., 'Ezekiel and the Mysteries', *JBL* 60 (1941), pp. 289-310.

Geiger, A., 'Der Baal in den hebräischen Eigennamen', *ZDMG* 16 (1862), pp. 728-32.

Genot-Bismuth, J., 'Pacifisme pharisien et sublimation de l'idée de guerre aux origines du rabbinisme', *ETR* 56 (1981), pp. 73-89.

George, A., *The Epic of Gilgamesh* (London: Penguin Books, 1999).

Gerstenberger, E., 'Covenant and Commandment', *JBL* 84 (1965), pp. 38-51.

Gide, André, *Saül* (Paris: Gallimard, 1896).

Ginzberg, L., *The Legends of the Jews* (8 vols.; Philadelphia: The Jewish Publication Society of America, 1954).
Gittin, S., D. Dothan and J. Naveh, 'A Royal Dedicatory Inscription from Ekron', *IEJ* 47 (1997), pp. 9-11.
Gitton, M., *Les épouses divines de la 18e dynastie* (Paris: Les Belles Lettres, 1984).
Glassner, J.-J., 'L'hospitalité en Mésopotamie ancienne: aspect de la question de l'étranger', *ZA* 80 (1990), pp. 60-75.
Glück, J.J., 'Merab or Michal', *ZAW* 77 (1965), pp. 72-81.
Goettesberger, J., 'Zu Ez. 9:8 und 11:13', *BZ* 19 (1931), pp. 6-19.
Goetze, A., *Kleinasien: Handbuch der Altertumwissenschaft* (Munich: Beck, 1933).
Goldschmit, M., *Jacques Derrida: une introduction* (Paris: Pocket, 2003).
Gordon, C.H., 'The Status of Woman Reflected in the Nuzi Tablets', *ZA* 43 (1936), pp. 146-69.
Gounelle, A., 'La frontière. Variations sur un thème de Paul Tillich', *ETR* 67 (1992), pp. 393-401.
Greenberg, M., 'Another Look at Rachel's Theft of the Teraphim', *JBL* 81 (1962), pp. 239-48.
—'Ezekiel', in M. Eliade (ed.), *The Encyclopedia of Religion* (New York: Macmillan, 1987), pp. 239-42.
—*Ezekiel 1–20* (AB, 22; Garden City, NY: Doubleday, 1983).
—*The Hab/piru* (AOS, 39; New Haven, CT: American Oriental Society, 1955).
Greenfield, J.C., 'Two Biblical Passages in the Light of their Eastern Background—Ezekiel 16.30 and Malachi 3.17', *IEJ* 16 (1982), pp. 56-61.
Greengus, S. 'The Old Babylonian Marriage Contract', *JAOS* 89 (1969), pp. 505-32.
Greenstein, E.L., 'Autobiographies in Ancient Western Asia', in J.M. Sasson (ed.), *Civilizations of the Ancient Near East* (4 vols.; New York: Charles Scribner's Sons, 1995).
Greenstein, E.L., and D. Marcus, 'The Akkadian Inscription of Idrimi', *JANES* 8 (1976), pp. 59-96.
Gressmann, H., *Die älteste Geschichtsschreibung und Prophetie Israels* (Die Schriften des Alten Testament, II/1; Göttingen: Vandenhoeck & Ruprecht, 2nd edn, 1921).
Grimal, N.-C., *Histoire de l'Egypte ancienne* (Paris: Fayard, 1988).
—*La stèle triomphale de Pi('nkh)y au Musée du Caire* (Cairo: Publications de l'Institut Français d'Archéologie Orientale, 1981).
Grønbaek, J.-H., *Die Geschichte vom Aufstieg Davids (1. Sam. 15–2. Sam. 5): Tradition und Komposition* (Acta Theologica Danica, 10; Copenhagen: Munksgaard, 1971).
Guichard, M., 'Les aspects religieux de la guerre à Mari', *RA* 93 (1999), pp. 27-48.
Gunn, D.M., 'Traditional Composition in the "Succession Narrative"', *VT* 26 (1976), pp. 214-29.
—*The Story of King David: Genre and Interpretation* (JSOTSup, 6; repr. Sheffield: JSOT Press, 1989 [1978]).
—*The Fate of King Saul* (JSOTSup, 14; Sheffield: JSOT Press, 1980).
Güterbock, H.G., and T. Jacobsen (eds.), *Studies in Honor of Benno Landsberger* (AS, 16; Chicago: The University of Chicago Press, 1965).
Haelewyck, J.-C., 'La mort d'Abner: 2 Sam. 3.1-39', *RB* 102 (1995), pp. 161-92.
—'L'assassinat d'Ishbaal (2 Samuel IV 1-12)', *VT* 47 (1997), pp. 145-53.
Hagan, H., 'Deception as Motif and Theme in 2 Sam. 9–20; 1 Kgs 1–2', *Bib* 60 (1979), pp. 301-26.

Hallo, W.W., 'The Birth of Kings', in J.H. Marks and R.M. Good (eds.), *Love and Death in the Ancient Near East: Essays in Honor of Marvin H. Pope* (Guilford, CT: Four Quarters Publishing Company, 1987), pp. 45-52.

Halpern, B., *David's Secret Demons: Messiah, Murderer, Traitor, King* (repr., Grand Rapids: Eerdmans, 2004 [2001]).

Hamilton, G.J., 'New Evidence for the Authenticity of *bšt* in Hebrew Personal Names and for its Use as a Divine Epithet in Biblical Texts', *CBQ* 60 (1998), pp. 228-50.

Hanning, R., and P. Vomberg, *Wortschatz der Pharaonen in Sachgruppen* (Hanning-Lexica, 2; Mainz: Verlag Philipp von Zabern, 1999).

Hanson, P.D., 'Masculine Metaphors for God and Sex-Discrimination in the Old Testament', *The Ecumenical Review* 27 (1975), pp. 316-24.

Harris, R., 'Inanna-Ishtar as Paradox and a Coincidence of Opposites', *History of Religions* 30 (1991), pp. 261-78.

Heintz, J.-G., 'Note sur les origines de l'apocalyptique judaïque à la lumière des "Prophétie akkadiennes"', in F. Raphaël et al. (eds.), *L'Apocalyptique* (Etudes d'Histoire des Religions, 3; Paris: Geuthner, 1977), pp. 77-87.

Herbig, R., 'Aphrodite Parakyptusa', *OLZ* 30 (1927), cols. 917-22.

Hertzberg, H.W., *I and II Samuel: A Commentary* (OTL; Philadelphia: Westminster Press, 1962).

Hillers, D.R., *Covenant: The History of a Biblical Idea* (Baltimore: The Johns Hopkins University Press, 1969).

Hoffmann, G., and H. Gressmann, 'Teraphim, Masken und Winkorakel in Ägypten und Vorderasien', *ZAW* 40 (1922), pp. 75-137.

Hoffner, H.A., Jr, 'Propaganda and Political Justification in Hittite Historiography', in H. Goedicke and J. J. M. Roberts (eds.), *Unity and Diversity: Essays in the History, Literature, and Religion of the Ancient Near East* (Baltimore: The Johns Hopkins University Press, 1975), pp. 49-62.

Horowitz, W., and V.(A.) Hurowitz, 'Urim and Thummim in Light of Psephomancy Ritual from Assur (LKA 137)', *JANES* 21 (1992), pp. 95-115.

International Congress for the History of Religions, *The Sacral Kingship: Contributions to the Central Theme of the VIIIth International Congress for the History of Religions (Rome, 1955)* (NumenSup, 4; Leiden: E.J. Brill, 1959).

Ishida, T., *The Royal Dynasties in Ancient Israel: A Study on the Formation and Development of Royal-Dynastic Ideology* (BZAW, 142; Berlin: W. de Gruyter, 1977).

—'The Story of Abner's Murder: A Problem Posed by the Solomonic Apologist', *ErIsr* 23 (1993), pp. 109*-13*.

Jacob, E., C.A. Keller and S. Amsler, *Osée, Joël, Amos, Abdias, Jonas* (CAT, 11a; Geneva: Labor & Fides, 1985).

Jacobsen, T., 'The Investiture and Anointing of Adapa', *AJSL* 46 (1930), pp. 201-203.

Jason, H., 'The Story of David and Goliath: A Folk Epic?', *Bib* 60 (1978), pp. 36-70.

Jastrow, M., *A Dictionary of the Targumim, Talmud Babli and Yerushalmi, and Midrashic Literature* (New York: Judaica Press, 1975).

Jaussen, J.-A., *Coutumes des Arabes au pays de Moab* (Paris: J. Gabalda, 1908).

Jenni, E., 'Fliehen im akkadischen und im hebräischen Sprachgebrauch', *Or* 47 (1978), pp. 351-59.

Johnson, R.F., 'Paltiel', in *IDB*, III, p. 647.

Jorgensen, E.W., and H.I. Jorgensen, *Eric Berne: Master Gamesman—A Transactional Biography* (New York: Grove Press, 1984).

Kaiser, O., 'Beobachtungen zur sogenannten Thronnachfolgeerzählung', *EThL* 64 (1988), pp. 5-20.
—'David und Jonathan', *EThL* 66 (1990), pp. 281-96.
Kapelrud, A.S., 'King David and the Sons of Saul', in International Congress for the History of Religions, *The Sacral Kingship*, pp. 294-301.
Kazantzakis, N., *Alexis Zorba* (Paris: Plon, 1954).
Keel, O., *Die Weisheit spielt vor Gott: Ein ikonographischer Beitrag zur Deutung des mesahäqät in Spr 8,30f* (Freiburg: Universitätsverlag, 1974).
Kelen, J., *Les femmes de la Bible* (Paris: A. Michel, 1985).
Keys, G., *The Wages of Sin: A Reappraisal of the 'Succession Narrative'* (JSOTSup, 221; Sheffield: Sheffield Academic Press, 1996).
Klengel, H., *Geschichte Syriens im 2. Jahrtausend v.u.Z.* II. *Mittel- und Südsyrien* (Berlin: Akademie Verlag, 1969), pp. 247-50.
Klíma, J., 'Le règlement du mariage dans les lois babyloniennes anciennes', in W. Meid and H. Trenkwalder (eds.), *Im Bannkreis des Alten Orients* (Festschrift Karl Oberhuber; IBK, 24; Innsbruck: Institut für Sprachwissenschaft der Universität, 1986), pp. 109-21.
—'La vie sociale et économique à Mari', in J.-R. Kupper (ed.), *La civilisation de Mari* (RAI, 15; Paris: Les Belles Lettres, 1967), pp. 39-50.
Knudtzon, J.A., *Die El-Amarna-Tafeln* (VAB, 2; 2 vols.; Leipzig: J.C. Hinrichs, 1915).
Köhler, L., 'Archäologisches', *ZAW* 36 (1916), pp. 21-28.
Koschaker, P., 'Eheschliessung und Kauf nach altem Recht, mit besonderer Berücksichtigung der ältesten Keilschriftrechte', *Archiv Orientálni* 18 (1950), pp. 210-96.
—'Zur Interpretation des Art. 59 des Codex Bilalama', *JCS* 5 (1951), pp. 104-22.
Kramer, S.N., 'BM 29616: The Fashioning of the *gala*', *Acta Sumerologica* 3 (1981), pp. 1-9.
Kraus, F.R., *Ein Edikt des Königs Ammi-ṣaduqa von Babylon* (Leiden: E.J. Brill, 1958).
—'Ein Edikt des Königs Šamšu-iluna von Babylon', in Güterbock and Jacobsen (eds.), *Studies in Honor of Benno Landsberger*, pp. 225-31.
Kruger, P.A., 'The Hem of the Garment in Marriage: The Meaning of the Symbolic Gesture in Ruth 3.9 and Ezek 16.8', *JNWSL* 12 (1984), pp. 79-86.
Kuhl, C., 'Die "Wiederaufnahme"—ein literarkritisches Prinzip', *ZAW* 64 (1952), pp. 1-11.
Kupper, J.-R., 'L'opinion publique à Mari', *RA* 58 (1964), pp. 79-82.
Lafont, B., 'Les filles du roi de Mari', in Durand (ed.), *La femme dans le Proche-Orient antique*, pp. 113-21.
Lafont, S., 'Le roi, le juge et l'étranger à Mari et dans la Bible', *RA* 92 (1998), pp. 161-81.
Lambert, W.G., 'Nabukadnezzar King of Justice', *Iraq* 27 (1965), pp. 1-11.
Lambert, W.G., and A.R. Millard, *Atra-Ḫasīs: The Babylonian Story of the Flood* (Oxford: Clarendon Press, 1969).
Lang, B., 'Du sollst nicht nach der Frau eines anderen verlangen', *ZAW* 93 (1981), pp. 216-24.
Langlamet, F., 'David, fils de Jessé, une édition prédeutéronomiste de l'Histoire de la Succession', *RB* 89 (1982), pp. 5-47.
—'De "David, fils de Jessé" au "Livre de Jonathan"', *RB* 100 (1993), pp. 321-57.
—'Pour ou contre Salomon? La rédaction prosalomonienne de 1 Rois I–II', *RB* 83 (1976), pp. 321-79, 481-529.
Lawrence, D.H., *David*, in *The Complete Plays of D.H. Lawrence* (New York: The Viking Press, 1966), pp. 63-154.

Lawton, R.B., 'I Samuel 18: David, Merob, and Michal', *CBQ* 51 (1989), pp. 423-25.
Lemaire, A., 'Cycle primitif d'Abraham et contexte géographico-historique', in Lemaire and Otzen (eds.), *History and Traditions of Early Israel*, pp. 62-75.
—' "Maison de David", "Maison de Mopsos", et les Hivvites', in C. Cohen, A. Hurvitz and S.M. Paul (eds.), *Sefer Moshe: The Moshe Weinfeld Jubilee Volume* (Winona Lake, IN: Eisenbrauns, 2004), pp. 303-12.
—'Mari, la Bible et le monde Nord-Ouest sémitique', *MARI* 4 (1985), pp. 549-58.
—'Traditions amorrites et Bible: le prophétisme', *RA* 93 (1999), pp. 49-56.
Lemaire, A., and B. Otzen (eds.), *History and Traditions of Early Israel: Studies Presented to Eduard Nielsen* (Leiden: E.J. Brill, 1993).
Lemche, N.P., 'David's Rise', *JSOT* 10 (1978), pp. 2-25.
Levenson, J.D., '1 Samuel 25 as Literature and as History', *CBQ* 40 (1978), pp. 11-28.
Levenson, J.D., and B. Halpern, 'The Political Import of David's Marriages', *JBL* 99 (1980), pp. 507-18.
Lévy, E. (ed.), *La femme dans les sociétés antiques* (Actes des colloques de Strasbourg, May 1980 and March 1981; Strasbourg: Université des Sciences Humaines de Strasbourg, 1983).
Lévy, I., 'Cultes et rites syriens dans le Talmud', *REJ* 43 (1901), pp. 183-201.
Lewis, C.S., *The Four Loves* (New York: Harcourt Brace Jovanovich, 1960).
Lewy, J., 'Studies in Akkadian Grammar and Onomatology', *Or* 15 (1946), pp. 361-415.
Liedke, G., '*jšr*', in *THAT*, I, pp. 790-94.
Lipiński, E., 'The Wife's Right to Divorce in the Light of Ancient Near Eastern Tradition', *The Jewish Law Annual* 4 (1981), pp. 9-28.
Liverani, M., 'Ṣuduk e Mišôr', in *Studi in onore di Eduardo Volterra* (Rome: Giuffrè Editore, 1969), VI, pp. 55-74.
—'Memorandum on the Approach to Historiographic Texts', *Or* 42 (1973), pp. 178-94.
Loretz, O., 'Die Teraphim als "Ahnen-Götter-Figur(in)en" im Lichte der Texte aus Nuzi, Emar und Ugarit', *UF* 24 (1992), pp. 133-78.
Luckenbill, D.D., *The Annals of Sennacherib* (OIP, 2; Chicago: The University of Chicago Oriental Institute Publications, 1924).
—*Ancient Records of Assyria and Babylonia*, I–II (Chicago: University of Chicago Press, 1926–27).
Luther, Martin, *Luther's Correspondence* (trans. and ed. P. Smith and C.M. Jacobs; 2 vols.; Philadelphia: United Lutheran Publication House, 1918).
MacDonald, E.M., *The Position of Women as Reflected in Semitic Codes of Law* (Toronto University Oriental Series, 1; Toronto: University of Toronto Press, 1931).
McCarter, P.K., *I Samuel: A New Translation with Introduction, Notes and Commentary* (AB, 8; New York: Doubleday, 1980).
—*II Samuel: A New Translation with Introduction, Notes and Commentary* (AB, 9; Garden City, NY: Doubleday, 1984).
—'The Apology of David', *JBL* 99 (1980), pp. 489-504.
—'The Historical David', *Int* 40 (1986), pp. 117-29.
McKane, W., *I and II Samuel: The Way to the Throne* (Torch Bible Commentaries; London: SCM Press, 1963).
—*Proverbs* (OTL; Philadelphia: Westminster Press, 1970).
Malamat, A., 'Doctrines of Causality in Hittite and Biblical Historiography: A Parallel', *VT* 5 (1955), pp. 1-12.

—*Mari and the Bible* (Studies in the History and Culture of the Ancient Near East, 12; Leiden: E.J. Brill, 1998).
—*Mari and the Early Israelite Experience* (Oxford: Oxford University Press, 1989).
Malbim, *Oṣar ha-Perushim: Debar Shemuel 1–2* (Tel Aviv: Mefarshei ha-Tanakh, n.d. [Hebrew]).
Mallowan, M.E.L., *Nimrud and its Remains* (London: Collins, 1966).
Meier, S.A., 'Women and Communication in the Ancient Near East', *JAOS* 111 (1991), pp. 540-47.
Mendenhall, G.E., *The Tenth Generation* (Baltimore: The Johns Hopkins University Press, 1973).
Merli, D., 'L'immolazione dei Saulidi (2 Sam. 21,1-14)', *Bibbia e Oriente* 9 (1967), pp. 245-51.
Mettinger, T.N.D., *King and Messiah* (Lund: G.W.K. Gleerup, 1976).
Meyer, E., *Geschichte des Altertums* (2 vols.; Stuttgart: J.G. Gotta, 1909).
Midrash Zuta (Berlin: Salomon Buber, 1894).
The Midrash on Psalms (Eng. trans. W.G. Braude; 2 vols.; New Haven: Yale University Press, 1959).
Midrash Rabbah, Genesis (ed. H. Freedman and M. Simon; Eng. trans. H. Freedman; London: The Soncino Press, 1961).
Midrash Rabbah, Leviticus (ed. H. Freedman and M. Simon; Eng. trans. J. Israelstam [chs. 1–9], J.J. Slotki [chs. 20–37]; London: The Soncino Press, 1961).
Midrash Rabbah, Numbers (ed. H. Freedman and M. Simon; Eng. trans. J.J. Slotki; London: The Soncino Press, 1961), I, pp. 133-34.
Midrash Shemuel (Lemberg: Solomon Buber, 1891 [Hebrew]).
Midrash Tehillim (Vilna: Solomon Buber, 1891 [Hebrew]).
Miller, P.D., and J.J.M. Roberts, *The Hand of the Lord: A Reassessment of the 'Ark Narrative' of 1 Samuel* (The Johns Hopkins Near Eastern Studies; Baltimore: The Johns Hopkins University Press, 1977).
Millet, O., and Ph. de Robert, 'David et Batshéba dans la littérature française', in W. Dietrich and H. Herkommer (eds.), *König David—biblische Schlüsselfigur und europäische Leitgestalt* (Stuttgart: W. Kohlhammer, 2002), pp. 777-93.
Miqra'ôt Gedolôt, Shemuel 1–2 (Jerusalem: Torah ha-Mefuarah, n.d. [Hebrew]).
Miscall, P.D., 'Michal and her Sisters', in Clines and Eskenazi (eds.), *Telling Queen Michal's Story*, pp. 246-60.
Mishnayot mevuaro't. Seder Neziqin 1991 (=5752) (Jerusalem: Hekal Shelomo, n.d.).
Moltmann, J., 'Die Bibel und das Patriarchat', *EvTh* 42 (1982), pp. 480-84.
Moran, W.L., *The Amarna Letters* (Baltimore: The Johns Hopkins University Press, 1992).
—'The Ancient Near Eastern Background of the Love of God in Deuteronomy', *CBQ* 25 (1963), pp. 77-87.
Morgenstern, J., '*Beena* Marriage (*Matriarchate*) in Ancient Israel and its Historical Implications', *ZAW* 47 (1929), pp. 91-110.
—'Additional Notes on *Beena* Marriage (*Matriarchat*) in Ancient Israel', *ZAW* 49 (1931), pp. 46-58.
—'David and Jonathan', *JBL* 78 (1959), pp. 322-25.
Mowinckel, S., 'General Oriental and Specific Israelite Elements in the Israelite Conception of the Sacral Kingdom', in International Congress for the History of Religions, *The Sacral Kingship*, pp. 283-93.

Murray, A.S., A.H. Smith and H.B. Walters, *Excavations in Cyprus* (London: British Museum, 1900).

Neirynck, F., 'Parakypsas blepei. Lc 24,12 et Jn 20,5', *EThL* 52 (1977), pp. 113-52.

Neusner, J., *History and Torah* (New York: Schocken Books, 1965).

—*The Mishnah: A New Translation* (New Haven: Yale University Press, 1988).

Niditch, S., 'The "Sodomite" Theme in Judges 19–20: Family, Community, and Social Disintegration', *CBQ* 44 (1982), pp. 365-78.

Nissinen, M., 'Akkadian Rituals and Poetry of Divine Love', in R.M. Whiting (ed.), *Mythology and Mythologies: Methodological Approaches to Intellectual Influences* (Melammu Symposium, 2; Helsinki: The Neo-Assyrian Text Corpus Project, 2001), pp. 93-136.

North, R., 'David's Rise: Sacral, Military, or Psychiatric?', *Bib* 63 (1982), pp. 524-44.

Noth, M., *The History of Israel* (New York: Harper & Row, 1960).

Nutkowicz, H., 'Concerning the Verb (*śn'*) in Judean-Aramaic Contracts from Elephantine' (forthcoming).

Olyan, S.M., 'Honor, Shame, and Covenant Relations in Ancient Israel and its Environment', *JBL* 115 (1996), pp. 201-18.

Orlinsky, H.M., '*Hā-rōqdīm* for *hā-rēqīm* in II Samuel 6.20', *JBL* 65 (1946), pp. 25-35.

Ornan, T., 'Ištar as Depicted on Finds from Israel', in B. Mazar (ed.), *Studies in the Archaeology of the Iron Age in Israel and Jordan* (JSOTSup, 331; Sheffield: Sheffield Academic Press, 2001), pp. 235-56.

Paul, S.M., 'Unrecognized Biblical Legal Idioms in the Light of Comparative Akkadian Expressions', *RB* 86 (1979), pp. 231-39.

Phillips, A., 'David's Linen Ephod', *VT* 19 (1969), pp. 485-87.

Picchioni, S.A., *Il poemetto di Adapa* (Assyriologia, 6; Budapest: Eötvös Loránd University, 1981).

Plautz, W., 'Die Form der Eheschliessung im Alten Testament', *ZAW* 76 (1964), pp. 298-318.

—'Zur Frage des Mutterrechts im Alten Testament', *ZAW* 74 (1962), pp. 9-30.

Podlecky, A.J., 'Quelques aspects de l'affrontement entre les hommes et les femmes chez Eschyle', in E. Lévy (ed.), *La femme dans les sociétés antiques*, pp. 59-71.

Polzin, R., '"HWQY" and Covenant Institutions in Early Israel', *HTR* 62 (1969), pp. 233-40.

Porten, B., and A. Yardeni, *Textbook of Aramaic Documents from Ancient Egypt*. II. *Contracts* (Winona Lake, IN: Eisenbrauns, 1989).

Porter, J.R., 'The Interpretation of 2 Samuel VI and Psalm CXXXII', *JTS* 5 (1954), pp. 161-73.

Poulssen, N., 'De Mikalscène 2 Sam. 6, 16, 20-23', *Bijdragen: Tijdschrift voor Filosofie en Theologie* 39 (1978), pp. 32-58.

Praag, A. van, *Droit matrimonial assyro-babylonien* (Archaeologisch-historische Bijdragen, 12; Amsterdam: N.V. Noord-Hollandsche Uitgevers Maatschappij, 1945).

Pury, A. de, and T. Römer (eds.), *Die sogenannte Thronnachfolgegeschichte Davids: Neue Einsichten und Anfragen* (OBO, 176; Freiburg: Universitätsverlag, 2000).

Pury, A. de, T. Römer and J.-D. Macchi (eds.), *Israël construit son histoire: L'historiographie deutéronomiste à la lumière des recherches récentes* (Geneva: Labor & Fides, 1996).

Qil, Y., *1–2 Shemuel* (2 vols.; Jerusalem: Mossad ha-Rav Kook, 1981).

Rad, G. von, 'The Beginnings of Historical Writing in Ancient Israel', in *idem*, *The Problem of the Hexateuch and Other Essays* (Edinburgh: Oliver & Boyd, 1966), pp. 166-204.
—*Old Testament Theology* (trans. by D.M.G. Stalker; 2 vols.; New York: Harper & Row, 1962).
Redford, D.B., *Egypt, Canaan, and Israel in Ancient Times* (Princeton, NJ: Princeton University Press, 1992).
Reiner, E., *Šurpu: A Collection of Sumerian and Akkadian Incantations* (*AfO* Beiheft, 11; Graz: Im Selbstverlage des Herausgebers, 1958).
Reisman, D., 'Iddin-Dagan's Sacred Marriage Hymn', *JCS* 25 (1973), pp. 185-202.
Renger, J., 'The Daughters of Urbaba: Some Thoughts on the Succession to the Throne During the 2. Dynasty of Lagash', in B.L. Eichler (ed.), *Kramer Anniversary Volume* (AOAT, 25; Neukirchen–Vluyn: Neukirchener Verlag, 1976), pp. 367-69.
Richardson, M.E.J., *Hammurabi's Laws: Text, Translation and Glossary* (The Biblical Seminar, 73; Semitic Texts and Studies, 2; Sheffield: Sheffield Academic Press, 2000).
Robert, Ph. de, 'Bayle and Voltaire devant la Bible', in P.-M. Beaude and J. Fantino (eds.), *Le discours religieux, son sérieux, sa parodie en théologie et en littérature* (Paris: Cerf, 2001), pp. 139-53.
—'David et ses enfants', in Desrousseaux and Vermeylen (eds.), *Figures de David à travers la Bible*, pp. 113-37.
—'Le roi David vu par Pierre Bayle', in *Pierre Bayle, citoyen du monde: de l'enfant du Carla à l'auteur du Dictionnaire* (ed. H. Bost and Ph. de Robert; Paris: H. Champion, 1999), pp. 187-98.
Rost, L., *The Succession to the Throne of David* (Historic Texts and Interpreters in Biblical Scholarship, 1; Sheffield: Almond Press, 1982).
—*Die Überlieferung von der Thronnachfolge Davids* (BWANT, III/6; Stuttgart: W. Kohlhammer, 1926).
—'Die Überlieferung von der Thronnachfolge Davids', in *idem, Das kleine Credo und andere Studien zum A.T.* (Heidelberg: Quelle & Meyer, 1965), pp. 119-253.
Roth, M., *Law Collections from Mesopotamia and Asia Minor* (SBL Writings from the Ancient World, 6; Atlanta: Scholars Press, 1995).
Rupprecht, K., *Der Tempel von Jerusalem: Gründung Salomos oder jebusitisches Erbe?* (BZAW, 144; Berlin: W. de Gruyter, 1977).
Saldarini, A., '"Form Criticism" of Rabbinic Literature', *JBL* 96 (1977), pp. 257-74.
Sasson, J.M., 'Biographical Notices on Some Royal Ladies from Mari', *JCS* 25 (1973), pp. 59-78.
Schechter, S.Z. (ed.), *Midrash ha-Gadol: Genesis* (Cambridge: Cambridge University Press, 1902 [Hebrew]).
Schroer, S., and T. Staubli, 'Saul, David und Jonathan—eine Dreieckgeschichte?', *Bibel und Kirche* 51 (1996), pp. 15-22.
Schulte, H., *Die Enstehung der Geschichtsschreibung im alten Israel* (BZAW, 128; Berlin: W. de Gruyter, 1972).
Schüssler Fiorenza, E., *In Memory of Her: A Feminist Theological Reconstruction of Christian Origins* (New York: Crossroad, 1987).
Seow, C.L., *Myth, Drama, and the Politics of David's Dance* (HSM, 44; Atlanta: Scholars Press, 1989).
Shearing, L.S., 'Palti', in *ABD*, V, p. 138.

Sheppard, G.T., 'Canonization: Hearing the Voice of the Same God in Historically Dissimilar Traditions', *Int* 36 (1982), pp. 21-33.

Silverman, H.J., *Derrida and Deconstruction* (Continental Philosophy, 2; New York: Routledge, 1989).

Smith, S., 'What Were the Teraphim?', *JTS* 33 (1932), pp. 33-36.

Soden, W. von, 'Der Mensch bescheidet sich nicht: Überlegungen zur Schöpfungserzählungen in Babylonien und Israel', in M.A. Beek *et al.* (eds.), *Symbolae biblicae et Mesopotamicae F.M.T. de Liagre Böhl dedicatae* (Leiden: E.J. Brill, 1973), pp. 349-58.

Soggin, J.A., 'Der offiziel gefördete Synkretismus in Israel während des 10. Jahrhunderts', *ZAW* 78 (1966), pp. 179-204.

—'The Davidic–Solomonic Kingdom', in J.H. Hayes and J.M. Miller (eds.), *Israelite and Judaean History* (Philadelphia: Westminster Press, 1977), pp. 332-80.

Stamm, J.J., *Die akkadische Namengebung* (MVAG, 44; Leipzig: J.C. Hinrichs, repr., 1968 [1939]).

—*Beiträge zur hebräischen und altorientalischen Namenskunde* (OBO, 30; Freiburg: Universitätsverlag, 1980).

Steinsaltz, A., *Talmud Babli, Meseket Megillah* (Jerusalem: Institute for Talmudic Publications, 1989 [Hebrew]).

Stoebe, H.-J., 'David und Mikal', in J. Hempel and L. Rost (eds.), *Von Ugarit nach Qumran: Beiträge zur alttestamentliche und altorientalishcen Forschung Otto Eissfeldt zum 1 September 1957 dargebracht* (BZAW, 77; Berlin: Alfred Töpelmann, 1958), pp. 224-43.

—*Das erste Buch Samuelis* (KAT, 8.1; Gütersloh: Gerd Mohn, 1973).

Suter, C.E., 'Die Frau im Fenster in der orientalischen Elfenbein-Schnitzkunst des frühen 1. Jahrtausends v. Chr.', *Jahrbuch der Staatlichen Kunstsammlungen in Baden-Württemberg* 29 (1992), pp. 7-28.

Tadmor, H., 'Autobiographical Apology in the Royal Assyrian Literature', in H. Tadmor and M. Weinfeld (eds.), *History, Historiography, and Interpretation: Studies in Biblical and Cuneiform Literatures* (Jerusalem: Magnes Press, 1983), pp. 38-41.

Le Talmud de Jérusalem (Talmud Yerushalmi) (ed. M. Schwab; Paris: Maisonneuve, 1960).

Talmud Yerušalmi (Jerusalem: Shiloh, 5729 = 1968 [Hebrew]).

Thimme, J., *Phönizische Elfenbeine: Möbelverzierungen des 9. Jahrhunderts v. Chr. Eine Auswahl aus den Beständen des Badischen Landesmuseums* (Bildhefte des Badischen Landesmuseums Karlsruhe; Karlsruhe: C.F. Müller, 1973).

Thomas, D.W., 'The Root *'āhēb* "Love" in Hebrew', *ZAW* 57 (1939), pp. 57-64.

Thompson, J.A., 'The Significance of the Verb LOVE in the David–Jonathan Narratives in 1 Samuel', *VT* 24 (1974), p. 334-38.

Thureau-Dangin, F., A. Barrois, G. Dossin and M. Dunand, *Arslan Tash* (Bibliothèque archéologique et historique, 16; 2 vols.; Paris: Geuthner, 1931).

Tidwell, N.L., 'The Linen Ephod', *VT* 24 (1974), pp. 505-507.

Toorn, K. van der, 'The Nature of the Biblical Teraphim in the Light of the Cuneiform Evidence', *CBQ* 52 (1990), pp. 203-22.

Towner, W.S., 'Form Criticism of Rabbinic Literature', *JJS* 24 (1973), pp. 110-18.

Trible, P., *God and the Rhetoric of Sexuality* (Philadelphia: Fortress Press, 1978).

—*Rhetorical Criticism* (Minneapolis: Fortress Press, 1994).

—*Texts of Terror: Literary-Feminist Readings of Biblical Narratives* (Philadelphia: Fortress Press, 1984).

Troeltsch, E., 'Ueber historische und dogmatische Methode in der Theologie', in *idem*, *Gesammelte Schriften* (4 vols.; Tübingen: J.C.B. Mohr, 1913–22), II, pp. 729-53.
Tsevat, M., 'Ishbosheth and Congeners: The Names and Their Study', *HUCA* 46 (1975), pp. 71-81.
—'Marriage and Monarchical Legitimacy in Ugarit and Israel', *JSS* 3 (1958), pp. 237-43.
Tuchman, B.W., *The March of Folly* (London: Abacus, 1984).
VanderKam, J.C., 'David's Complicity in the Deaths of Abner and Esbaal: A Historical and Redactorial Study', *JBL* 99 (1980), pp. 521-39.
Vannier, G., 'Balzac', in D. Couty, J.-P. de Beaumarchais and A. Ray (eds.), *Dictionnaire des littératures de langue française* (3 vols.; Paris: Bordas, 1984), I, pp. 120-43.
Vanschoonwinkel, J., 'Mopsos: légendes et réalité', *Hethitica* 10 (1990), pp. 185-211.
Vaux, R. de, *Ancient Israel* (2 vols.; New York: McGraw–Hill, 1965).
Veijola, T., *Die ewige Dynastie: David und die Entstehung seiner Dynastie nach der deuteronomistischen Darstellung* (Annales Academiae Scientiarum Fennicae B, 193; Helsinki: Suomalainen Tiedeakatemia, 1975).
Vermeylen, J., *La loi du plus fort: Histoire de la rédaction des récits davidiques de 1 Samuel 8 à 1 Rois 2* (BETL, 154; Leuven: Peeters, 2000).
—'La Maison de Saül et la Maison de David. Un écrit de propagande théologico-politique de 1 S 11 à 2 S 7', in Desrousseaux and Vermeylen (eds.), *Figures de David à travers la Bible*, pp. 34-74.
Weidner, E.F., 'Der Staatsvertrag Assurniraris VI von Assyrien mit Mati'ilu von Bît-Agusi', *AfO* 8 (1932), pp. 17-34.
Weinfeld, M., 'Traces of Hittite Cult in Shiloh and Jerusalem', *Shnaton* 10 (1986–89), pp. 107-14 (Hebrew) + xvii-xviii (English abstract).
Weiser, A., 'Die Legitimation des Königs David', *VT* 16 (1966), pp. 325-54.
Welch, J.W. (ed.), *Chiasmus in Antiquity* (Hildesheim: Gerstenberg Verlag, 1981).
Wellhausen, J., *Einleitung in das Alte Testament* (Berlin: F. Bleek, 4th edn, 1878).
—*Reste arabischen Heidentums gesammelt und erläutert* (Berlin: W. de Gruyter, 3rd edn, 1961).
Wenham, G.J., 'The Restoration of Marriage Reconsidered', *JJS* 30 (1979), pp. 36-40.
Westbrook, R., 'Old Babylonian Marriage Law' (2 vols.; unpublished PhD dissertation, Yale University, 1982; UMI Microfilms, Ann Arbor no. 8221763).
Westendorf, W., 'Beschneidung. A.', in W. Helck (ed.), *Lexikon der Ägyptologie* (6 vols.; Wiesbaden: Otto Harrassowitz, 1975–), I, pp. 727-29.
Whedbee, J.W., 'On Divine and Human Bonds: The Tragedy of the House of David', in G.M. Tucker *et al.* (eds.), *Canon, Theology and Old Testament Literature* (Festschrift B.S. Childs; Philadelphia: Fortress Press, 1990), pp. 147-65.
Whybray, R.N., *The Succession Narrative: A Study of II Sam. 9–20 and 1 Kings 1 and 2* (SBT, 2/9; London: SCM Press, 1968).
Widengren, G., 'Quelques remarques sur l'émasculation rituelle chez les peuples sémitiques', in *Studia orientalia J. Pedersen dicata* (Copenhagen: E. Munksgaard, 1953), pp. 377-84.
Wilson, J.A., *The Culture of Ancient Egypt* (Chicago: The University of Chicago Press, 1958).
Winter, U., *Frau und Göttin: Exegetische und ikonographische Studien zum weiblichen Gottesbild im Alten Testament und in dessen Umwelt* (OBO, 53; Freiburg: Universitätsverlag, 1983).
Wiseman, D.J., 'Law and Order in Old Testament Times', *Vox Evangelica* 8 (1973), pp. 5-21.

—'The Vassal Treaties of Esarhaddon', *Iraq* 2 (1958), pp. 1-99.

Yalquṭ Shimoni, Nebi'im u-ketubim (Jerusalem: H. Vegeschel, n.d. [Hebrew]).

Yaron, R., *The Laws of Eshnunna* (Jerusalem: Magnes Press, 1969 [2nd edn 1988]).

Yaron, Y., 'The Restoration of Marriage', *JJS* 17 (1966), pp. 1-11.

Yee, G.A., '"Fraught with Background": Literary Ambiguity in II Samuel 11', *Int* 42 (1988), pp. 240-53.

Zehnder, M., 'Exegetische Beobachtungen zu den David-Jonathan-Geschichten', *Bib* 79 (1998), pp. 153-79.

Zevit, Z., 'The Use of *'ebed* as a Diplomatic Term in Jeremiah', *JBL* 88 (1969), pp. 74-77.

Ziegler, N., *Le harem de Zimrî-Lîm: La population féminine des palais d'après les archives royales de Mari* (Mémoires de NABU, 5; Florilegium marianum, 4; Paris: Société pour l'étude du Proche-Orient ancien, 1999).

Zimmern, H.,'Die babylonische Göttin im Fenster', *OLZ* 31 (1928), cols. 1-3.

INDEXES

INDEX OF SELECT REFERENCES

Hebrew Bible

Genesis

2.18	142
19	24
23.4	30
24.22	81
24.53	81
26.8	47, 125
28.15	131
29.18	136
29.26-28	66
31.4	136
31.32	27
31.34	102, 136
39.12	113
39.14	47
39.17	47, 125
46.19	136

Exodus

28.42-43	49
32.6	47

Leviticus

18.18	93
21.7	78
25.38	129

Numbers

25.7	113
30.10	78

Deuteronomy

11.19	140
17.15	29
17.17	131
22.13	76
22.19	78
22.29	81
23.3	30
24.1	78
24.3	76
24.4	38
24.5	98
33.8	26

Joshua

2.15	25

Judges

4.18	113
5.28	42
14.16	76
14.18	111
15.2	76
16.1-2	24
17.5	26
18.14	26
18.17	26
19	24
21.25	17

1 Samuel

15	7, 20
15.23	103
15.23b	26
16.8-11	21
16.21	13
16.22	35
16.23	13
17.12	21
17.18	107
17.25	89, 93
18.1	14
18.3	15
18.7	15
18.16	15
18.17-19	57, 64
18.17	95
18.19	93
18.20-28	11, 60
18.20-26	22
18.20	12, 16, 141
18.21	89, 95, 97
18.22	90, 94
18.23	95, 96
18.25	97
18.26	16, 19, 97
18.27	20
18.28-30	98
18.28	16
19.10	101
19.10d	23
19.10d-18a	22, 100
19.11-12	101
19.11	25
19.12	25, 103
19.13-16	102, 136
19.13	23, 100
19.15	101
19.16	102
19.18a	23
22.17	106
23.1-4	26
23.9-12	26
25.3	30, 31, 137

25.7	32
25.10	30
25.13	28
25.17	127
25.28	33
25.39	142
25.42-45	28
25.42	33
25.44	103, 108, 109, 112, 113, 115, 136
26.19	129
27	31
27.8-9	31
28	12
2 Samuel	
1.26	15, 91, 142
2.8	35
2.14	125
3.5	111, 132, 133, 135, 138
3.12-16	34
3.12	19
3.13	37, 99
3.14	39, 66, 110, 112
3.15	66, 104, 112, 113
3.16	112, 115
5	7
6.6-23	8
6.11	123
6.12	45, 121, 123
6.14	48, 117
6.14a	117
6.15	123
6.16-23	40
6.16	12, 25, 48, 118, 120, 123
6.18-19	118
6.19	49, 124
6.20-22	124, 126
6.20	45, 46, 117, 124
6.21	47
6.23	111, 120, 131, 133, 135
7.14	41
9–20	7
11	60
11.2	137
11.3	107
11.15	107
11.26	116
12.8	92
13.14	113
16.5-8	127
16.7	127
16.21	105
19.30	128
20.3	111
21.1-10	133
21.6	54
21.8-9	6, 53
21.8	57, 109, 115, 133, 134
21.9-10	54
21.12-14	56
1 Kings	
1–2	7
2.9	127
5.15	14
12.26	128
2 Kings	
9.30	42
1 Chronicles	
3.3	111
15.29	117, 120, 121, 125
26.8	122
Psalms	
59.1	91
81.5	113
89.14	18
89.15 Heb	18
97.2	18
104.35	141
113.9	136
119.54	121
119.141	96
131.1a	126
Proverbs	
7.6	42
16.12	18
18.22	91
20.28 LXX	18
25.5	18
31.25	140
31.29	114
31.30	114
Ecclesiastes	
7.26	113
Song of Songs	
2.5	50
Isaiah	
16.7	50
62.2	51
Jeremiah	
22.3	18
Ezekiel	
17.19-20	56
21.21	102
21.26	26
48.35	51
Hosea	
2.18	115, 116
3.1	50, 118

Amos
5.12 33

Zechariah
10.2 102

Mishnah
Sanhedrin
2.4 131

Soṭah
8.7 98

Talmuds
b. Berakot
63b-64a 122

b. 'Erubin
96a 137, 139

b. Giṭṭin
26b 107

b. Ketubot
9a-b 107

b. Qidduššin
6b 93
47a 93

b. Šabbat
17a 104
55b-56a 130
55b 128
56a 106
88a 120
105a 127

b. Sanhedrin
2.2 91
19 108
19b-20a 104
19b 92-94, 109, 112, 114, 134
21a 131, 132, 140
69b 105

b. Soṭah
11.8 134
35a-35b 121
44b 98, 99

b. Yebamot
63a 142
77a 104
79a 133

b. Yoma
84 116

b. Zebaḥim
54b 105

y. Berakot
6a 140
12b 139
13.2 140
14b 140

y. 'Erubin
59a 137, 139, 140

y. Qiddušin
42b 133

y. Sanhedrin
10 106
12.1 117
29b 133

y. Sukkah
5.4 133
24.1 117

t. 'Aboda Zara
4.5 129

t. 'Erubin
96a 137, 139

t. Megillah
3.38 130

t. Rosh ha-Shanah
331 139

t. Soṭah
11.8 134

Midrash
Sifre Devarim
53 129

Canticles Rabbah
2.18 122

Genesis Rabbah
17.3 142
32.1 105, 106
64.5 125
82.7 135

Leviticus Rabbah
23.10 112
37.4 89

Mek. Mishpatim, Tractate Neziqin
20 103

Midrash Bereshit
82.13 140

Midrash Mishle
31.22 101

Midrash Shemuel
11.3 135, 140
22.2 98, 99
22.4 138
25.4 91, 141
25.6 117

Midrash Tehillim
6.2 91
9.8 91
52.4 106

59.3 91, 100
59.4 100, 138

Numbers Rabbah
4.20 117, 119, 122, 126
8.4 133

Oṣar ha-Midrashim Hupat Eliahu
Chapter 5 139

Pirkei de Rabbi Eliezer
12 142

Pesikta Rabbati
22.7 139, 140

Qoheleth Rabbah
7.39 113

Sifre
51 129

Sifrei Behalotkha
41 137

Tanna Devi Eliahu Rabbah
10.6 142

Yalquṭ Shimoni
19 101

Akkadian and Hittite Literature
ARMT
1 77.8-13 82
2 40 81
2 109.9-10 75
10 5.3 72
10 31.7′-13′ 73
10 31.7-11 73
10 32.11′-14′ 74
10 32.15′ 74
10 32.20′-28′ 74
10 33.5,18 75
10 34.8′-13′ 74
10 94.3-7 72
10 113.6-11 74
12 322 81
22 154.5 81
22 232.5′ 81
22 322.58 82
26 no. 303 71
26 no. 351.24 74

Adapa Fragment A, BRM
4.18 42

Annals of Sennacherib
OIP 2, p. 46 col. VI 9–12 21

Apology of Hattušiliš
— 61

Codex Hammurabi
I 32-34 46
V, 20 46
135 38
142 77

El Amarna
1.15 46
1.18 46
17.27-28 14
88.46-47 46
138.71-73 14
244 29
245.36 46
246.6 29

Emar
369 52

Inscriptions
Karatepe
A 1.16 67

Sefire
I A 11 67

Index of Authors

Abecassis, A. 44
Abrabanel, I. 94
Ackroyd, P.R. 8, 16, 30
Ahlström. G.W. 49
Alster, B. 12
Alter, R. 9, 25, 27, 39, 44, 60
Amsler, S. 50
Anbar, M. 6, 18
Andersen, F.I. 50, 115
Arnaud, D. 52
Astour, M.C. 6, 70
Auld, A.G. 62, 64
Auzou, G. 45
Avishur, Y. 49

Badalì, E. 67
Badinter, E. 59
Bailey, R.C. 46
Barnett, D. 42
Barrois, G. 42
Barthélemy, D. 57, 64
Barton, G. 51
Barton, J. 8
Batto, B.F. 71
Bayle, P. 144
Ben-Barak, Z. 38, 39
Berlin, A. 11, 58
Bernado, G. di 67
Bernard, J. 128, 129
Biga, M.G. 67
Bleeker, C.J. 20
Bodi, D. 19, 47, 55, 79, 103
Boecker, H.J. 5, 6
Bottéro. J. 10
Breasted, J.H. 19
Brenner, A. 10
Briand, J. 65
Brueggemann, W. 55
Brunner, H. 18
Buccellati, G. 28
Buren, E.D. van 41
Çambel, H. 67
Caquot, A. 49, 51, 66, 118
Carena, O. 67
Carlson, R.A. 7, 40, 53
Caspari, W. 27
Cazelles, H. 17, 54
Chalier, C. 6
Charpin, D. 68, 70, 71, 74, 85, 86
Clines, D.J.A. 5, 7, 9, 12
Conrad, J. 7
Contenau, G. 43
Crowfoot, G.M. 42
Crowfoot, J.W. 42
Crüsemann, F. 46
Cryer, F.H. 35
Culi, J. 95

Dahood, M. 16
Dalglish, E.R. 34
Decamp de Mertzenfeld, C. 42
Delekat, L. 5
Derrida, J. 3, 7
Desnoyers, L. 22
Desroches-Noblecourt, C. 83, 84
Dieterlé, C. 54
Dietrich, W. 9, 11, 52
Donner, H. 18
Dossin, G. 29, 42, 68
Dothan, D. 31
Draffkorn Kilmer, A. 32, 76
Driver, G.R. 17, 76, 81
Dunand, M. 42, 43
Durand, J.-M. 10, 35, 37, 69-76, 82, 85

Edelman, D.V. 13
Edzard, D.O. 70
Ehrlich, E.L. 36
Eisenberg, J. 44
Erman, A. 21

Eskenazi, T.C. 5, 7
Exum, J.C. 25, 58

Farber-Flügge, G. 32
Fauth, W. 42
Fensham, F.C. 55
Fergusson, M.A. 44
Fields, W.W. 24
Finet, A. 38, 68, 75, 80
Finkelstein, J.J. 17, 18
Fishbane, M. 15
Fitzmyer, J. 55
Flanagan, J.A. 53
Fleming, D.E. 52, 85
Fokkelman, J.P. 8, 68
Frankfort, H. 18
Freedman, D.N. 50, 115
Frye, N. 58

Gadamer, H.-G. 146
Gadd, C.J. 26
Gardiner, A. 19
Garvie, A.F. 79
Gaster, T.H. 51
Geiger, A. 38
Genot-Bismuth, J. 99
George, A. 32
Gerstenberger, E. 15
Gide, A. 15, 58
Ginzberg, L. 106
Gittin, S. 31
Gitton, M. 84
Glassner, J.-J. 32
Glück, J.J. 56
Goettesberger, J. 34
Goetze, A. 55, 81
Goldschmit, M. 59
Gooding, D.W. 64
Gordon, C.H. 81
Gounelle, A. 26
Grapow, H. 21
Greenberg, M. 26, 28, 51, 81
Greenfield, J.C. 81
Greengus, S. 76
Greenstein, E.L. 28
Gressmann, H. 23, 26
Grimal, N.-C. 21, 85
Grønbaek, J.-H. 7, 66
Guichard, M. 86
Gunn, D.M. 8, 15, 22, 37, 45, 60, 68, 145

Haelewyck, J.-C. 35
Hagan, H. 68
Hallo, W.W. 52
Halpern, B. 11, 33, 145
Hamilton, G.J. 38
Hanning, R. 21
Hanson, P.D. 60
Harris, R. 13
Hawkins, J.D. 67
Heintz , J.G. 17
Herbig, R. 43
Herdner, A. 49, 51, 118
Hertzberg, H.W. 20
Hillers, D.R. 59
Ho, C.Y.S. 64
Hoffmann, G. 26
Hoffner, H.A. 61
Horowitz, W. 26
Hurowitz, V.(A.) 26

Ishida, T. 20, 35, 56

Jacob, E. 50
Jacobsen, T. 32
Jason, H. 64
Jastrow, M. 137
Jaussen, J.-A. 31
Jenni, E. 23
Johnson, R.F. 34
Jorgensen, E.W. 60
Jorgensen, H.I. 60

Kaiser, O. 7, 8
Kapelrud, A.S. 54
Kazantzakis, N. 44
Keel, O. 47
Kelen, J. 11, 27
Keller, C.A. 50
Keys, G. 8
Klengel, H. 29

Klíma, J. 80
Knudtzon, J.A. 14
Köhler, L. 24
Koschaker, P. 77
Kramer, S.N. 13
Kraus, F.R. 18
Kruger, P.A. 76
Kuhl, C. 6
Kupper, J.-R. 17

Lafont, B. 69
Lafont, S. 83
Lambert, W.G. 17, 42
Lang, B. 7, 38
Langlamet, F. 5, 47, 65, 67
Lawrence, D.H. 58
Lawton, R.B. 57
Lemaire, A. 30, 67, 68
Lemche, N.P. 28
Levenson, J.D. 33
Lévy, E. 10
Lévy, I. 51
Lewis, C.S. 11
Lewy, J. 69
Liedke, G. 17
Lipiński, E. 78
Liverani, M. 18, 67
Loretz, O. 26
Luckenbill, D.D. 21
Lust, J. 64
Luther, M. 9

Macchi, J.-D. 5
MacDonald, E.M. 81
Malamat, A. 55, 68
Mallowan, M.E.L. 42
Marcus, D. 28
Margueron, J. 37
McCarter, P.K. 14, 20, 22, 44, 49, 50, 61
McKane, W. 30, 42
Meier, S.A. 68
Mendenhall, G.E. 28
Merli, D. 54
Mettinger, T.N.D. 7, 41
Meyer, E. 21
Miles, J.C. 17, 76, 81
Millard, A.R. 42
Miller, P.D. 40
Millet, O. 58
Miscall, P.D. 19
Moltmann, J. 59
Monsarrat, M.V. 54
Moran, W.L. 14, 29, 46
Morgenstern, J. 36, 53
Mowinckel, S. 62
Murray, A.S. 43

Naveh, J. 31
Neirynck, F. 42
Neusner, J. 3, 91, 92, 99
Niditch, S. 24
Nissinen, M. 52, 53
North, R. 13
Noth, M. 31, 66
Nutkowicz, H. 78

Olyan, S.M. 46
Orlinsky, H.M. 48
Ornan, T. 50

Paul, S.M. 17
Phillips, A. 49
Picchioni, S.A. 42
Plautz, W. 53
Podlecky, A.J. 79
Polzin, R. 55
Porten, B. 78
Porter, J.R. 41, 52, 63
Poulssen, N. 44
Praag, A. van 76
Pury, A. de 5, 8

Qil, Y. 90, 91, 97, 101, 102, 111, 119, 124, 126, 136, 138

Rad, G. von 58, 62, 67
Redford, D.B. 21
Reiner, E. 43
Reisman, D. 51
Renger, J. 20
Richardson, M.E.J. 17, 38, 77

Rienzo, S. di 67
Robert, Ph. de 36, 37, 58, 66, 144
Roberts, J.J.M. 40
Röllig, W. 18, 67
Römer, T. 5, 8
Rost, L. 7-9, 41, 45, 67
Roth, M. 39
Rupprecht, K. 41

Saldarini, A. 4
Sasson, J.M. 37, 69
Schechter, S.Z. 140
Schroer, S. 15
Schulte, H. 7, 47, 58
Schüssler Fiorenza, E. 146
Seow, C.L. 52
Shearing, L.S. 34
Sheppard, G.T. 17, 57
Silverman, H.J. 145
Smith, A.H. 43
Smith, S. 26
Soden, W. von 79
Soggin, J.A. 31, 63
Stamm, J.J. 11, 34
Staubli, T. 15
Steinsaltz, A. 137
Stoebe, H.-J. 24, 27, 56, 65
Stol, M. 70
Suter, C.E. 43
Sznycer, M. 49, 51, 118

Tadmor, H. 61
Thimme, J. 43
Thomas, D.W. 16
Thompson, J.A. 14, 16
Thureau-Dangin, F. 42
Tidwell, N.L. 49
Toorn, K. van der 26
Tov, E. 64
Towner, W.S. 4
Trible, P. 9, 59
Troeltsch, E. 66
Tsevat, M. 36, 38
Tuchman, B.W. 10

VanderKam, J.C. 54
Vannier, G. 145
Vanschoonwinkel, J. 67
Vaux, R. de 80
Veijola, T. 47, 67
Vermeylen, J. 9, 31, 61, 144
Vitali, P. 67
Vomberg, P. 21

Walters, H.B. 43
Weidner, E.F. 55
Weinfeld, M. 49
Weiser, A. 61
Welch, J.W. 37
Wellhausen, J. 49, 67
Wenham, G.J. 39
Westbrook, R. 77
Westendorf, W. 21
Whedbee, J.W. 58
Whybray, R.N. 8
Widengren, G. 21
Wilson, J.A. 83
Winter, U. 42, 48
Wiseman, D.J. 15, 39

Yardeni, A. 78
Yaron, R. 39
Yaron, Y. 39
Yee, G.A. 146

Zehnder, M. 15
Zevit, Z. 14
Ziegler, N. 68-70, 78
Zimmern, H. 43

www.ingramcontent.com/pod-product-compliance
Lightning Source LLC
Chambersburg PA
CBHW071426160426
43195CB00013B/1823
9781905048748